Identity in Adolescence

The author writes in a manner that is both scholarly and engaging. She is truly an expert in the topic of adolescent identity, and her depth of knowledge shines through. I love this book!
(Susan Moore, Swinburne University of Technology, Australia)

Fully updated to include the most recent research and theoretical developments in the field, the third edition of *Identity in Adolescence* examines the interaction of individual and social context in the process of identity formation. Setting the developmental tradition in context, Jane Kroger begins by providing a brief overview of theoretical approaches to adolescent identity formation currently in use. This introduction is followed by a discussion of five developmental models which reflect a range of attempts, from the oldest to among the most recent, to describe this process; works of Erik Erikson, Peter Blos, Lawrence Kohlberg, Jane Loevinger and Robert Kegan are included in this volume. Although focusing on each theorist in turn, this volume also compares and integrates the varied theoretical models and research findings and sets out some of the practical implications for social response to adolescents. Different social and cultural conditions and their effects on the identity formation process are also covered, as are contemporary contextual, narrative and post-modern approaches to understanding and researching identity issues.

Jane Kroger is Professor of Psychology, University of Tromsø, Norway. Her previous publications include *Discussions on Ego Identity* and *Identity Development: Adolescence through Adulthood*.

Adolescence and Society
Series editor: John C. Coleman

The Trust for the Study of Adolescence

The general aim of the series is to make accessible to a wide readership the growing evidence relating to adolescent development. Much of this material is published in relatively inaccessible professional journals, and the goals of the books in this series will be to summarise, review and place in context current work in the field so as to interest and engage both an undergraduate and a professional audience.

The intention of the authors is to raise the profile of adolescent studies among professionals and in institutions of higher education. By publishing relatively short, readable books on interesting topics to do with youth and society, the series will make people more aware of the relevance of the subject of adolescence to a wide range of social concerns.

The books will not put forward any one theoretical viewpoint. The authors will outline the most prominent theories in the field and will include a balanced and critical assessment of each of these. Whilst some of the books may have a clinical or applied slant, the majority will concentrate on normal development.

The readership will rest primarily in two major areas: the undergraduate market, particularly in the fields of psychology, sociology and education; and the professional training market, with particular emphasis on social work, clinical and educational psychology, counselling, youth work, nursing and teacher training.

Also available in this series:

Adolescent Health
Patrick C.L. Heaven

**The Nature of Adolescence
(second edition)**
John C. Coleman and Leo Hendry

The Adolescent in the Family
Patricia Noller and Victor Callan

**Young People's Understanding of
Society**
Adrian Furnham and Barrie Stacey

Growing up with Unemployment
*Anthony H. Winefield, Marika
Tiggermann, Helen R. Winefield and
Robert D. Goldney*

Young People's Leisure and Lifestyles
*Leo B. Hendry, Janet Shucksmith,
John G. Love and Anthony Glendinning*

Sexuality in Adolescence
Susan Moore and Doreen Rosenthal

Adolescent Gambling
Mark Griffiths

**Youth, AIDS and Sexually
Transmitted Diseases**
*Susan Moore, Doreen Rosenthal and
Anne Mitchell*

Fathers and Adolescents
*Shmuel Shulman and
Inge Seiffge-Krenke*

Adolescent Coping
Erica Frydenberg

Young People's Involvement in Sport
*Edited by John Kremer, Karen Trew
and Shaun Ogle*

The Nature of Adolescence
John C. Coleman and Leo B. Hendry

**Social Networks and Social Influences
in Adolescence**
John Cotterell

Identity in Adolescence
The Balance between Self and Other

Third Edition

Jane Kroger

Routledge
Taylor & Francis Group

LONDON AND NEW YORK

First published 2004 by Routledge
27 Church Road, Hove, East Sussex BN3 2FA

Simultaneously published in the USA and Canada
by Routledge
270 Madison Avenue, New York, NY 10016

Routledge is an imprint of the Taylor & Francis Group

Copyright © 2004 Psychology Press

Typeset in Times by RefineCatch Ltd, Bungay, Suffolk
Printed and bound in Great Britain by TJ International Ltd, Padstow,
Cornwall
Paperback cover design by Hybert Design

This publication has been produced with paper manufactured to strict
environmental standards and with pulp derived from sustainable
forests.

British Library Cataloguing in Publication Data
A catalogue record for this book is available from the British Library

Library of Congress Cataloging-in-Publication Data
Kroger, Jane, 1947–
    Identity in adolescence : the balance between self and other / Jane
Kroger.—3rd ed.
        p. cm.
    Includes bibliographical references and index.
    ISBN 0-415-28106-7 (hardcover)—ISBN 0-415-28107-5 (pbk.)
    1. Identity (Psychology) in adolescence.   I. Title.
    BF724.3.I3K76 2004
    155.5′182—dc22   2004008029

ISBN 0-415-28107-5 (PBK)
ISBN 0-415-28106-7 (HBK)

This book is again dedicated to those who search and to those who assist along the way.

True 'engagement' with others is the result and the test of firm self-delineation.

(Erik Erikson 1968: 167)

Contents

Preface to the third edition   xiii

1   **Adolescence and the problem of identity:**
    Historical, socio-cultural and developmental views   1

    Historical approaches to adolescent identity 2
    Socio-cultural approaches to adolescent identity 3
    Developmental approaches to adolescent identity 7
    The developmental approach detailed 8
    Identity as the balance between self and other 10
    Further reading 14

2   **Adolescence as identity synthesis: Erikson's**
    psychosocial approach   15

    Erikson the person 16
    The nature of ego identity 18
    Identity: development and resolutions 19
    An optimal sense of identity 23
    Identity as a stage in the life-cycle scheme 23
    Criticism of Erikson's identity concept 34
    Measuring ego identity 35
    Historical backdrop to Erikson's and Marcia's
        psychosocial schemes 38
    Research findings on adolescent identity formation 39
    Criticism of Marcia's identity status construct 46
    Implications for social response 47
    Summary 51
    Further reading 52

3   Adolescence as a second individuation process: Blos's psychoanalytic perspective and an object relations view   53

Blos the person 54
The nature of character formation 55
The challenges detailed 57
Character formation through adolescence 66
A healthy character structure 68
Criticism of Blos's identity construct 69
Elaborations on the second individuation process of adolescence 71
Measuring the adolescent separation–individuation process 74
Historical backdrop to Blos's separation–individuation challenge 77
Research findings on adolescent separation– individuation 77
Implications for social response 84
Summary 88
Further reading 88

4   Identity through a cognitive-developmental lens: Kohlberg's contributions   90

Kohlberg the person 91
Kohlberg's view of identity 93
Moral reasoning development 94
An optimal level of moral reasoning 101
Measuring moral reasoning 103
Historical backdrop to Kohlberg's moral reasoning model 105
Criticism of Kohlberg's construct 106
Research findings on the development of moral reasoning 111
Implications for social response 116
Summary 121
Further reading 122

**5   Ego development in adolescence: Loevinger's
     paradigm**   123

*Loevinger the person 124
The nature of the ego 125
The ego and its development 127
An optimal level of ego development 137
Measuring ego development 138
Historical backdrop to Loevinger's model of ego
     development 139
Criticism of Loevinger's construct 141
Research findings on ego development 143
Implications for social response 149
Summary 154
Further reading 155*

**6   Identity as meaning-making: Kegan's constructive-
     developmental approach**   156

*Kegan the person 157
Kegan's view of identity 158
The evolution of meaning-making 163
An optimal mode of meaning-making 173
Measuring of meaning-making balance 174
Historical backdrop to Kegan's constructive-
     developmental model 175
Criticism of Kegan's construct 176
Research findings on the evolving self 178
Implications for social response 182
Summary 188
Further reading 188*

7   Towards integration and conclusions   190

*Commonalities across theoretical models 191
Contrasts across theoretical models 194
Commonalities and contrasts in implications for
     social response 198
Empirical comparisons across models 200
Development in context 201*

*Balance between self and other: new directions for
   identity theory and research* 203
Conclusions 208

Bibliography   210
Name Index   243
Subject Index   249

Preface to the third edition

In an age of contextual, narrative, and post-modern influences in psychology, I have sometimes been asked why retain a developmental focus to the question of how identity forms and changes over the time of adolescence. Of course, there are many approaches one might take to understand how adolescents come to construct themselves in a world that is constructing them, and different research emphases have gained and lost favor throughout various historical eras. My retention of a developmental focus in this volume was made for a number of reasons. First, I regard Erik Erikson's theory as one of the earliest examples of developmental contextualism in the study of adolescent identity development. Developmental contextualism is an approach currently popular in developmental psychology. It stresses that understanding developmental change lies neither in the individual alone nor in the social context alone, but rather in an interaction between the two over time (Lerner 1993). Erikson (1968) exemplified this contemporary approach, as he examined ways in which individual biological processes, psychological needs, defenses and desires interact with the demands, expectations and responses of a social context to create change in both the individual and society over time. Additionally, each of the five developmental models reviewed in the pages ahead has generated a wealth of empirical literature since the second edition of this volume was produced, raising a number of fascinating, new questions. Furthermore, the five models have also now been examined in a multitude of cultural and/or social contexts, and these investigations provide valuable new insights into how development and context interact to affect the course of the identity formation process over and beyond the years of adolescence.

A further purpose of this volume is to highlight the time of adolescence in selected theories of self, ego and identity development. When I wrote the first edition of *Identity in Adolescence*, published in

1989, studies of adolescent development in general and adolescent identity development in particular were in their infancy. In the interval since that time, there has been an enormous increase in research attention directed to issues of both normative and non-normative development during life's second decade. Overview textbooks on adolescent development continue to flourish and a number of new journals devoted to the study of adolescence have appeared. There has, however, been an additional demand for more specialized texts as well as journals dealing with specific issues during the adolescent passage. The present volume and others included in the *Adolescence and Society* series edited by John Coleman reflect this important trend. The present volume focuses specifically on identity during adolescence. Identity has also become the central theme of at least four new journals in psychology, all of which have appeared since the second edition of this volume was produced. Alongside this increasing interest in the study of identity, there has also been a growing concern among many social scientists to integrate their varied theoretical models and research findings with some discussion of practical implications for social response to adolescents in the identity formation process. The present volume, again, reflects this ambition. Finally, a desire to understand identity issues for adolescents growing up in a diversity of cultural, ethnic and social class contexts has also been emerging. The present volume reflects the importance of contextual-developmental interactions in the adolescent identity formation process.

The third edition of *Identity in Adolescence* examines some of the ways in which young people may mature to reinterpret and make sense of their important relationships and their surrounding environments, as their environments come to recognize, acknowledge and make sense of them. The five developmental models selected for coverage in this volume reflect a range of attempts from the oldest to among the most recent efforts to describe this process. This volume also addresses how different social and cultural conditions may be associated with varied resolutions to the identity formation process, as late adolescents prepare to enter adult life. Chapter 1 sets the developmental tradition in context by providing a brief overview of alternative contemporary theoretical approaches to adolescent identity formation currently in use. In this chapter, assumptions of selected historical, socio-cultural and developmental orientations are elucidated and a more detailed rationale for the volume's present focus is presented. Theoretical chapters then turn to the writings of five major developmental theorists addressing identity issues: Erik Erikson, Peter Blos, Lawrence Kohlberg, Jane Loevinger and Robert Kegan. These theorists have all grappled with the

nature of the 'I' and the special transformations it normatively undergoes during adolescence, as well as the social conditions associated with
varied resolutions. While taking different avenues of approach, each
theorist maps a model of identity that allows one to formulate culturally appropriate, facilitative individual, group and institutional
responses for those undergoing the identity formation process of adolescence. The final chapter focuses on comparisons and contrasts across
these models. It also provides a response to various contextual, narrative and post-modern approaches to understanding and researching
identity issues at the present time.

Since this work may be serving as an introduction to the field of
adolescent identity formation for many readers, introductory sections
to key theoretical concepts of each chapter have been retained from
earlier editions. Where theoretical modifications have been made, I
have drawn upon the most recent publications available and have
changed theoretical summaries accordingly. I have retained and
updated earlier sections on the theorist's biography, alongside sections
devoted to criticism, researches, current research directions and implications for social response for each of the five developmental models
of identity. I have also included an expanding body of recent research
on social and cultural forces impacting on each development framework presented in this volume. At the same time, I have provided
more subheadings within major sections that I hope will assist the
reader to follow key themes under review. In addition, I have added
two new sections to each chapter: one details the measures most
commonly and currently in use for identity assessment, while the second overviews the historical backdrop to each model. I have also
provided a list of additional recommended reading at the conclusion
of each chapter. I hope the reader will find these new additions helpful
in both understanding and responding to the identity formation process
of adolescence.

This volume has again been sparked by my concern over adults' frequent failure to recognize, meet and respond optimally to the special
needs of adolescents in their various stages of identity development.
While each young person is unique in personal history, talents and
attributes, there do appear to be certain underlying and predictable
structural reorganizations that comprise the identity formation process.
Once recognized and addressed, opportunity exists for supporting the
process of change, when it occurs, in facilitative and culturally
appropriate ways. Rather than chance occurrence, effective developmental intervention can be a planned event. It is hoped that an understanding of the developmental and contextual approaches to identity

presented in this volume might promote more effective social responses to adolescents undergoing the identity formation process.

Acknowledgments

Thoughts and observations presented in the pages ahead are the product of many stimulating discussions with colleagues, students and friends as well as many solitary ruminations over the past four decades of my life. As a university teacher and researcher in lifespan development, I continue to learn by all that my students, research interviewees and colleagues teach me.

Since publication of the first edition of *Identity in Adolescence*, I have had several periods of sabbatical leave which have enabled me to meet and interact with many of the theorists and researchers covered in the pages ahead. Time in 1988–1989 as a visiting research associate at the Erik H. and Joan M. Erikson Center, Cambridge Hospital, Harvard Medical School, provided me with opportunities for many engaging conversations with both of the Eriksons as well as others in the Cambridge community. I spent a semester in 1993 as a visiting scholar at the Henry A. Murray Research Center for the Study of Lives at Radcliffe College, which again enabled me to engage in many stimulating interactions. At that time, I received the thoughtful feedback of Drs Gil Noam, Gus Blasi and John Levine as I worked toward integrating theoretical models. Dr Bob Kegan provided many wonderful learning opportunities through his teachings on adult development. Dr Anne Colby, Director of the Murray Research Center, provided me with access to the many rich resources of data archived there. A further semester of leave spent with Dr James Marcia and his graduate students in 2001 at Simon Fraser University in Vancouver, Canada, also gave me many rich experiences that have enhanced the third edition of this volume.

The University of Tromsø has also been generous in its provision for leave and other supports for the completion of this current edition. I am particularly grateful to Jan-Are Johnsen for his assistance in the preparation of this edition. Friends and colleagues both here in Tromsø and on more distant shores have again been patient with me and the time and effort this current volume has demanded.

Finally, I would again like to thank Dr John Coleman, Director of the Centre for the Study of Adolescence in the UK and Psychology Press for their support in producing this volume. Over the years since *Identity in Adolescence* was first produced, I have also had the opportunity to meet and correspond with a number of readers, and many of your very helpful ideas have once again been incorporated in this volume. To you, I also express my grateful thanks.

Jane Kroger
Havnes, Håkøya
Eidkjosen, Norway
January 2004

1 Adolescence and the problem of identity

Historical, socio-cultural and developmental views

'Listen,' F. Jasmine said. 'What I've been trying to say is this. Doesn't it strike you as strange that I am I, and you are you? I am F. Jasmine Addams. And you are Berenice Sadie Brown. And we can look at each other, and touch each other, and stay together year in and year out in the same room. Yet always I am I, and you are you. And I can't ever be anything else but me, and you can't ever be anything else but you. Have you ever thought of that? And does it seem to you strange?'

(F. Jasmine Addams, in Carson McCullers'
Member of the Wedding, 1946)

When and how does [one] develop a sense of 'I'?

(Erik Erikson, *Infancy and the Rest of Life*, 1983)

F. Jasmine (alias Frankie) Addams's ruminations address a question that adolescents and social scientists alike have pondered over preceding decades: When and how does one develop a sense of 'I'? While the foundations of 'I' are formed in infancy through the interactions of caretakers and child, adolescence does seem to be a time, at least in many contemporary, technologically advanced western cultures, when one is confronted with the task of self-definition. 'I can't ever be anything else but me,' begins Frankie. However trying to find out who 'me' is becomes Frankie's task in Carson McCullers' (1946) novel, *Member of the Wedding*. The process of self-definition is something which scholars have attempted to understand from a variety of perspectives – historical, socio-cultural and developmental. While Frankie, herself is not concerned with all of these issues, she eloquently gives voice to some of the forces that help shape her 'I', her sense of identity, her place in the world.

Frankie's story is set during the Second World War in a small, rural US southern town during a seemingly endless summer. Frankie is about to turn 'twelve and five-sixths', feeling very much betwixt and between meaningful social niches (which summer has a way of exacerbating), and wrestling with the matter of belonging. Given an option, Frankie would have been a boy and gone to war as a marine. However, this was not to be her fate, so she decided instead to give blood (at least a quart a week). In this way, a part of her would be in the veins of Allies fighting all over the world (the reddist and strongest blood ever – a true medical wonder). Soldiers would return, saying they owed their lives to 'Addams' (not 'Frankie'). But this scenario was not to be her fate either, for Frankie was too young, and the Red Cross would not take her blood. Thinking about the war for very long made Frankie afraid, not because of the fighting but because the war refused to include her, to give her a place in the world. Actually, thinking for very long, at all, made Frankie afraid as well, for it brought up questions of who she was, of what she would be in the world, of why she was standing where she was at that moment – alone. Through the trials of trying to adopt a new name (F. Jasmine Addams), a new family, a new town, Frankie struggled to establish her sense of 'I' and where she belonged.

Frankie's identity struggles may be understood through a variety of theoretical lenses. Historical, socio-cultural, and developmental traditions have all arisen to account for various dimensions of human development, including identity. Under these broad rubrics, a number of specific approaches have arisen. It is my intention below to note only the general emphases given within each tradition and to refer the reader to further resources that can provide more specific details at the conclusion of this chapter.

Historical approaches to adolescent identity

Were Frankie born in an earlier *historical* era, her story would probably not have given rise to a novel, for self-definition would not have been a problem. As Erikson (1975) has noted, the issue of identity holds historical relativity. Erikson suggested that identity only became a matter of concern in the United States late in the nineteenth century because a new generation of immigrants were attempting to define themselves in a land far removed from their ancestral homes. Baumeister (1986, 1987) has provided an excellent and more extensive overview of how the problematic nature of identity for many adolescents has evolved and intensified over the course of history.

Baumeister noted that medieval adolescent and adult identities were defined in a very straightforward manner. The social rank and kinship network into which one was born determined one's place for life. While some changes of title or role were inevitable over the course of time, general possibilities were circumscribed by the clan. In the early modern period, the rise of a middle class began a shift in the standard for self-definition when wealth rather than kinship ties became the new measure of social status and hence self-definition. The later Protestant split and subsequent decline of the Christian faith gave rise to an era in which individuals became able at least to accept or reject the religious traditions of their forebears. During the romantic era, most still espoused Christian beliefs, but these held less influence over their daily lives. Furthermore, society was often perceived to be oppressive and the need to reject some of its demands was recognized. By the Victorian era, late adolescents and adults increasingly began to reject Christian dogma and a focal concern was whether or not morality could survive without religion. Thus, Victorian adolescents had to define their adult identities without clear guidelines in the midst of general cultural uncertainty on issues of appropriate values.

Such difficulties for adolescents continued into the twentieth and twenty-first centuries, as the process of self-definition and identity formation became normative developmental tasks (Erikson 1968). Cushman (1990) further suggests that at least in the United States absence of community, tradition and shared meaning has created the conditions for an 'empty self'; a sense of 'I' which experiences chronic emotional hunger for adolescents and adults alike. Cushman argues that the 'empty self' attempts to be soothed, to be 'filled up' by consumer products. Advertising and psychotherapy are the two professions that Cushman cites as being most involved in individuals' attempts to heal the 'empty self'. Viewed historically, the process of identity formation and the process of self-definition, at least for many youths in western contexts, is a relatively recent phenomenon.

Socio-cultural approaches to adolescent identity

In her efforts toward self-definition, Frankie voices her intense desire to break free – free of her family, town and many of the socio-cultural conditions that constrain her. Berenice, the black housekeeper, attempts to understand:

> 'I think I have a vague idea what you were driving at,' [responds Berenice]. 'We all of us somehow caught. We born this way or that way and we don't know why. But we caught anyhow. . . . We each one of us somehow caught all by ourself. Is that what you was trying to say?'

'I don't know,' F. Jasmine said. 'But I don't want to be caught.'
'Me neither,' said Berenice. 'Don't none of us. I'm caught worse
than you is.'
F. Jasmine understood why she had said this, and it was John
Henry who asked in his child voice: 'Why?'
'Because I am black,' said Berenice.

(McCullers 1946: 113)

Frankie is 'caught' by her social class and ethnicity as well as the
technological influences, societal norms and legal requirements for adolescents in her culture. The socio-cultural conditions of her society,
some would contend, create her problems of identity and self-definition.

A variety of theoretical orientations to identity are represented under
this general socio-cultural approach, ranging from proposals that identity is a reflection of individual adaptation to context (e.g. Baumeister
and Muraven 1996; Côté and Levine 2002) or a reciprocal interaction
between person and context (e.g. developmental contextualism, Lerner
1993) to more radical suggestions that one's identity is merely an
imprint of one's social and cultural surroundings. Baumeister and
Muraven (1996) exemplify the initial stance that identity is formed
as one's adaptations to social, cultural and historical contexts. This
suggestion does not imply that identity acquisition is merely a passive
response by individuals to their social contexts but neither is identity an
entirely self-determined event. Rather, people are active agents in
choosing, altering and modifying their identities in ways that will provide greatest satisfaction within their social and cultural situations.
'People do not simply turn out the way society dictates, but neither can
they develop identity without regard to the socio-cultural context. The
self constructs for itself a definition that allows it to get along reasonably well in its social environment' (Baumeister and Muraven 1996:
415). Similarly, Adams and Marshall (1996) review and reflect on a
wide range of literature to propose more specific macro- and micro-
levels of influence on identity, mediated through inter- and intra-
personal processes. Macro-levels of influence on identity development
include cultural ideologies as reflected in various social institutions,
while micro-levels of influence reflect dialogue, conversation, interactions between individuals. In approaching Frankie's dilemma from
this person-in-context orientation, cultural conditions that give individuals a freedom of choice also restrict Frankie's desires for self-
expression due to restrictions of age, gender and social class. With the
individual qualities of determination, perseverance, an understanding
of causal relationships, openness to new experiences, internal locus of

control and many personal characteristics, Frankie seeks an adaptation and place in the world that results in more personal satisfaction than she now finds.

Another means by which social scientists have been attempting to understand identity formation in context has come through an orientation known as *developmental contextualism* (Lerner 1993). This approach is based on two key ideas:

1 There are factors from numerous, qualitatively distinct levels of analysis involved in human development.
2 Factors within these various levels of analysis exist in reciprocal relationships.

'In short, in developmental contextualism the person-context relation is understood as an organization of mutually influential variables . . . changing over time (Lerner 1993). It is not the study of person in context, but rather study of the interaction among many individual and contextual systems and their influences on one another. Thus, a developmental contextualist would look at how different personal and contextual factors in Frankie's world reciprocally interact and influence one another to create change in Frankie's sense of identity over time.

A further group of writers has focused more strongly on contextual implications that such conditions hold for individual identity formation. Triandis (1989), for example, differentiated 'tight' from 'loose' societies on the basis of how much opportunity for individual choice a society would allow. Thus, enormous variation may be seen across cultural contexts in how much latitude youth are given for creating or realizing their identity interests. Adolescents in collectivist societies are not faced with the choices and decisions that youths in contemporary western cultures must make in defining their own identities (Côté and Levine 2002). Tupuola (1993) interviewed New Zealand and Samoan-born youths living in New Zealand about their experiences of adolescence. One Samoan-born participant summarized the responses of many as follows:

I feel I still can't answer the adolescent thing. As a Samoan born, I had never heard of it [adolescence] until I came to New Zealand. I don't think it was part of my life because it is a western concept, and from a non-western society all those development stages didn't relate to me. All I know is that my aiga [family] and my community and my culture are important. They determine the way I behave, think, and feel.

Sometimes I think that we [in Samoa] are children for most of our lives, and it can take a very long time for us to become adults. It does not matter how old you are, [for] if you are not considered worthy or responsible enough by your elders then you will not be treated as an adult. You really have to earn your place in the Samoan culture. So adolescence as a developmental stage is foreign to our culture.

(Subject #3, Tupuola 1993: 308, 311)

Cultural conditions for this young woman made the issue of identity formation and finding her place in the societal milieu a rather straight-forward process. While some of the roles that she was expected to fulfill were not easy, the actual process of identifying suitable roles for herself within the larger society was not in itself a complex problem. Tupuola further reports that a number of participants in her study consulted Samoan dictionaries over the course of their interviews and were unable even to find a Samoan word meaning 'adolescence'.

The most radical of approaches to the person-in-context dilemma has come from the post-modernists. There are again many different schools of thinking within this approach, but common to all is the denial of any general pattern of development across individuals, a de-legitimizing of anything structural or hierarchical in form, of anything that is consistent across situations. Post-modernists consider this to be 'the end of the age of development' (e.g. Gergen 1991), a denial that there is any depth and design to the course of change over time. When addressing issues of identity, post-modernists argue for the existence of multiple identities that are assumed in different contexts. Post-modernity emphasizes fragmentation, discontinuity and only local rather than general themes. In the words of Rattansi and Phoenix (1997), identity is fluid and fragmented and not something that exists within the individual. Thus, we all have a range of identities, each having salience in a different context. Identity is also conceptualized by post-modernists as a culturally appropriated mode of discourse (Slugoski and Ginsburg 1989). Many post-modernists would hear Frankie's narrative as an example of a teenager with fragmented iden-tities, created through the language that she uses to tell her story. That story reflects identities created in the whims of the moment, lacking any central core or continuity across situations. Great discrepancies in the demands of various contexts induce 'situated' identities, ultimately leading to a sense of no self at all (Gergen 1991). While such radical positions are not widespread in the study of adolescent identity, they present a view in direct contrast to assumptions of the developmental approach described below. This approach is used as a framework for the remainder of this volume.

Developmental approaches to adolescent identity

Social and historical circumstances have undoubtedly left teenagers from technologically advanced cultures with ambiguous role prescriptions to struggle with the problem of self-definition. A number of social scientists, however, have focused more intently on what Frankie describes as a changing sense of 'I' – on an internal, *developmental* transformation of the sense of self and consequent ways of filtering and making sense of one's life experiences. Intrapsychic restructuring during adolescence brings identity questions to the surface. While socio-cultural factors undoubtedly may accelerate, delay or even arrest this developmental process, sequential stages in the transformation of the self and its way of understanding exist, according to this developmental perspective. Transformations in cognitive and affective processes or qualitative change in some self (ego) structure which subtends both of these facets of identity have been held accountable for alterations to the subjective sense of 'I' frequently experienced during life's second decade – at least in societies where adult identities for youth are not prescribed.

While acknowledging the contributions of society to creating the phenomenon of adolescence with its concomitant questions of identity, this book focuses on five developmental models addressing the intrapsychic potential emergence of the self within certain social and cultural frames of reference. All approaches attend carefully to the period of adolescence with the internal reorganization it may bring. However, all respect the process of identity formation as a lifelong enterprise and are reviewed in this volume in a manner reflecting this understanding. Just as the significance of a painting cannot be fully grasped without knowledge of its contextual origins and resulting influences on later art, so identity formation during adolescence cannot be fully appreciated without knowledge of its childhood antecedents and consequent adult states.

Until the 1960s, much of the literature on adolescent psychology came from psychoanalytic treatment centers. There was often a stress on the 'universality of ego weakness' in adolescence, and the depiction of an ego 'besieged by the drives and unable to rely on the now-dangerous parental ego for support' (Josselson 1980: 188). Such portrayals lay at the heart of the 'turmoil' theory of adolescent development which presented storm and stress as normative features of the teenage years. It was only when researchers of the 1960s and 1970s (e.g. Douvan and Adelson 1966; Offer and Offer 1975) began to find little evidence of psychopathology or even much storm and stress among large samples of adolescents in the general population of the United States that attention began to shift from clinical to more normative populations for an understanding of developmental processes occurring during adolescence. Literature on adolescent development has mushroomed in the last four decades, with the creation of at least six new North American and European journals and two professional societies in these locales devoted solely to research on this stage of the life cycle. Additionally, the field of adolescence has witnessed greater specialization in its textbook and journal offerings. A number of supplementary textbooks now deal with selected issues of adolescence, including the current volume on identity. Interest in identity has also been evidenced by the emergence of at least four new journals in the past decade devoted to themes of self or identity (Côté and Levine 2002). It is the intention of this book to examine, through critical analysis, the contributions of five theories related to identity development during adolescence. While the task of identity formation, revision and maintenance is a lifelong challenge, it is the intention of this volume to highlight adolescence and the identity issues normatively encountered when societies generally demand an initial resolution. While some less than optimal identity resolutions will be presented, the focus rests primarily on those normative though 'cataclysmic [adolescent] ego changes that hardly make a sound' (Josselson 1980: 190).

The developmental approach detailed

As developmental models, the theories of Erik Erikson, Peter Blos, Lawrence Kohlberg, Jane Loevinger and Robert Kegan presented in the pages ahead all have certain features in common. Rather than depicting change in a linear fashion, *quantitative* in nature, these approaches all focus on change more *qualitative* in kind, developmental in form. The linear or non-stage view of change holds that something which exists early in life becomes merely bigger or more pronounced through time, while the developmental orientation attempts to detail how that which existed at earlier life stages 'becomes transformed into something related to, but also different than, what existed earlier' (Breger 1974: 3). Some approaches to identity are non-developmental in nature. The ancient Greeks defined personality in terms of character type; an individual was merely one of four basic personality types, never undergoing qualitative change. More recent efforts to describe personality in terms of body build (such as endomorph, mesomorph, ectomorph), character disposition (such as introvert, extrovert), or psychiatric diagnostic classification (such as sociopath, schizophrenic, manic depressive) are all examples of linear or non-developmental views of identity. These labels simply assume that 'a person's type resides within and is stimulated to unfold with experience' (Breger 1974: 6). In developmental models of identity, by contrast, it is possible to detect qualitatively different stages of organization, each with its own unique features that will never again exist in the same form. Once stage reorganization has occurred, it is simply not possible to go back to view the world through earlier, less complex modes of organization (however much one may wish to do so at times). Developmental stages exist in a hierarchical and invariant sequence, each building on that which has gone before, incorporating yet transcending the last stage to provide a foundation for the next (Loevinger 1987).

Theorists reviewed in this volume all describe identity as a developmental process of qualitative stage reorganization rather than a mere unfolding of static personality characteristics. While theorists reviewed in the pages to follow are not the only writers holding a developmental perspective on identity development during adolescence, their writings have been both central to theory construction as well as fundamental to later researches on the adolescent identity formation process. Researches generated by theorists and later investigators reviewed here have also contributed to an increased understanding of the role that context plays in shaping the developmental course. With growing interest over the last 15 years in the relation between identity development and context, a variety of studies has addressed social and cultural circumstances associated with facilitating identity development as well as arrest. Such researches are included in each chapter and highlighted in the conclusion, which summarizes circumstances associated with developmental progression, regression and stability. It is my view that an appreciation of developmental processes, in combination with contextual forces, provides the best means of understanding issues involved in the identity formation task of adolescence at the present time.

When identity is viewed as a developmental phenomenon, some important implications for social response become apparent. Rather than being a collection of static traits, identity is conceptualized as a structural organization more responsive to opportunities that will obviate developmental arrest as well as promote further movement toward maturity. For example, no longer do we need to consider an individual with the label 'sociopathic personality disorder' as having a static personality trait unamenable to change, but rather as someone with a condition of childhood developmental arrest who, with appropriate intervention, may be helped to embark on a more normative developmental course in varied life contexts (Kegan 1986a). A discussion of the implications that each model holds for social response in the promotion of optimal identity formation is thus an important feature of each chapter presented in this volume.

Identity as the balance between self and other

The terms 'identity', 'self', 'ego', 'I' and 'me' have all held very specific meanings for various social scientists interested in addressing the issue of self-definition. Each theorist reviewed in the pages ahead attaches a somewhat unique meaning to the nature of the 'I' at particular phases of the lifespan. However, despite usage of different concepts, a further basic commonality seems present as we look across these developmental approaches to the essence of identity. In some way, shape or form, identity invariably gets defined (at various stages of the life cycle) as a balance between that which is taken to be self and that considered to be other. The means by which we differentiate ourselves from other people in our lives as well as from our own organic functions constitutes the very core of our experiences of personal identity. American novelist Thomas Wolfe struggled through his life to differentiate his own identity from that internalized image of his primary caretaker. This intrapsychic battle was replayed in many of his adolescent and adult relationships: 'His popularity [as a writer] is partially due to his being a chronicler of the human aspirations for individuation, for the establishment of a real self, as well as of the feelings of loss associated with this search' (Masterson 1986: Tape 4). Though using differing terms and concepts, Erikson, Blos, Kohlberg, Loevinger and Kegan all provide descriptions of how the internal balancing and rebalancing of boundaries between self and other produce more differentiated subjective experiences of identity as well as relationships with other people at various life stages. Adolescence encompasses one phase of heightened activity for most in this intrapsychic and interpersonal juggling act.

From psychodynamic beginnings, Erikson's work was the first to appreciate the psycho*social* nature of identity with the important role played by the community in recognizing, supporting and thus helping to shape the adolescing ego. As a developmental theorist, he distinguishes the identity solutions of *introjection* during infancy and *iden-tification* in childhood from the process of *identity formation* during adolescence. It is during the adolescent phase of the lifespan that Erikson sees opportunities for identity resolution through a synthesis that incorporates yet transcends all previous identifications to produce a new whole, based upon yet qualitatively different from that which has gone before:

> The final identity, then, as fixed at the end of adolescence, is superordinated to any single identification with individuals of the past: it includes all significant identifications, but it also alters them in order to make a unique and reasonably coherent whole of them.
>
> (Erikson 1968: 161)

Here the new balance between self and other involves a reorganization of the means to identity itself. That self of childhood, derived from significant identifications with important others, must during adolescence give way to a self derived from yet transcending those foundations – to a new whole greater than the sum of its parts. Others now become important not merely as potential sources of identification but rather as independent agents, helping to recognize the 'real me'. Erikson, however, appreciated the importance of context to this process. He saw identity development also as a reciprocal relationship between individual and context, a process of recognizing and being recognized by 'those who count'.

Blos, more strongly than Erikson, has maintained his alliance with classic psychodynamic theory. However, Blos's portrayal of adolescence as a second individuation process has paved the way for a new approach to the study of adolescent individuation and identity. Blos built upon the groundbreaking work of Margaret Mahler, who detailed the infant separation and individuation processes. He noted that while the successful establishment of an autonomous self in life's earliest years rests with the toddler's ability to incorporate or internalize an image of its primary caretaker, such intrapsychic organization hinders further development during adolescence. During the second individuation process, it is this very internalized parent which must be relinquished if development is to progress. Blos sees adolescence as a time spent unhinging the old intrapsychic arrangement of that which has been considered self (the parental introjects) and that taken to be other. He finds regressive thoughts and actions to be necessary for further development and to be common phenomena accompanying this loss of the childhood 'I'. A sense of heightened distinctiveness from others is the subjective experience following successful adolescent individuation. Now others can be recognized as agents in their own right rather than merely as internalized orchestrators of one's responses to life. Certain interpersonal and contextual features associated with this process are described in Chapter 3.

Kohlberg, unlike other theorists in the pages ahead, does not address the formation of identity directly. Rather, he conceptualizes identity (or in his terms, ego) as an entity which can only be approached through specific subdomains of ego functioning. These subdomains (for example, cognition, moral reasoning) develop alongside one another, often exhibiting only conditional links. Thus, a certain stage of cognitive development seems to be a necessary but not sufficient condition for reasoning at a more advanced level of moral judgment. Kohlberg has been particularly interested in the evolution of moral reasoning, and an understanding of his developmental model does enable one to view a particular aspect of identity in formation. Normatively over the course of adolescence, one can see movement from moral reasoning driven by self-interest and later by the need for social approval to moral reasoning motivated by a desire to uphold the law for its own sake. It is only beginning in late adolescence that one can sometimes hear a logic based on internalized ethical principles which may transcend the written law. Through Kohlberg's stage sequence, one can again see an internal developmental reorganization of self and other in the logic of decision making on matters moral. Where self-interest and then social approval were once necessary cornerstones of the self's architecture, both organizations may give way in late adolescence to a more differentiated and autonomous self, the author of its moral decisions based on a universal respect for human life. While responses to Kohlberg's dilemmas have been found to vary across contextual circumstances, the chapter illustrates how such findings can still be understood as part of an underlying, developmental process.

Loevinger views identity in a more holistic manner as that 'master trait of personality'. The ego, to Loevinger, is a screening device which allows us to perceive (or misperceive) reality in such a way as to reduce anxiety. Based on extensive psychometric studies of responses to her projective Sentence Completion Test, Loevinger has described a series of developmental stages in the formation of the ego or the experience of self. Taking great care to clarify her concept of the ego as one which is distinct from most earlier psychoanalytic usages of the term, Loevinger proceeds to detail stages through which this master trait of personality comes into being during infancy and develops to (or becomes arrested at) more mature stages of functioning during late adolescence and adulthood. In so doing, she examines common forms of impulse control, interpersonal style, conscious preoccupations and cognitive style at each stage. Normatively during adolescence, one can view the shift from an impulsive organization, where self-interest is the primary motivator, to one of conformity to dictates of the immediate social group. A more mature state of self-awareness seems to be the modal organization (at least within the United States) of the late adolescent and adult ego. At this level, some degree of self-awareness and appreciation of the multiple possibilities of situations exists. Loevinger's paradigm thus traces stages of self–other differentiation during adolescence from one of self-interest or conformity to others' attitudes and behaviors to an organization of self more distinct from others, appreciative of individuality and capable of greater mutuality in relationship.

Lastly, Kegan views the formation of identity as a lifelong evolutionary process of meaning-making. His developmental scheme draws upon Piagetian, Kolbergian and object-relations theories to conceptualize identity as an holistic process that subtends both cognition and affect. Identity formation is about how that which is regarded as self (or subject) is structured, lost and then re-formed. At various stages of the lifespan, the self is intrapsychically embedded in particular contexts from which it is unable to gain distance. Thus, the young child *is* its impulses, and only later does the self differentiate so as to *have* its impulses and desires. That which is regarded as other (or object) undergoes transformation as development proceeds to a new stage of self–other (subject–object) balance. The young adolescent's self is normatively embedded in its own needs and interests, unable to distance from or gain a perspective on them. Only later is this outworn self 'thrown away' so that that which was once subject (needs and interests) becomes object in a new subject–object balance. When such change occurs, the mid-adolescent can now reflect upon his or her own interests and coordinate them with those of other people. The limitation of this new normative mid-adolescent balance lies, however, in the self's embeddedness in its own interpersonal context: now one *is*, rather than *has*, his or her relationships. It is only during late adolescence that the self–other balance may tilt once again; if it so moves, the self comes to *have* its friendships (the new object) while becoming embedded in its institutional roles such as work (the new subject). Kegan's construct depicts identity development (or meaning-making) as an ongoing process of finding, losing and creating new balances between that which is regarded as self and that taken to be other in the social context. Normative adolescent development encompasses a time of increased movement in the balancing and rebalancing of subject and object.

The general aim of this volume is to understand how adolescents navigate through life, more or less successfully, to develop a sense of who they are and how they can best find personal satisfaction in the adult worlds of love and work. It also aims to highlight the ways in which context interacts with individual factors to shape individual identity trajectories. Five developmental models of the identity formation process are presented, accompanied by critical comment, reviews of related research, and a discussion of the implications that each theory holds for social response. Each model is based on particular assumptions, focuses on specific understandings of identity, adopts particular research methods, holds particular views about the role of context in development, describes mechanisms for change and differing implications for social response. Einstein once noted it is the theory that decides what we can observe. It is hoped that this theoretical overview, however, will in no way set limits to future ways of understanding and responding to the identity formation process of adolescence.

Further reading

Adams, G. R. and Marshall, S. (1996) 'A developmental social psychology of adolescence: understanding the person-in-context', *Journal of Adolescence* 19: 429–442.

Baumeister, R. F. and Muraven, M. (1996) 'Identity as adaptation to social, cultural, and historical context', *Journal of Adolescence* 19: 405–416.

Côté, J. E. and Levine, C. G. (2002) *Identity Formation, Agency, and Culture: A Social Psychological Synthesis*, Mahwah, NJ: Lawrence Erlbaum Associates.

Lerner, R. M. (2003) 'Applying developmental science for youth and families: Historical and theoretical foundations', in R. M. Lerner, F. Jacobs, and D. Wertleib (eds) *Handbook of Applied Development Science: Promoting Positive Child, Adolescent, and Family Development through Research, Policies, and Programs*, vol. 1, Newbury Park, CA: Sage.

2 Adolescence as identity synthesis

Erikson's psychosocial approach

> Siddhartha reflected deeply as he went on his way. He realized that he was no longer a youth; he was now a man. He realized that something had left him, like the old skin that a snake sheds. Something was no longer in him, something that had accompanied him right through his youth and was part of him: this was the desire to have teachers and to listen to their teachings. He had left the last teacher he had met, even he, the greatest and wisest teacher, the holiest, the Buddha. He had to leave him; he could not accept his teachings.
>
> (Hermann Hesse, *Siddhartha*, 1980)

In his novel, *Siddhartha*, Hermann Hesse movingly recounts the journey of a man in search of his own identity. The story opens in an idyllic communal setting along a sunny and tranquil river bank (complete with fig tree), as Siddhartha senses the first nuances of inner discontent. Family and friends alike love and admire the handsome and supple Siddhartha, and his destiny as a prince among Brahmins is the fate envisaged by all for this great Brahmin's son. For Siddhartha, however, knowledge of such a future brings no satisfaction or peace of mind. After a final meditation, the young man announces his intention of joining the Samanas, a wandering group of ascetics who practice a lifestyle in all ways contrary to the values held dear by childhood friends and mentors. Through such action, Siddhartha's single goal is to let the self die, to become empty, to become something other than himself. Despite all efforts of self-denial through pain, hunger, thirst, and fatigue, however, Siddhartha cannot escape his own existence. After several unsatisfying years with the Samanas, Siddhartha once more finds new hope for peace by testing the way of the Buddha in conquering the self. After a short time it becomes clear, however, that such efforts will also fail to bring salvation, and it is at this point that we meet

Siddhartha ruminating on his newfound learnings as he leaves the grove of the Buddha. It seems that neither complete identification with childhood's teachers nor their complete banishment from his existence help Siddhartha to solve the riddle of the self and so structure an identity that will see him through (or at least into) adult life. Perhaps no piece of literature so adequately and accurately anticipates the themes central to Erikson's writings on identity formation during adolescence, and it is to Siddhartha we shall later return for illumination of Erikson's concepts.

Erik Erikson was the first psychoanalytic writer to enquire seriously into the phenomenon of identity formation during adolescence. His approach was based upon, but diverged in important ways from, Freud's biologically based psychosexual orientation to personality development. Erikson moved beyond classic psychoanalysis with its focus on the id and libidinal drivers of development to emphasize the ego and its adaptive capacities in the environment. Rather than viewing others as objects of cathexis important to intrapsychic functioning as did Freud, Erikson saw others as interacting with and regulating the ego to provide a context in which the self can find meaning and cohere. Moving beyond Freud's goal of raising human misery to mere unhappiness, Erikson painted not only a more optimistic picture of human capabilities, but also shifted the emphasis of psychoanalysis from pathology to healthy functioning. Finally, Erikson recognized that personality development did not end in adolescence but rather continued to evolve throughout the lifespan.

Erikson the person

Erikson was born in Germany in 1902 to Danish parents. His birth was the result of an affair his mother had following the break-up of her first marriage. Erikson was raised by his mother and German pediatrician stepfather, whom his mother had met when Erik was 3 years old. Erikson did not learn of the circumstances of his parentage until adolescence. However, a sense of being 'different' both as a stepson in a reconstituted family and as a blond, blue-eyed Dane growing up in a German Jewish community pervaded much of Erikson's childhood. From adolescence, the search for his biological father occupied Erikson's attentions throughout much of his remaining life (Friedman 1999). In late adolescence, the young Erikson was drawn to the role of an artist, a 'passing' identity providing some income while still allowing the young man a much needed psychosocial moratorium before choosing his life's work. Additionally, sketching gave training in the recording of impressions, a skill vital to his later profession. (The artist's vocational choice also made a definitive statement to his step-father about the role in medicine the elder physician had envisaged for his stepson.) Throughout his late adolescence, Erikson drifted from one European city to another until his mid-twenties (Hopkins 1995). He later responded to Robert Coles' questioning about his youth: 'Yes, if ever an identity crisis was central and drawn out in somebody's life, it was so in mine' (Coles 1970: 180).

It was eventually the invitation of childhood friend Peter Blos to join the staff of a small school in Vienna which placed Erikson in a position to meet Freud's inner circle (Friedman 1999). In Vienna, he was invited by Anna Freud to become a training analysand and undertake training in child psychoanalysis. Again, not quite belonging to Freud's com-munity of medical rebels, Erikson's stepson relationship to the psycho-analytic profession did not furnish him with a more settled sense of vocational identity until much later, when his own artistic talents could be integrated with his psychoanalytic practice through theoretical writ-ing – the sketching of impressions through linguistic rather than visual form. It was there in Vienna that Erikson also married Canadian Joan Serson, who became his intellectual partner and editor for the rest of his life (Hopkins 1995).

Erikson and Joan left Vienna with their two young sons as Hitler came to power in Germany, and they eventually migrated to Boston where a psychoanalytic association had recently been founded. It was in this social context that Erikson, one of the society's few non-medical members, found a professional niche as one of the area's first practicing child analysts (Friedman 1999). Throughout his impressive career, Erikson accepted appointments at Yale, the University of California, Berkeley, the Austin Riggs Center and Harvard, all without accruing a single earned academic degree. It was in 1950 that Erikson's theoretical framework was adopted in total by the White House Conference on Children, which provided a national charter for child and adolescent development in the United States. In 1978, Harvard University awarded Erikson an honorary doctorate and later established the Erik H. and Joan M. Erikson Center to provide a forum for interdisciplinary studies of the life cycle. Erikson died in 1994 following a brief illness just prior to his ninety-second birthday.

It is not surprising that the theme of identity so central to Erikson's own life became central in his writings on life cycle development. Now, with at least ten books and a collection of individual papers dedicated to examining the nature of identity formation during adolescence and the life cycle, Erikson's contributions seem an appropriate starting point for enquiries into adolescent identity development.

The nature of ego identity

What then is identity and how does it develop during adolescence? Erikson first used the term 'ego identity' to describe a central disturbance among some returning Second World War veterans who were experiencing a loss of sameness and continuity in their lives:

> What impressed me most was the loss in these men of a sense of identity. They knew who they were; they had a personal identity. But it was as if subjectively, their lives no longer hung together – and never would again. There was a central disturbance in what I then started to call ego identity.
>
> (Erikson 1963: 42)

He continued by noting that it was often a decisive yet innocent moment in the lives of these soldiers wherein the needs of a man's social group, those of his biological organism, and those idiosyncratic to his own development and family history met in irreconcilable conflict, heralding the breakdown of personal meaning and life continuity.

Several concepts basic to Erikson's later work emerged from the observation of these veterans. First, identity seems to be most easily definable through its absence or loss; it is only when one can no longer take for granted the fabric of one's unique existence that its foundation threads become exposed and more clearly apparent. It is through such loss of ego identity or its developmental failure that opportunity does exist for understanding more normative modes of identity formation and the means by which society can provide for optimal development. Erikson's clinical experience sensitized him to questions of how identity forms and develops for the wider non-patient population.

Furthermore, the soldiers' tales brought the tripartite nature of identity into view. Freud had left psychoanalysis focused on the role played by biology in personality development. However, for a somewhat dissatisfied Erikson, 'traditional psychoanalytic method . . . cannot quite grasp identity because it has not developed terms to conceptualize the environment' (Erikson 1968: 24). While biology is important to individual biography, so too are an individual's life history and the presiding cultural and historical context, argued the analyst. For one medical officer veteran who came to Erikson's attention, it was the combination of lowered group morale in his unit followed by group panic over loss of leadership (social and historical context), physical fatigue and illness (biological state) and his lifelong denial of anger following a traumatic childhood incident (individual life history) which culminated in his loss of ego identity. Erikson conceptualizes and defines identity in an interdisciplinary way; biological endowment, personal organization of experience, and cultural milieu all conspire to give meaning, form and continuity to one's unique existence.

Following his initial statement on identity, Erikson was persuaded to expand and elaborate the construct. As a psychosocial phenomenon, he saw identity rooted both within the individual as well as within the communal culture (Erikson 1970). Subjectively, the theorist suggests what it feels like to have a sense of identity by citing a letter from William James to his wife:

> A man's character is discernible in the mental or moral attitude in which, when it came upon him, he felt himself most deeply and intensely active and alive. At such moments there is a voice inside which speaks and says: '*This* is the real me!'
>
> (James, cited in Erikson 1968: 199)

One knows when identity is present, in greater or lesser degree. For the individual, identity is partly conscious and partly unconscious. It gives one's life a feeling of sameness and continuity, yet also a 'quality of unselfconscious living', and is taken for granted by those in possession. Identity involves conflict and has its own developmental period during adolescence and youth, when biological endowment and intellectual processes must eventually meet societal expectation for a suitable display of adult functioning. Identity depends upon the past and determines the future; rooted in childhood, it serves as a base from which to meet later life tasks (Erikson 1970). Erikson does not elaborate in similar detail on the 'social' side of the psychosocial partnership, though he does stress the importance of the social context in providing 'something to search for and ... be true to' (Erikson 1968: 235). Erikson also views identity as a generational issue, pointing to the responsibility of the parent generation for providing an ideological framework for its youth (if only for the purpose of giving adolescents a structure against which to rebel and forge their own values).

Identity: development and resolutions

Perhaps Erikson's most concise account of how identity develops is to be found in *Toys and Reasons:* '[T]he process of identity formation depends on the interplay of what young persons at the end of childhood have come to mean to themselves and what they now appear to mean to those who become significant to them' (Erikson 1977: 106). This deceptively simple statement is based upon a number of developmental principles basic to Erikson's concept of identity. The theorist distinguishes identity formation, which generally occurs during adolescence, from the childhood processes of introjection and identification. That first sense of 'I', he suggests, emerges only through the trustful interplay with a parental figure during infancy (Erikson 1968). It is in the experience of a safe relationship that the child comes to know itself as distinct from its beloved developmental partner. At this point, *introjection* or the incorporation of another's image operates and prepares the way for more mature forms of identity resolution. During childhood 'being like' admired others and assuming their roles and values reflects the mechanism of *identification* as the primary means by which the self is structured. It is only when the adolescent is able to select some and discard others of these childhood identifications in accordance with his or her interests, talents and values that *identity formation* occurs. Identity formation involves a synthesis of these earlier identifications into a new configuration, which is based on but different from the sum of its individual parts. It is a process also dependent on social response; identity formation relies on the way society 'identifies the young individual, recognizing him as somebody who had to become the way he is and who, being the way he is, is taken for granted' (Erikson 1968: 159). Thus, identity does not first emerge during adolescence, but rather evolves through earlier stages of development and continues to be reshaped throughout the life cycle.

Erikson uses the term *epigenesis* to describe this property of identity development as well as broader aspects of personality change. Meaning literally 'upon' (*epi*) 'emergence' (*genesis*), epigenesis implies that 'one item develops on top of another in space and time' (Evans 1967: 21–22). Suffice it to say at this point that identity formation during adolescence emerges from what youngsters (through their introjections and identifications) at the end of childhood come to know as their selves. Yet it also transcends these earlier forms in the individual's realization and society's recognition of personal interests and talents.

To return now to Siddhartha and his beleaguered quest: in his journey, this Brahmin's son tries many means by which Erikson suggests identity resolution is possible. Through his childhood years, Siddhartha appears successfully to have internalized and identified with his father and the later vocational, ideological and sexual roles he is expected to play as an up-and-coming Brahmin priest. We are told of his father's happiness in watching the son 'growing up to be a great learned man, a priest, a prince among Brahmins' (Hesse 1980: 339). A psychosocial *foreclosure* appears well on the way, whereby Siddhartha seems prepared to step into predetermined roles in his family and culture. While Erikson does not detail this identity solution, it has been elaborated through empirical research which will be presented in a later section of this chapter.

Soon, however, shadows pass across Siddhartha's eyes and a 'restlessness of the soul' makes its presence known as he begins to 'feel the seeds of discontent within'. The late adolescent's decision to join a group of wandering ascetics whose values present a diametric contrast to all those of his own heritage seems to be a choice of *negative identity*. Such a solution for Siddhartha illustrates the ego's attempt to adhere to something distinctly other than its past, to go beyond the bounds of given experience and begin anew. Here there is no synthesis of previous identifications to give some foundation to later identity, but rather an effort to jettison all identifications and start the task of creating a self completely different from its origins. Siddhartha attempts to cancel his previous self through denial of physical needs and the self-destructive infliction of pain. Erikson comments on such a form of negative identity resolution:

> Such vindictive choices of a negative identity represent, of course, a desperate attempt at regaining some mastery in a situation in which the available positive identity elements cancel each other out. The history of such a choice reveals a set of conditions in which it is easier for the patient to derive a sense of identity out of a total identification with that which he is least supposed to be than to struggle for a feeling of reality in acceptable roles which are unattainable with his inner means.
>
> (Erikson 1968: 176)

For some troubled adolescents, it is better to be somebody totally other than what existed during childhood rather than struggle to reintegrate the past into a present and future having some continuity with one's previous existence. There is often much relief following the choice of a negative identity, however destructive that solution may ultimately be.

For Siddhartha, however, that relief did not come. We are told of his realization that complete immersion in the 'contra-culture' of the Samanas' community and later Buddhist collective fail to solve the riddle of his existence. He departs, and it is at this point that we meet the young man continuing his ruminations presented at the beginning of this chapter:

The reason why I do not know anything about myself, the reason why Siddhartha has remained alien and unknown to myself is due to one thing, to one single thing – I was afraid of myself, I was fleeing from myself. . . . I wished to destroy myself . . . in order to find in the unknown innermost, the nucleus of all things. . . . But by doing so, I lost myself on the way. . . . [Now] I will learn from myself, be my own pupil; I will learn from myself the secret of Siddhartha.

(Hesse 1980: 359)

At this point Siddhartha enters a *moratorium* that carries him in search of different roles that would seem to allow greater possibilities for synthesizing and integrating all that has gone before. Anxiety, however, soon becomes his companion:

[A]n icy chill stole over him. Previously when in deepest meditation, he was still his father's son, he was still a Brahmin of high standing, a religious man. Now he was only Siddhartha . . . he was overwhelmed by a feeling of icy despair, but he was more firmly himself than ever. That was the last shudder of his awakening, the last pains of birth. Immediately he moved on again . . . no longer homewards, no longer back to his father, no longer looking backwards.

(Hesse 1980: 360)

Siddhartha's 'awakening' or resolution to one part of his identity riddle brings with it a new challenge for development: to *achieve* an identity, a sense of self that synthesizes earlier identifications into a new whole that is now uniquely his own.

Siddhartha's life is a case study of the evolution of identity from adolescence into old age. After experiencing many roles and building various lifestyles that fit his innermost needs at the time, Siddhartha returns in his old age to the river over which many of his earlier life journeys had crossed and beside which he eventually finds peace. Through many inward and external travels in adult life, Siddhartha demonstrates how the achievement of an identity does not remain fixed, resolved once and for all, but rather is constantly open to change through shifting needs and circumstances:

Such a sense of identity is never gained nor maintained once and for all. Like a good conscience, it is constantly lost and regained, although more lasting and more economical methods of maintenance and restoration are evolved and fortified in late adolescence.

(Erikson 1956: 74)

An optimal sense of identity

If soma, ego and society have done their jobs, what should be present by the end of adolescence and the beginnings of early adulthood? Subjectively, there should be a sense of well-being: 'Its most obvious concomitants are a feeling of being at home in one's body, a sense of "knowing where one is going" and an inner assuredness of anticipated recognition from those who count' (Erikson 1968: 165). With its psychosocial connotation, optimal identity formation should show itself through commitment to those work roles, values and sexual orientations that best fit one's own unique combination of needs and talents. It is this more directly observable commitment feature of ego identity that has been at the heart of most empirical attempts to address some of its properties.

Identity as a stage in the life-cycle scheme

As hinted previously, identity has a past. Erikson portrays identity as the fifth stage in an eight-act sequence of life conflicts one encounters along the road from birth to death in old age. While the primary focus in this chapter is on identity, it nevertheless is important to appreciate the contribution that both earlier and later acts make to the complete life drama.

Erikson conceptualizes the life cycle as a series of stages, critical periods of development which involve bipolar conflict that must be addressed and resolved before one can proceed unhindered. According to the epigenetic principle, each stage has 'its time of special ascendancy, until all parts have arisen to form a functional whole' (Erikson 1968: 92). There is a proper rate and sequence of development; the child must crawl before she can walk.

The polarity of each stage presents a crisis, a crucial turning point where development must make a move for better or for worse as one orients to the physical environment and social and historical context: 'Each successive stage and crisis has a special relation to one of the basic elements of society, and this for the simple reason that the human life cycle and man's institutions have evolved together' (Erikson 1963: 250). The developmental possibilities of each stage do not demand 'either/or' resolutions, but rather some dynamic balance of 'more or less' between the poles; hopefully that balance will favor the positive end. Erikson describes his fifth stage, which comes to the fore during adolescence, as that of *identity versus role confusion*. Here, as mentioned earlier, the young person is faced with the psychosocial dilemma of synthesizing yet transcending earlier identifications of childhood to realize aptitudes in social roles, while the community in turn provides its recognition and contribution to an individual's sense of self. Ironically, it may be one's willingness to undergo times of temporary uncertainty that gives the achievement resolution its ultimate strength. Stage resolutions should not be regarded as achievement scales based only on the more positive pole; they represent a balance between positive and negative poles that determines an individual's characteristic mode of adapting to the environment. One does not, however, enter the life drama during the fifth identity formation act. Identity versus role confusion has been preceded by four earlier stages, each having a necessary place in the unfolding chain of life-cycle tasks. All of Erikson's eight stages are now briefly reviewed to illustrate their relationships to the identity crisis of adolescence.

Trust versus mistrust/hope

As the opening scene in the life-cycle production, *trust versus mistrust* sets the stage for all that is to follow. It is during infancy that the developmental crisis of trust is met, based in part on Freud's biological concern with early oral experience. Through the mutual regulation and interaction between caretaker and infant, a rudimentary sense of ego identity is born. The child comes to know itself in relation to another and gains a sense of inner continuity, sameness and trust in itself and its developmental partner.

In her short story, 'The Door of Life', Enid Bagnold recounts the fine-tuning of responses between a mother and her 4-day-old infant that reflect the building blocks of basic trust:

> [M]other and child [were] on the rails of development with fine movements, [caretaker] setting order into the baby's life, creating peace, keeping off the world, watching, reflecting, adjusting, jockeying the untidiness of civilization into perfection, teaching even so tiny a baby manners and endurance; to cry at the proper time for exercise, to sleep at the proper hour.
>
> (Bagnold 1972: 7)

This heightened sensitivity of both players to the nuances of the partner's movements illustrates the importance of mutuality to development. The quality of the caretaker's messages gives the infant a sense that it is all right to be, to be oneself, and to become 'what other people trust one will become' (Erikson 1963: 249).

Somewhere in between the polar extremes of trust and mistrust, most of us find an adaptive balance; neither complete trust nor complete mistrust of the world is ultimately beneficial. An optimal resolution to this infant crisis will find scales tipped more firmly toward the trusting pole, leading to *hope*, which in turn is the basic ingredient of later survival. It is also through this dynamic balance that a sense of 'I', as one who can hope, emerges to serve as the very rudimentary foundation for identity in adolescence.

Autonomy versus shame and doubt/will

Following the sense of basic trust, life's next developmental hurdle during the second and third years is that of developing autonomy. Again finding a biological base in Freud's anal stage of development, Erikson's sense of autonomy is characterized by the child's increasing awareness of its self through control of bodily functions and expression of other motor and linguistic skills (performing in concert with the expectations of important others in the social milieu).

Holding on or letting go of body wastes is one of the child's earliest opportunities to exercise complete control over the outcome of events, regardless of parental desire. Such auspicious occasions as toilet-training episodes provide toddlers with an experience of *will*, something originating from within in response to social conditions and highlighting the issue that wills of developmental partners can differ. With *trust* in order, it is now possible to risk one's own *will* against the response that such self-expression may bring. This 'counterpointing of identities' again carries the rudiments of later adolescent identity.

Newfound linguistic and locomotor skills conspire to aid the development of autonomy during toddlerhood. By the age of two and a half years, the child is using the personal pronoun 'I' (as well as the declarative 'no') to give further evidence of will. Now possessing the motoric status of 'one who can walk', one is also in a position to encounter social response, for better or worse. The account of socialization experiences for a young Papago Indian girl cited by Erikson illustrates again the role the social environment plays in aiding and abetting this developmental task:

> [T]he man of the house turned to his three-year-old granddaughter and asked her to close the door. The door was heavy and hard to

shut. The child tried, but it did not move. Several times the grand-father repeated: 'Yes, close the door'. No one jumped to the child's assistance. No one took the responsibility away from her. On the other hand, there was no impatience, for after all the child was small. They sat gravely waiting until the child succeeded and her grandfather gravely thanked her. It was assumed the task would not be asked of her unless she could perform it, and having been asked, the responsibility was hers alone just as if she were a grown woman.

(Erikson 1963: 236)

Such an experience of personal autonomy in completing a difficult task is met with a social response that can only convey a sense of respect for and recognition of the child's developing 'I'.

Like all of Erikson's stages, an adaptive balance between the two extremes is necessary for optimal development. When the scale is weighted towards shame and doubt, one retains a sense of inferiority, of being 'not good enough' through all life's later stages. As a corollary, however, it is knowledge that one is fallible and capable of evoking a less than favorable social response that tempers absolute autonomy and serves to regulate the self in a social order.

Initiative versus guilt/purpose

The third act of Erikson's life drama is met during the preschool years and coincides with Freud's phallic stage of development; pleasure in infantile genitality gives rise to Erikson's social as well as sexual sense of being 'on the make' in the stage of *initiative versus guilt*. Now adept at mastering such skills as playing batman on a tricycle and more com-plicated sex roles, the preschooler possesses the ability to imagine. This capacity, so central to early childhood play, carries with it the seeds for *initiative* in the translating of thoughts to action. Only from an autonomous position is it possible to initiate; in knowing *that* one is, it is then possible to learn *what* one is. Issues such as what kind of person to become and what kind of sex role to adopt now become critical questions. From initiative grows a sense of purpose and ambition vital to tasks of adolescence and adulthood. It is initiative that 'sets the direction toward the possible and the tangible which permits the dreams of early childhood to be attached to the goals of an active adult life' (Erikson 1963: 258).

Locomotor skills and language continue to develop. One is now able to move and expend energy finding out what this status of one who walks means and of how moving can be used for purposes other than pleasure alone to accomplish more far-reaching goals. Language becomes a tool for communication with others in sorting out the often complex and confusing state of world affairs, or a least those of the preschool playground. The following conversations, recorded by Welker (1971), illustrates not only this new linguistic function but also the young child's fascination with sexual differences and roles in later life:

> Laura got her hair cut very short. She and Tony were on the swings.
> *Laura:* Tony, do I look like a boy?
> *Tony:* No.
> *Laura:* Look at the back of my head where my hair is so short.
> *Tony:* No, you're a girl.
> *Laura:* You know I'm a girl cause you saw me before I got my hair cut.
> *Tony:* I know you're a girl cause you have curly hair . . .
>
> Laurie, playing with Marian, said: 'When I grow up, I'm going to be a daddy.'
> Marian replied, 'You can't. Girls grow up into ladies.'
> 'Yes I can too,' retorted Laurie, 'Look, I've got big hands, and daddies have big hands.'
>
> (Welker 1971: 67–68)

Thus, identity in adolescence has roots in the purposeful activities of early childhood. Out of initiative comes the ability to fantasize about and experiment with social and sexual roles of critical importance to adolescent and young adult life.

At this stage, however, the potential for guilt exists. A tip of the scales toward this negative end may leave the individual immobilized in taking future action through guilt or fear. An optimal balance would see boundless sexual and social initiative tempered by an awareness of the possibilities for social criticism and sanctions. Such a balance can best be obtained by a social environment aware of its role in fostering curiosity within the limits of cultural convention.

Industry versus inferiority/competence

According to Freud, the primary school years are marked by a shift from libidinal energy focused on bodily zones to a time of sexual latency; attention becomes channeled outward towards the world of the school yard and neighborhood. In contrast to Freud's focus on sexual latency, Erikson views the primary school years as ones in which the practicing of skills and the completion of tasks, anticipating those of later adult work roles, is life's main focus. Industry has been described as an apprenticeship to life; feelings of competence and achievement are the optimal results here. Thus, it is only through the *initiative* of an *autonomous* self which *trusts* the social milieu that the challenge of *industry versus inferiority* can be addressed. Social recognition for a job well done is the milieu's contribution to fostering development at this stage.

In her short story, 'Prelude', Katherine Mansfield illustrates an optimal response to industry in a brief interchange between young Kezia and her grandmother:

> [S]he decided to go up to the house and ask the servant girl for an empty match-box. She wanted to make a surprise for the grandmother. . . . First she would put a leaf inside with a big violet lying on it, then she would put a very small white picotee, perhaps, on each side of the violet, and then would sprinkle some lavender on the top, but not to cover the heads. She often made these surprises for the grandmother, and they were always most successful.
>
> 'Do you want a match, my granny?'
>
> 'Why, yes, child, I believe a match is just what I'm looking for.'
>
> The grandmother slowly opened the box and came upon the picture inside.
>
> 'Good gracious, child! How you astonished me!'
>
> 'I can make her one every day here,' she thought, scrambling up the grass on her slippery shoes.
>
> (Mansfield 1972: 90)

Such wisdom in social response can only serve to strengthen the sense of accomplishment in making and giving experienced by this young girl. Crucial to this sense of industry is the 'positive identification with those who know things and know how to do things' (Erikson 1968: 125). One special teacher in the lives of many gifted individuals has often been credited as the spark which ignited outstanding later achievements (Erikson 1968). Finding one's special skills and talents during the phase of industry may have long-range implications for later vocational identity. Wise parents, teachers or other important identification figures play a critical role in fostering a sense of industry or inferiority.

Erikson (1968: 124) notes the child's possible negative resolution of this stage, 'the development of an estrangement from himself and from his tasks'. A home environment insufficiently preparing the child for life outside its boundaries, or failure of the wider cultural milieu to recognize and reward real accomplishments of its younger members, may be perpetrators of inferiority. Again, healthy resolution to the industry versus inferiority conflict would see a ratio favoring industry. At the same time, feelings of limitless competence must be checked by an awareness of one's genuine limitations in order for optimal development to occur.

Identity versus role confusion/fidelity

Moving away from Freud's biological orientation to personality development during puberty, Erikson saw physiological change as only one aspect of a more pervasive adolescent dilemma: 'But even where a person can adjust sexually in a technical sense and may at least superficially develop what Freud called genital maturity, he may still be weakened by the identity problems of our era . . . fully developed genitality is not a goal to be pursued in isolation' (Erikson, cited in Evans 1967: 29). Identity, to Erikson, incorporates yet transcends the endocrinological revolution of puberty to include psychosocial issues. It is finding a 'feeling of reality' in socially approved roles.

Drawing upon resolutions to earlier stages, one must now approach the task of identity formation. Erikson suggests fidelity is the essence of identity. To become faithful and committed to some ideological world view is the task of this stage; to find a cause worthy of one's vocational energies and reflecting one's basic values is the stuff of which identity crises are made. It is ultimately to affirm and be affirmed by a social order that identity aspires.

We have already seen and described some possible ways of negotiating life's conflicts during the fifth act through Siddhartha's quest. Suffice it to say here that the stage of *identity versus role confusion* is one of life's critical crossroads in the transition to adult life; not only must this stage incorporate a *trustworthy* 'I' who has evolved as an *autonomous* individual capable of *initiating* and completing satisfying tasks modeled by significant others, but it must also transcend such identifications to produce an 'I' sensitive to its own needs and talents and capable of chipping its own niche in the surrounding social landscape.

In contrast to Freud, the curtain on development for Erikson does not fall at this point. With a favorable resolution to the identity crisis of adolescence, it is now and only now possible to proceed to the stage of *intimacy* – that meeting of an 'I' with an 'I', each firm on its own unique identity foundations. The remaining three acts of the life-cycle production, however, involve a shift of developmental focus from 'I' to 'we'.

Intimacy versus isolation/love

For Erikson, intimacy in young adulthood encompasses far more than sexual fulfillment; in fact, sexual activity may be used in the service of identity conflict rather than as a reflection of *love*. 'Intimacy is the ability to fuse your identity with somebody else's without fear that you're going to lose something yourself' (Erikson, cited in Evans 1967: 48). Intimacy involves the desire to commit oneself to a relationship, even when such commitment may call for personal sacrifice or compromise. Intimacy involves communion and can occur in a variety of forms – in same and opposite sex friendships, in love, in sexual union and even in relationship with oneself or one's life commitments (Evans 1967).

To Erikson, genuine intimacy is not possible until issues of identity are reasonably well resolved. Relationships of earlier adolescence often serve only the purpose of self-definition rather than intimacy; another may be used merely as a mirror to reflect a form less visible to its owner. Relationships may also involve attempts to find one's own identity through merger with another – efforts which similarly preclude intimacy. Indeed some marriages serve such a function for those in whom identity issues remain unresolved: 'Many young people marry in order to find their identity in and through another person, but this is difficult where the very choice of partner was made to resolve severe unconscious conflict' (Erikson, cited in Evans 1967: 49). Ultimately, there is only enough identity for one.

Drawing upon Martin Buber's concepts of 'I' and 'Thou', Moustakas captures the character of genuine intimacy in the following passage:

> Growth of the self requires meetings between I and Thou, in which each person recognizes the other as he is; each says what he means and means what he says; each values and contributes to the unfolding of the other without imposing or manipulating. And this always means some degree of distance and independence. It does not depend on one revealing to another everything that exists within, but requires only that the person be who he is, genuinely present.
>
> (Moustakas 1974: 92)

Here the identities of 'I' and 'Thou' must be assured in order for such a relationship of mature, unselfish love to occur.

Isolation is the psychosocial alternative creating conflict at this stage. If true 'engagement' with another is elusive, one may 'isolate himself and enter, at best, only stereotyped and formalized interpersonal relations; or one may, in repeated hectic attempts and dismal failures, seek intimacy with the most improbable partners' (Erikson 1968: 167). Isolation can occur in the context of relationship just as intimacy can exist in the physical absence of a partner. '[T]here are partnerships which amount to an isolation *à deux*, protecting both partners from the necessity to face the next critical development – that of generativity' (Erikson 1963: 266). An ideal balance between intimacy and isolation results through a relationship which allows time for both withdrawal and communion between partners. It is the recognition of one's ultimate aloneness which gives intimacy its base, and it is one's capacity for security in that aloneness which makes genuine intimacy possible.

Generativity versus stagnation/care

The next task for that 'we' to meet during adulthood is taking a place in society at large and *caring* – for one's offspring, productions, social contributions and future generations. Erikson again notes the limitations of Freud's psychosexual scheme with its emphasis on genital maturity as the epitome of development:

> I would go even further than that and say that Freud, by paying so much attention to the prepubertal impediments of the genital encounter itself, underemphasized the procreative drive as also important to man. I think this is a significant omission, because it can lead to the assumption that a person graduates from psychoanalytic treatment when he has been restored to full genitality. As in many movies, where the story ends when lovers finally find one another, our therapies often end when the person can consummate sexuality in a satisfactory, mutually enriching way. This is an essential stage but I would consider generativity a further psychosexual stage, and would postulate that its frustration results in symptoms of self-absorption.
>
> (Erikson, cited in Evans 1967: 52)

Erikson's concept here does not imply that generativity can be met only in parenting; it resides also in the desire of an *autonomous* 'I' as part of an *intimate* 'we' to contribute to the present and future well-being of other life cycles. Such generative individuals provide the models needed for introjection and identification by younger members of the society.

The counterpart of generativity is stagnation or self-absorption, whereby personal comfort becomes the primary motivator for action. When this resolution occurs, individuals 'often begin to indulge themselves as if they were their own – or one another's – one and only child; and where conditions favor it, early invalidism, physical or psychological, becomes the vehicle of self-concern' (Erikson 1963: 267). Alternatively, procreation or other forms of production are not necessarily the expression of generativity; true care must take root for generativity to flourish.

Again, an optimal balance between generativity and self-absorption is necessary. One must be selective of those people and projects to nurture in the interests of self-preservation; unlimited energy and resources are not available to one through life's passages and some attention to self-interest is crucial in perpetuating a generative life attitude. As in all previous life stages, the ratio needs to favor the more positive pole for healthy development to proceed, however.

Integrity versus despair/wisdom

The final act of the life drama requires facing the developmental task of balancing *integrity* with *despair*. More difficult to define than preceding stages, integrity 'is the acceptance of one's one and only life cycle as something that had to be and that, by necessity, permitted of no substitutions. . . . In such final consolidation, death loses its sting' (Erikson 1963: 268). One gauge of integrity is the ability to accept one's own mortality. A life lived in contributing one's guidance, gifts and talents to future generations is not regretted, and death is not feared as time shortens before the last curtain call. An old age favoring integrity is characterized by the *wisdom* of mature judgment and a reflective understanding of one's own 'accidental' place in the historical scheme of things.

On the other hand, the potential for despair in old age exists to counterpoint integrity. A life culminating in despair finds remaining time too short to locate a different path toward a more comfortable and satisfying conclusion. In his 'Reflections on Dr Borg's Life Cycle', Erikson (1976) illustrates the conflict of the final stage of development through a character study of Dr Borg, the leading figure in Ingmar Bergman's film *Wild Strawberries*. In a car journey to Lund to receive the highest honor of his medical profession, an aged and retired Dr Borg also departs on a psychological journey back in time through his own development. Borg's precarious psychosocial balance as the scene opens is tipped toward despair:

At the age of seventy-six, I feel that I'm much too old to lie to myself. But of course I can't be too sure. My complacent attitude toward my own truthfulness could be dishonesty in disguise, although I don't quite know what I might want to hide. . . . I have of my own free will withdrawn almost completely from society. . . . I have found myself rather alone in my old age.

(Bergman, cited in Erikson 1976: 2)

One of the car's passengers, Borg's daughter-in-law Marianne, takes it upon herself to drive the old man's despair to the surface. Through her doings, Borg is offered some opportunity for salvation through the journey by rebalancing solutions to earlier psychosocial stages that enable him to find a more fulfilling old age. Identity themes are carried forward for Borg as he reworks his sense of self to become more intimate with and caring about that which he will soon leave behind.

So identity themes are met again in old age, where the sense of the 'I' that has developed and established itself in social contexts through earlier stages of development must rest content (or not) on what it *is*. Unlike Dr Borg in Bergman's film fantasy, such opportunities for change are limited for most:

[A] sense of 'I' becomes a most sensitive matter again in old age, as an individual's uniqueness gradually and often suddenly seems to have lost any leeway for further variations such as those which seemed to open themselves with each previous stage. Now, non-Being must be faced 'as is'.

(Erikson 1984: 102)

The favorable balance of integrity with despair again gives wisdom its ultimate strength. Remaining open to existential issues of being and non-being as well as Kierkegaard's sense of dread, present very real opportunities for despair. Willingness to address sobering questions such as the meaning of one's existence makes deeper the tranquility that integrity brings.

Identity is thus an ingredient of all stages of the human life cycle. Having roots in infant trust, identity is also present in the *integrity* versus *despair* conflict of old age. Identity formation during adolescence reflects developmental resolutions to all preceding stages and serves as base for personality developments that lie ahead. In adolescence, however, identity assumes a change in form. Through a process different from the internalizations and identifications of earlier psychosocial stages, its configuration now evolves into a new structure, different from (but related to) the sum of its parts. Through the synthesis and resynthesis of all earlier childhood identifications, the 'I', like Siddhartha's sense of self, is now ready to move forward, 'no longer homewards . . . no longer looking backwards'.

Criticism of Erikson's identity concept

Erikson's definition of identity has been criticized on a number of grounds. Unclear or imprecise formulations of identity have been the source of numerous difficulties for many readers of Erikson. The analyst himself suggests that the concept should be defined 'from different angles', and proceeds to use the term for emphasizing different issues at different points. At times, identity refers to a structure or a configuration; at other points it refers to a process. Still on other occasions, identity is viewed as both a conscious subjective experience as well as an unconscious entity. In a rather candid comment given during a radio interview, Erikson stated, 'I think one could be more precise than I am, or than I am able to be. I very much feel that scientific training and logic would have helped a lot' (Erikson, cited in Stevens 1983: 112). Yet it is this very breadth of phenomena captured through Erikson's formulation of identity that social scientists have argued make the construct more amenable to research than much of psychodynamic theory.

Empirical validation of the psychosocial issues addressed at different stages that were described by Erikson has been questioned by some critics. Ciaccio (1971) was one of the first investigators to test whether or not conflicts purported by Erikson to be inherent in some of the early developmental stages were actually at issue for groups of boys aged 5, 8 and 11 years. Although psychosocial strengths or attitudes did seem to progress with age in the sequence described by Erikson, the negative aspects (or crises) of the stages did not find such confirmation. Additional research using Constantinople's (1969) Inventory of Psychosocial Development has raised questions regarding Erikson's proposed timing of development; issues of focal concern at given ages have varied across samples, possibly reflecting the influence of different cultural and/or historical factors (Waterman and Whitbourne 1981). While finding empirical support for central propositions of Erikson's theory, Côté and Levine (1989) have argued that longitudinal studies are necessary that address problems of causation from a wider social psychological perspective.

Erikson's views on womanhood and the inner space have drawn equally sharp responses from critics. To Erikson, anatomy is destiny and initially determines the style of engagement with the social milieu;

reflecting sexual morphology, boys emphasize outer space in their predominantly aggressive and intrusive play, while girls focus on the inner space in their more peaceful, passive activities. The scientific validity of this observation has been called into question by Caplan (1979), who failed to replicate results from Erikson's single experiment in any findings from a series of studies. Caplan further notes that the statistical grounds of Erikson's claim to significant sex differences in play configurations accounted for less than 2 per cent of the total variance in the analyst's results. Furthermore, many have attacked Erikson's statement that the problem of identity definition for women must wait until a suitable partner is found and 'welcomed to the inner space'. Still others have argued that stages of identity and intimacy in Erikson's scheme may be reversed or at least coexist for women (e.g. Gilligan 1982a). Additional critics have indicated Erikson needs either to add new stages or substantially modify existing ones to portray accurately both male and female development (Vaillant and Milofsky, 1980; Franz and White, 1985; Logan 1986).

Additionally, Erikson's epigenetic scheme of identity formation may reflect cultural bias. It would seem that only in cultural contexts which allow choice as to social, ideological and vocational roles are conditions for identity crises ripe. While Marcia (1983) argues that such social conditions of choice promote ego development at puberty, they may not reflect the cultural norm for the majority of the world's teenage population. Furthermore, Bettelheim (1969) argues that Erikson's model of psychosocial development needs modification when applied to development of children growing up in extended family circumstances. The continuity and sameness important to basic trust between mother and child takes on a different slant in the communal child rearing experiences for the kibbutz infant. Despite such criticism, however, Erikson's model continues to offer important insights and has sparked an array of empirical inquiries into identity formation during adolescence.

Measuring ego identity

Erikson's vivid descriptions of the adolescent identity formation process have presented a challenge to researches attempting to examine and understand the phenomenon empirically. In a frequently cited definition of ego identity, Erikson (1959: 116) describes many different dimensions of identity's structure and functions: '[Ego identity is] an evolving configuration of constitutional givens, idiosyncratic libidinal needs, favored capacities, significant identifications, effective defenses, successful sublimations, and consistent roles'. It is not surprising, then, that different research traditions have emerged to examine different dimensions of the identity formation experience. Erikson himself never wished to undertake empirical research to validate his theory of personality development. He devised no single measure of ego identity to enable researchers to explore its many properties.

Three general approaches have arisen to study the identity formation process as conceptualized by Erikson. One stream has focused on the place that 'identity versus role confusion' holds in Erikson's larger, eight-stage epigenetic scheme. Investigators working within this framework have argued that by focusing on only one psychosocial stage, identity research fails to do full justice to Erikson's model of life-cycle development (Constantinople 1967, 1969; Hamachek 1988, 1989; Markstrom-Adams *et al.* 1994; Rosenthal *et al.* 1981). A second orientation has focused on the 'identity versus role confusion' task alone. From this perspective, identity is defined as a resolution that lies somewhere on a continuum between identity and role confusion, and measurement scales developed within this tradition have explored identity scores in relation to other personality variables (for example, Simmons 1983). A third general approach has focused on one of the specific dimensions of identity described by Erikson. Van Hoof (1999), for example, has studied issues of spatial and temporal continuity during adolescence, while Blasi and his colleagues (Blasi 1988; Blasi and Glodis 1995) have investigated subjective aspects of identity. However, it is the element of fidelity which has attracted greatest research attention, and it has been through studies initiated by James Marcia (1966, 1967) that the process of identity exploration and commitment have been most fully examined. Marcia's elaboration of Erikson's fifth psychosocial stage has now generated over 500 published studies of the identity formation process, and this approach will be the focus for researches overviewed later in this chapter.

Marcia's ego identity statuses

On the basis of Erikson's writings on identity, Marcia (1966, 1967) developed the Identity Status Interview (ISI). This interview has been revised over the past 30 years, and current early and mid-adolescent forms, late adolescent and adult versions are available with interview guidelines and scoring instructions (Marcia *et al.* 1993). The interview consists of domains deemed to be salient to the adolescent in question. For the late adolescent, areas commonly probed are vocational plans, religious and political values, sexual expression and sex role beliefs.

Semi-structured questions are designed to assess any current commitments the individual may hold, how stable they may be and how the commitments have been undertaken. Interviews generally last 30 to 45 minutes and are taperecorded for later assessment. Interrater reliability has generally been about 80 per cent agreement between two raters. Among studies that have corrected for chance agreements, this percentage far exceeds agreements expected by chance. Expected patterns of relationships with other variables have helped to establish construct validity of the ISI (Marcia *et al.* 1993).

Marcia reasoned that fidelity or commitment to a vocation, a set of meaningful values (religious and political beliefs) and a sexual identity (sexual expression and sex role values) are the observable cues indicative of a more or less successful identity resolution during late adolescence for those in western contexts. From Marcia's observations, however, commitment or fidelity comes in several forms. While Erikson saw identity as some balance between commitment and confusion about one's roles in society, Marcia identified two distinct types of commitment and two of non-commitment. Individuals adopting an achievement or foreclosure orientation have both made commitments to various social roles. However, identity achieved individuals have done so following a crisis or decision-making period, while foreclosures have bypassed the identity formation process and merely adopted roles and values of childhood identification figures. Similarly, moratoriums and diffusions are both lacking commitment to a place in the social order. However, moratoriums are undergoing an evaluative process (ego synthesis) in search of suitable social roles, while diffusions are not. These commitment types or identity statuses have been empirically validated as four distinct modes of dealing with identity defining issues of late adolescence.

A further popular measure of identity status has been developed by Adams (1999) and Adams *et al.* (1989). This paper and pencil Objective Measure of Ego Identity Status-II (EOM-EIS-II) is comprised of 64 items presented in a Likert-scale format that assess the degree of identity achievement, moratorium, foreclosure and diffusion an individual demonstrates within eight identity defining domains. Occupational, political, religious and philosophy of life values constitute the general ideological domain, while friendship, dating, sex role and recreational values comprise a general interpersonal domain. Reliability has been established over a number of studies via measures of internal consistency. Cronbach alphas have generally been around 0.66. Test–retest reliability studies have shown an average correlation of 0.76. Efforts to establish construct, predictive and concurrent validity have generally produced moderate to high relationships between the EOM-EIS-II and associated measures (Adams 1999).

Historical backdrop to Erikson's and Marcia's psychosocial schemes

Erikson's theoretical writings on identity and personality development emerged from origins in psychoanalysis. Erikson (1959), however, was among the early psychoanalysts to focus on ego rather than id processes in personality development. Classic psychoanalysts had also focused primarily upon the Oedipal phase of development, when the superego (conscience) was formed, and balances among the personality structures of id, ego and superego were established (Marica 1994). Interest in pre-Oedipal development and the structuralization of the self had received little attention until Erikson's writings. Freud had used the concept of identity only once to refer to his Jewish heritage (Erikson 1959). However, as a student and analysand of Anna Freud, Erikson was undoubtedly influenced by the adaptive processes of the ego and its mechanisms of defense. Hartmann (1958) had also focused upon the ego and formulated concepts of primary and secondary autonomy and ego epigenesis, while Rapaport (1960) and White (1959), respectively, had contributed work on the role of the ego in development and in the drive toward competence. However, it was Erikson (1959) who focused attention on the adaptive processes of ego development across the entire life cycle. Erikson's writings, however, were never well integrated into the psychoanalytic mainstream, nor was he adequately credited with his early influence on the field of psychoanalytic ego psychology (Wallerstein 1998). Indeed, it was only Rappaport (cited in Erikson 1959) who delineated the contributions of but two men, Hartmann and Erikson, pointing out the profound influences each had on the field of ego psychoanalytic psychology (Wallerstein 1998).

A number of contemporary object relations approaches emerged from Erikson's writings, laying varied emphases on the role of relationships in the development of the self and on elements of the surrounding milieu in individual identity development. Jacobson (1964), Bowlby (1969) and Mahler (Mahler *et al.* 1975) all examined the role of internal representations of relationships during infancy and early childhood in the development of an autonomous sense of self and other, while Winnicott (1953) described the role of transitional objects in this process. Blos (1967) examined further changes to these internal representations during the course of adolescence. However, it was Jacobsen (1964) who unfortunately set the rather dismissive tone for Erikson's writings on the development of the self. Thus, Erikson's influence as a fore-runner to later object relations and ego psychoanalytic theory has only rarely been acknowledged (Wallerstein 1998).

James Marcia (2004) describes how his interest in Erikson's (1959) concept of identity arose during his clinical internship. Marcia, under the supervision of David Gutmann (Erikson's former teaching assistant at Harvard), was assigned to undertake a psychodiagnostic review on a 16-year-old boy, a new admission to the hospital. The boy's psychological tests indicated a severe thought disorder, indicative of schizophrenia. However, six months later, the youth was released from the hospital with no signs of this illness. Marcia reflected on this experience as he selected a dissertation topic: the construct validation of Erikson's identity construct. With many false starts and amused skepticism from peers and professors, Marcia constructed the identity statuses. Over the years of his career, Marcia has wished to make Erikson more accessible to the social science community. With his construct now appearing in virtually every major textbook on adolescence, he has certainly succeeded in accomplishing that mission.

Research findings on adolescent identity formation

While identity and its development during adolescence have been examined from many angles, the review below will focus on those investigations using Marcia's (1966; Marcia *et al.* 1993) identity status paradigm. Early research with the identity statuses focused primarily on individual personality, cognitive and relational differences across the various identity status positions, while more recent work has examining developmental and contextual processes associated with identity status change.

Identity achievement

Marcia (1979, 1994) has suggested what it might be like to sit down with a young person in each of the identity statuses through brief character sketches based on his own observations of university students. For the identity achieved, flexible strength describes their manner of relating to the world. Thoughtful and introspective, they do not become immobilized by their reflections and function cognitively very well under stress. They may or may not be aware that their identity defining commitments may very likely undergo future change. A sense of humor as well as openness to new experiences accompany a willingness to listen and judge according to their own inner standards.

From empirical studies, identity achieved youths have scored consistently higher on measures of autonomy and are less reliant on the opinions of others to make their decisions. In terms of cognitive capacities, the identity achieved function well under stress and use more planful, rational and logical decision-making strategies than other identity statuses (Blustein and Philips 1990; Boyes and Chandler 1992; Marcia 1966, 1967). No significant differences in intelligence have appeared across the identity statuses as assessed in various studies by at least six different measures (Marcia *et al.* 1993). The identity achieved have demonstrated the highest levels of ego development (Berzonsky and Adams 1999). They engage in intimate relationships and are androgynous in sex role attitudes (Fitch and Adams 1983; Kacerguis and Adams 1980). Identity achievements function most frequently at the highest level of post-conventional moral reasoning (Rowe and Marcia 1980; Skoe and Marcia 1991). The identity achieved, along with foreclosed individuals, are satisfied with the way they are (Makros and McCabe 2001). The identity achieved are intrapsychically more differentiated from others and more secure in their attachment patterns (Ginsburg and Orlofsky 1981; Josselson 1987; Kroger and Haslett 1988; Papini *et al.* 1989). The identity achieved are able to perceive parental strengths and weaknesses and have come from families which have parents supporting adolescent autonomy (Grotevant and Cooper 1985; Willemsen and Waterman 1991).

Moratorium

From Marcia's (1979, 1994) character portraits, some moratoriums may be animated and anxious in their identity struggles, while others are more quietly thoughtful. Moratoriums do not yield easily to demands for conformity and have a stable sense of self-esteem. Although able to describe what intimacy must be like, moratoriums are not as a rule *in* such a relationship. Intrapsychically, they have difficulties detaching themselves from parents, particularly the parent of the opposite sex. This difficulty may underlie reluctance for relationship commitment. Moratoriums may use the identity status interview as a kind of therapy in an effort to disentangle their conflicting identity elements: 'Ambivalent struggle characterizes the moratorium' (Marcia 1979: 8).

Empirical studies have found moratoriums to be consistently more anxious than achievement or foreclosure individuals (Marcia 1967; Podd *et al.* 1970; Sterling and Van Horn 1989). Moratoriums may be volatile and intense in their interpersonal relationships. While possessing the capacity for intimacy, they shy away from the commitment demanded by such a relationship (Dyk and Adams 1990; Josselson 1987; Orlofsky *et al.* 1973). In many ways, however, moratoriums resemble achievements in their cognitive complexity, higher levels of moral reasoning, information processing style and failure to conform or rely on judgments of others for making decisions (Skoe and Marcia 1991; Slugoski *et al.* 1984). Moratoriums have demonstrated greater degrees of skepticism than other identity statuses (Boyes and Chandler 1992), as well as greater openness to experience and experiential orientation (Stephen *et al.* 1992; Tesch and Cameron 1987). Intrapsychically, moratoriums are in the process of disengaging from parental introjects and have more mixed attachment profiles (Kroger and Haslett 1988). Again, however, parents of moratorium youths tend to emphasize independence in their child-rearing practices (Frank *et al.* 1990; Grotevant and Cooper 1985).

Foreclosure

According to Marcia's (1979, 1994) profiles, foreclosures may appear very similar to the identity achieved in their initial interview impressions; however, their inflexibility and defensiveness soon become apparent. Foreclosures are happy and may be smugly self-satisfied; they are very authoritarian and unbending in their opinions of 'the right way'. Conventional in their moral reasoning and very committed to vocational and ideological values, foreclosures are particularly drawn to the values of a parent or strong leader who can show them this 'right way'. 'The strength of the foreclosure is a rigid and brittle strength, rather like glass; if you push at it in one way, it is very strong; if you push at it in a different way, it shatters' (Marcia 1979: 9). In some contexts where communal values are stressed as necessary for group survival, however, foreclosure is the most adaptive identity status (Marcia *et al.* 1993).

Empirical studies have consistently found foreclosures of both sexes to be the identity status most authoritarian in attitude (Côté and Levine 1983; Marcia 1966, 1967; Schenkel and Marcia 1972). Such individuals tend to be very approval seeking and base actions on the opinions of others; measures of foreclosures' autonomy have consistently produced low scores (Marcia 1966, 1967, Marcia *et al.* 1993). Perhaps as a result of their rigid adherence to authoritarian values, foreclosures are also the least anxious of the identity groups (Marcia 1966; Marcia and Friedman 1970; Schenkel and Marcia 1972) and least open to new experiences (Stephen *et al.* 1992; Tesch and Cameron 1987). If there is no openness or willingness to question life commitments, there is little room for anxiety to enter. Foreclosures also use less integratively complex cognitive styles and are pre-conventional or conventional in their levels of moral judgment (Rowe and Marcia 1980; Skoe and Marcia 1991; Slugoski *et al.* 1984). Furthermore, along with diffusions, foreclosures show greater realist and defended-realist epistemic stances in comparison with moratorium and achievement statuses (Boyes and Chandler 1992). In interpersonal relationships, foreclosures are 'well-behaved', placid individuals engaged in stereotypic or merger styles of interaction (Dyk and Adams 1990; Josselson 1987; Levitz-Jones and Orlofsky 1985; Orlofsky *et al.* 1973). Along with diffusions, they show very strong similarilities in friendship choices (Akers *et al.* 1998). Still undifferentiated intrapsychically from parental introjects, youths who remain foreclosed during late adolescence are more non-secure (anxious or detached) in attachment profiles than youths of any other identity group (Kroger and Haslett 1988; Papini *et al.* 1989). They report very close relationships with parents, while parents in turn encourage conformity and adherence to family values (Frank *et al.* 1990; Grotevant and Cooper 1985; Willemsen and Waterman 1991).

Diffusion

From Marcia's (1979, 1994) character sketches, diffusions are less homogeneous as a group than individuals of other identity statuses. Encompassing a range of individuals unable to make identity commitments, the diffusion status may result from cultural conditions (producing few viable identity options) as well as developmental deficits. Diffusion males tend to be either 'superficial or unhappy' (Marcia 1979: 9). Some diffusions may drift through life in a carefree, uninvolved way, while others may evidence severe psychopathology with great loneliness. Diffusions are not involved in intimate relationships and seem to lack any real sense of self to contribute to a dyad or group. Generally, diffusions give the sense of lacking any central core.

From empirical studies, diffusions evidence low self-esteem and autonomy (Marcia *et al.* 1993). They function at pre-conventional or conventional levels of moral reasoning and use less complex cognitive styles than moratoriums and achievements (Podd 1972; Skoe and Marcia 1991; Slugoski *et al.* 1984). They have scored highest of all identity statuses on hopelessness (Selles *et al.* 1994). In terms of interpersonal relationships, diffusions tend to be distant and withdrawn, most likely to be stereotyped or isolated in their dealings with others (Orlofsky *et al.* 1973). Their reports of parents' child-rearing practices indicate caretakers who were distant and rejecting (Josselson 1987). Such individuals are likely to have had great difficulty internalizing a parental introject during early childhood.

Developmental change in identity status

A number of longitudinal investigations during the years of adolescence have indicated clear patterns of progressive movement from foreclosure and diffusion positions to moratorium and achievement stances for those who do change identity status positions (e.g. Costa and Campos 1989; Cramer 1998; Fitch and Adams 1983; Foster and La Force 1999; Goossens 1991; Josselson 1987; Kroger 1988; 1995; Marcia 1976a; Meeus and Dekovic 1994; Phinney and Chavira 1992; Streitmatter 1993; Waterman *et al.* 1974; Waterman and Goldman 1976; Wires *et al.* 1994). The moratorium status has generally been the least stable of the identity groups, indicative perhaps of the discomfort in prolonging identity conflict. From a moratorium position in late adolescence, movement to the achievement status appears most likely from those longitudinal studies cited above in which it is possible to trace individual change. From these same investigations, however, approximately 50 per cent of individuals remained stable in less mature identity positions at the end of late adolescence. Anthis (2002), Bosma and Kunnen (2001), Dunkel and Anthis (2001) and Kroger and Green (1996) are among those who have been exploring conditions associated with identity status change. It appears that perceived conflict and/or stressful life events, the ability to generate possible future selves and readiness for change are key elements in the identity exploration process.

Gender and ethnicity issues in identity status research

Questions are frequently asked about the possibility of gender and ethnic differences in the adolescent identity formation process. Recently I conducted a narrative analysis of empirical investigations (Kroger 1997) using Marcia's identity status model and asked three questions related to gender:

1 Are there gender differences in the identity status distributions of adolescents and adults to deal with identity defining roles and values?
2 Are there gender differences in the identity domains most important to self-definition?

3   Are there gender differences in the developmental process of identity formation?

It was interesting to find that surprisingly few gender differences appeared in response to these three questions. There were few significant gender differences in identity status distributions over some 42 testings; these differences were not consistent across the six studies where they appeared. Some gender differences did appear within individual identity domains, yet these were not consistent across studies. No gender differences occurred in developmental pathways undertaken. A promising line of research suggests, however, that gender–role orientation, rather than gender per se is an important predictor of resolution to questions of identity, moral reasoning and intimacy (Bartle-Haring and Strimple 1996; Dyk and Adams 1990; Skoe 1993; Sochting *et al.* 1994).

Phinney (1989, 1996) and her associates have developed a model of ethnic identity formation that is consistent with Marcia's (1980) ego identity statuses and widely used in research on ethnic identity development during adolescence. An understanding of ethnic identity formation is important, as it impacts on the adjustment of minority group adolescents. Phinney's (1989) measure enables the assignment of an adolescent to one of three stages of ethnic identity development:

- an initial stage with little or no questioning of ethnic identity and its meaning (foreclosure/diffusion)
- a moratorium stage which questions preexisting ethinic attitudes and the place of one's ethnicity in present life circumstances
- an achieved ethnic identity, in which one attains a secure, positive sense of one's identity as a member of an ethnic group, with an acceptance of other groups.

Phinney's model has been used to understand the ethnic identity formation process for adolescents of a number of diverse ethnic groups. Longitudinal work indicates a significant change to more complex levels of ethnic identity development over time (Perron *et al.* 1998; Phinney and Chavira 1992; Phinney 1996).

Current directions in identity status research

Within recent years, a number of issues have continued to be examined within the tradition of identity status research that Marcia (1966, 1967) began. Two domains of identity development, in particular, have received increased attention: the roles of religious and vocational identity to the adolescent identity formation process. In general, identity achieved individuals have integrated more effectively their religious faith maturity with their services to self and community than foreclosures, while diffusions have shown the least mature forms of religious commitments compared with all other identity statuses; the foreclosed have avoided circumstances that might threaten their religious beliefs and have been indiscriminately pro-religious in their religious orientation (Hunsberger *et al.* 2001; Markstrom-Adams and Smith 1996; McKinney and McKinney 1999; Sanders 1998). Career indecision has also been associated with the identity statuses (e.g. Flum and Blustein 2000; Vondracek *et al.* 1995). Membership in a specific identity status has been linked to the nature and amount of career indecision. In retrospective work, Skorikov and Vondracek (1998) have found a developmental progression in adolescent vocational identity that parallels findings discussed earlier in longitudinal studies of identity status change. Additionally, identity statuses in religious, lifestyle and political domains are related to but lag behind identity status in the vocational domain.

A number of issues related to contexts for identity development have also begun to be examined. The role of contexts, generally, in the identity formation process has been described at both theoretical and empirical levels. Coté (1996) has attempted theoretically to link ways in which culture and identity are interrelated. He has constructed a framework that links macro-sociological factors through micro-interactional ones to psychological factors. Furthermore, he has begun testing the relationship between agency and identity formation, possibly paving the way for a more interdisciplinary approach to understanding the identity formation process (Coté and Schwartz 2002).

From a somewhat different perspective, Yoder (2000) has used the concept of 'barriers' to describe external influences on adolescent identity exploration and commitment processes. By describing possible barriers for each identity status, she has developed an innovative means of assessing socio-cultural factors that may impact on individual psychological functioning.

Issues in the assessment and meaning of the identity statuses have been a further area of development in identity status research. Goossens (2001) has been examining the usefulness of global vs. domain-specific identity status ratings, while Schwartz *et al.* (2000) have been examining empirical links across multiple theoretical constructs. Marcia (2002) has been attempting to understand the meaning of the identity status model when applied to transitions in adult development.

Criticism of Marcia's identity status construct

Over the past 15 years, there have been several critical commentaries of the identity status approach (Blasi and Glodis 1995; Côté and Levine 1988; van Hoof 1999). One focus of criticism has been on whether or not Marcia's identity status construct captures Erikson's theoretical understanding of identity. Blasi and Glodis (1995) argue that the identity statuses fail to capture the phenomenological dimensions of identity, while Côté and Levine (1988) indicate that Marcia has focused on only one small element of Erikson's identity concept, ignoring the impact of developmental contexts. Similarly, van Hoof (1999) argues that Marcia ignores what she believes to be central to identity – spatial and temporal continuity. However, at no time has Marcia claimed that his attempt to operationalize identity captures all identity dimensions described by Erikson. Any such effort would be unwieldy, if not impossible. Berzonsky and Adams (1999) have noted that in order to operationalize a construct there is a trade-off between theoretical richness and amenability to scientific study. The identity statuses are an attempt to expand some but not all of Erikson's meanings of the term identity.

The ability of the identity statuses to capture identity development has also come under fire from van Hoof (1999). Virtually all longitudinal studies of identity status change over late adolescence or early adulthood have shown approximately 50 per cent of individuals remaining stable in foreclosure or diffusion positions. Among those adolescents who have changed, however, movement has primarily been from foreclosure or diffusion to moratorium or achieved identity statuses. Van Hoof argues that because the identity status model fails to record progressive changes for such a large percentage of late adolescents, the model is not sensitive enough to capture identity change. However, the failure of many individuals to progess to more complex stages of identity development cannot be used as an argument against a model's sensitivity to change. There may simply be a large percentage of late adolescents who do not attain more complex levels of identity development. This finding is entirely consistent with results from longitudinal studies of ego development, moral reasoning and meaning-making to be described later in this volume.

Additionally, van Hoof (1999) has argued that there is little evidence of construct validity for the identity status positions. She bases her arguments on the conservative position that each of the four identity statuses must be statistically different from every other identity status on the variable in question. However, on many variables used to help establish construct and predictive validity, one would not expect statistically significant differences between each identity position and every other one (although some data do discriminate among the four identity positions; see Berzonsky and Adams 1999). Rather, one would expect a distinctive pattern of responses for the identity statuses on dependent variables, and such patterns of responses have generally been found. Indeed, few developmental paradigms in psychology would meet van Hoof's (1999) stringent critieria for the establishment of construct validity. See Kroger (2003) for a more thorough critique of the identity status paradigm.

Implications for social response

Social response is intimately linked to identity development through all eight of Erikson's life-cycle stages. From the mutual recognition and regulation of infant and caretaker to the definition of self through social role in adolescence to reflection over social participation in the integrity of old age, recognition from both a developmental partner and a larger social group is critical to resolving the conflict of each stage in the favorable direction. Assuming more or less favorable solutions have been found to the conflicts of preceding eras, parents, close associates and the educational, employment, recreational, religious, health, political and legal systems of one's cultural context have a vital role to play in the formation of identity during adolescence. All such orders regulate attitudes and behavior of their younger members, and all are capable of becoming too cooperative in the provision of labels that may not ultimately serve the best interests of youths seeking self-definition. It is through social willingness *not* to predetermine roles and to allow youth a moratorium that identity formation can best be facilitated; it is social tolerance for role experimentation without labeling that eventually benefits all concerned.

Erikson himself cites numerous examples of ways in which the psychiatric profession and legal system can provide youths with labels that offer a ready identity to troubled adolescents but do not allow optimal resolution to the conflict of this stage. Just as an adolescent psychiatric patient may 'choose the very role of patient as the most meaningful basis for an identity formation' (Erikson 1968: 179), others might gratefully adopt the 'criminal' or 'delinquent' roles that courts and psychiatric agencies could so easily and cooperatively confer. Society's *refusal* to provide ready role definitions for such adolescents and *not* to treat their experimentations as the final identity are in the best interests of the entire community.

In social response to the formation of identity, the importance of the community's recognition has been emphasized. Such recognition, however, must extend beyond a mere response to accomplishment alone. Social lip service to adolescent achievement cannot replace genuine opportunities provided by society for individual talents to be both realized and recognized. It is beyond the scope of this chapter to examine the means by which a variety of different social institutions might facilitate the identity formation process for its youth (see Archer 1994 for an excellent examination of such issues). However, comment will be made on how educational and therapeutic intervention might best serve adolescents in each of Marcia's four identity statuses; each identity status reflects a time of special need requiring differential social response.

Resolution of identity issues for the identity achieved makes need for psychotherapeutic intervention unlikely. Self-definition has been constructed through the identity formation process and resolution to the conflicts of preceding stages has been successful in order for identity achievement to occur. The need for counseling might arise for such an individual only in situations of crisis and would involve short-term intervention techniques (Marcia 1986, 1993). Educational settings must continue to provide new opportunities for insight and exploration, meet genuine needs and allow opportunity for individual talent to be expressed and channeled into real social roles. Experimental schools such as those described in Rogers's (1983) *Freedom to Learn for the 80's* and Neill's (1972) *Summerhill* would initially appear to offer the ideal in educational opportunity for identity achievements. In such settings, encouragement is given students to pursue curricula of relevance to their own interests and talents. However, Erikson would seek a less radical solution to the curriculum dilemma, at least during the stage of industry:

> 'Teacher, *must* we do today what we *want* to do?' Nothing could better express the fact that children at this age [industry] do like to be mildly but firmly coerced into the adventure of finding out that one can learn to accomplish things which one would never have thought of by oneself, things which owe their attractiveness to the very fact that they are not the product of play and fantasy but the product of reality, practicality, and logic; things which thus provide a token sense of participation in the real world of adults.
>
> (Erikson 1968: 127)

Schools with flexible curricula designed both to address changing student and social need and also to provide challenge and conflict situations are best suited to enhancing later identity development, according to Erikson. It is the job of the school and other social institutions to provide avenues for enhancing the identity achieved's way of 'having an effect on the world and on others'.

Moratoriums, very much in the throes of the identity formation process, often appear in psychotherapeutic or counseling settings. Ironically, they probably need direct intervention less than foreclosure or diffusion youths, who are less likely to request assistance (Marcia 1986). A sympathetic 'other' who does not become aligned with various aspects of the moratorium's struggle, but rather acts in a Rogerian way to reflect prospective identity elements in the interests of identity synthesis, would seem the best form of assistance here. It is important that therapist or counselor not be allied with one side of the moratorium's conflict. Such a therapeutic attitude merely 'externalizes the conflict into the therapeutic relationship and delays its resolution' (Marcia 1979: 16). Educational environments similar to those proposed for the identity achieved individual would best help the moratorium to explore vocational, ideological and sexual roles available in his or her society and find a social niche that matches individual interests and endowments. A curriculum relevant to the genuine needs of adolescents (for example, human sexuality, peace education, education for parenting, vocational skills, international relations) have been the focus for many programs of psychological education (Blustein *et al.* 1989; Ivey 1976). Opportunities for adolescents to become exposed to and 'try out' a variety of work roles through work-study programs at high school or college, as well as having interested and sympathetic adults available for listening, also facilitate resolution to a psychosocial moratorium period. Raskin (1994) provides further discussion of interventions that may promote career exploration in secondary and tertiary educational contexts.

For the foreclosed individual, identity has been reached through mechanisms of introjection and identification rather than ego synthesis. Much has been vested in 'being loved and cared for' by childhood identification figures at the expense of self-definition and ego development. Appearing to proceed smoothly along the track toward occupational goals and steadfast in their ideological beliefs, these youths have avoided any form of serious exploration. As a consequence, rigid identity structures are formed which are impervious to challenge from new life situations. Confidence and security have been the foreclosure's reward for adhering to prescribed role expectations. These youths rarely come for counseling or psychotherapy except when such beliefs have been threatened. Foreclosures would seem to be the most neglected status for psychotherapeutic, counseling, or educational intervention in cultural contexts where *identity formation* is adaptive (Kroger 1985).

Counseling or psychotherapy with foreclosed adolescents must recognize the rigidity of this identity structure and the security it provides, while striving slowly to provide new models for identification and introducing greater alternatives for choice. It should be noted that direct challenge to foreclosure commitments are likely to result in a further solidifying of defenses and closure to new possibilities (Marcia 1986). Vocational or personal counseling should proceed very slowly, with gradual encouragement to consider new options and identify with potentially new role models. Marcia (1994) points out that people cannot be 'taught' to explore alternatives; the process of considering alternatives for many foreclosures becomes laden with fears of rejection from significant others; adults, rather should provide safety, structure, facilitation, and some direction. An educational environment which supports open exploration of occupational and ideological alternatives rather than rewarding premature commitment could do much to foster identity development among the adolescent foreclosed. However, it must be recognized that a safe context is essential for those who might begin to question internalized roles and standards and move toward self-determined choice.

The diffusion status captures the greatest range of individuals having difficulty in finding a social niche. Here, failure to resolve favorably conflicts of preceding psychosocial stages may be primarily responsible for adolescent identity difficulties. For some diffusions, early massive ego failure makes 'being something' beyond the realm of the possible; just being, and developing some feeling of coherence, represents their main developmental task. Intervention efforts with such individuals would occur primarily in a psychiatric setting. Difficult though it may be, therapeutic aims would address issues of basic trust in relationship and ultimately in oneself (Erikson 1968). It is only through a return to this basic developmental conflict that any possibility exists for the emergence of an autonomous sense of self. If a diffusion's difficulties begin no earlier than the stage of industry, a facilitative psychotherapeutic or educational response might assist the individual in finding or reconnecting with interests and talents that have lain dormant through childhood (Brenman-Gibson 1986; Marcia 1986). Efforts should be made to help the diffusion become aware of his or her own unique attributes and experiences. Some forms of structured choice in the therapeutic or educational arenas might eventually be presented to diffusions in the interests of providing an experience of self through choosing an alternative best suited to personal preferences and competencies (Kroger 1985). Jones (1994) has noted that most if not all school-based prevention and intervention efforts for adolescents have focused on specific, isolated problem behaviors (such as substance abuse). Jones points out that if intervention programs were designed to address specific underlying developmental deficits at an individual level, then reduction of problem behaviors would be a side effect of a generally more effective developmental intervention.

Some intervention programs have been designed to facilitate progressive identity status movement. Markstrom-Adams *et al.* (1993) provide evidence that short-term intervention training strategies in social perspective taking may facilitate ideological identity achievement. Kaly (2000) designed a short-term, ship-based adventure program, to enhance self-esteem and encourage self-exploration through various water sports. The investigation found that adolescent participants did decrease foreclosure and diffusion global identity scores over the course of one month. Dreyer (1994) offers a comprehensive review of identity enhancing curricula which promote responsible, self-determined choice. Recent work by Berzonsky and Kuk (2000) suggests that identity measures may be useful in identifying students likely to have difficulty in negotiating the transition to university and raises some interesting intervention possibilities. However, much research remains to be undertaken in order to assess the effectiveness of specific intervention programs with individuals of varied identity statuses in various target groups.

Summary

Ego identity as conceptualized by Erik Erikson is a psychosocial construct which can be understood only through the interaction of biological need, ego organization and social context. During adolescence, features of identity which have formed through more or less favorable resolutions to earlier stages of developmental conflict must now evolve into a new configuration, different from yet based upon the earlier introjections and identifications of childhood. Furthermore, the balance achieved during the identity conflict of adolescence will affect all developmental stages encountered during adult life. James Marcia has empirically elaborated Erikson's identity versus role confusion conflict and describes four identity resolutions based on attitudes of crisis and commitment toward social roles. These identity statuses are characterized by different styles of personality organization which must be appreciated for effective educational, counseling, or psychotherapeutic intervention.

Further reading

Adams, G. R. (1999) 'The objective measure of ego identity status', unpublished manuscript, University of Guelph, Ontario, Canada.

Bosma, H. A. and Kunnen, E. S. (2001) 'Determinants and mechanisms in ego identity development: a review and synthesis', *Developmental Review* 21: 39–66.

Erikson, E. H. (1968) *Identity, Youth and Crisis*, New York: Norton.

Kroger, J. (2003) 'Identity in adolescence', in G. R. Adams and M. D. Berzonsky (eds) *Blackwell Handbook of Adolescence*. Oxford: Oxford University Press.

Marcia, J. E., Waterman, A. S., Matteson, D. R., Archer, S. L. and Orlofsky, J. L. (eds) (1993) *Ego Identity: A Handbook of Psychosocial Research*. New York: Springer-Verlag.

3 Adolescence as a second individuation process

Blos's psychoanalytic perspective and an object relations view

My mother packed a little bundle of clothes. . . . At last came the after-noon when I was to leave . . . she put her arms round my neck, weeping and unable to utter a word . . . and so we parted. . . . It was a lovely sunny afternoon, and soon my fickle childish mind forgot its sadness. I rejoiced in all the new things I was seeing . . . however, [before long] I realized how alone and left to my own resources I was, and how I had no other than God in heaven. . . . It was all so strange, that I seemed to be far out in the wide world.

(Hans Christian Andersen, in da Ponte *Memoirs*, 1929)

A mother's job is to be there to be left.

(Anna Freud, in Furman, *Mothers Have to be There to be Left*, 1982)

Another sunny afternoon setting of mixed emotion marked not only home-leaving for Hans Christian Andersen but also a milestone in his personal identity development. That Andersen persisted towards his own dream of a career in Copenhagen theaters with much joy and determination, despite contrary pressure and the awesome reality of a big wide world beyond Odense, attests to the young man's healthy indi-viduation process. Anna Freud's whispered aside captures the essence of optimal conditions for the development of identity, according to both psychoanalytic and object relations traditions: a parent–child partnership that enables not only an adolescent's confident, guiltless physical departure from the home of childhood both to love and to work in the wide world beyond, but also an intrapsychic departure from an internalized parental image that has to this point been one's source of guidance, support and self-esteem. Hans Christian Andersen's actions are possible through both reduction of his need for an intra-psychic parental representation as well as the gradually unfolding individuation process, concepts elaborated by Peter Blos in his psychoanalytic account of identity development (or in his terms, character formation) during adolescence.

Through a complex labyrinth of psychoanalytic routes, Blos's work emerges and marks an interesting crossroads in the evolution of psychodynamic theory itself. While retaining many contours of classic psychoanalytic maps that stress the resolution of Oedipal conflict for healthy personality development, Blos also appreciates the significance of pre-Oedipal experience in determining modes of later interpersonal relatedness. An awareness of the potentially productive rather than unconditionally maladaptive role played by regression in adolescent character formation is also critical to Blos's modification of orthodox psychoanalytic theory. Although retaining an appreciation of the place of adolescence on the road to genital maturity, Blos is one of the few psychodynamic theorists to focus almost exclusively on developments taking place during this youthful transition.

In line with most psychodynamic contributions, Blos's notions come to us via the experiences of troubled individuals seeking relief from distress. While developmental difficulty is of enormous value in highlighting normative psychodynamic processes, the deviant foundations of Blos's theoretical architecture must be remembered. In this chapter, particular effort will be made to select and describe psychodynamic processes central to Blos's conceptualization of *normative* character formation during adolescence. Later in the chapter, Blos's contributions will be elaborated with recent insights from object relations theory and research on the second individuation process of adolescence derived primarily from non-clinical populations.

Blos the person

Peter Blos, was born in 1903 in Karlsruhe, Germany, and was a lifelong friend of Erik Erikson. Blos undertook his initial training in biology, a field in which he was awarded a PhD from the University of Vienna in 1934. In the very early years of his career, he was greatly stimulated by his associations with Anna Freud and August Aichhorn at the Vienna Psychoanalytic Institute. There, he began his psychoanalytic studies and directed the now famous Experimental School in association with Anna Freud, August Aichhorn, Dorothy Burlingham and Erik Erikson. From these early experiences arose Blos's lifelong professional commitment to the welfare of youth (Esman 1997).

Blos (like Erikson) migrated to the United States with Hitler's rise to power. He settled in New York to further a career that eventually spanned six decades. A gifted teacher and clinician, Blos held several faculty and supervisory positions at the New York Psychoanalytic Institute and the Columbia University Center for Psychoanalytic Training and Research prior to his retirement from active teaching in 1977. Among his later professional honors was receipt of the Heinz Hartmann Award from the New York Psychoanalytic Institute. Blos's lifelong interests in psychodynamic processes of adolescence are reflected in some of his book titles: *On Adolescence* (1962); *The Young Adolescent: Clinical Studies* (1970); and *The Adolescent Passage* (1979). His last volume, *Son and Father: Before and Beyond the Oedipus Complex* (1985), traces the reciprocity of the son–father relationship over the course of the generations, as son becomes a father in turn. Peter Blos died in 1997 at the age of 93. He is regarded by many as one of the last in a great generation of clinical scholars who helped form the foundations of contemporary psychoanalysis (Esman 1997).

The nature of character formation

Where Erikson uses the term 'ego identity', Blos prefers the use of 'character' to denote that entity which restructures and consolidates during adolescence. However, the nature of that entity, which forms at the end of adolescence, differs for the two psychoanalysts. Character, to Blos, is that aspect of personality which patterns one's responses to stimuli originating both within the environment as well as within the self. Blos does not focus primarily on ego processes in the formation of character but rather on the dynamic balance between id, ego and superego structures.

Blos (1968) posits four challenges which are related to the formation of character; without addressing and favorably resolving each of these issues, adolescents retain a character deficient in the structure necessary to healthy functioning during adult life.

> The credentials of character are to be found in the postadolescent level which, if attained, renders character formation possible . . . The extent to which the four preconditions have been fulfilled . . . will determine the autonomous or defensive nature of the character that ensues.
>
> (Blos 1968: 259)

Failure to resolve adolescent challenges may or may not be based on earlier developmental arrest.

Blos's four character challenges of adolescence, detailed in the next section, are

- the second individuation process
- reworking and mastering childhood trauma
- ego continuity
- sexual identity.

The second individuation process of adolescence involves the relinquishing of those very intrapsychic parental representations which were internalized during toddlerhood and have formed the structure of childhood identity. Blos finds regression to be a normative feature among adolescents as they disengage from early object ties. In reworking childhood trauma, adolescents must return to, rather than avoid, the scene of early organismic insult and re-experience the injury so that it may be mastered rather than defended against through adult life. Similar to Erikson's suggestion of the need for a sense of inner continuity and sameness to healthy identity formation, Blos's notion of ego continuity refers to the need for a sense of personal history; one cannot have a future without a past. In line with orthodox psychoanalytic theory, Blos sees the reactivation of childhood Oedipal issues and the formation of a sexual identity as the final critical challenge to adolescent character formation. It is the young person's ability to seek romantic relationships outside the original family constellation that indicates successful resolution to this challenge.

These four challenges, central to adolescent character formation, rest on a history of individual antecedents – from constitutional givens to infant interpersonal experience to resolution of early childhood Oedipal conflict. Like ego identity, character can be conceptualized only in developmental terms; its origins begin in infancy and its stabilization appears at the end of adolescence. Blos does not trace its development through adulthood, however. Character formation involves progressively higher levels of differentiation and independence from the environment. Subjectively, one's character is one's sense of self: 'Psychic life cannot be conceived without it [character], just as physical life is inconceivable without one's body. One feels at home in one's character. . . . If must be, one dies for it before letting it die' (Blos 1968: 260). The four character formation challenges should be regarded as components of a total process; their integrated resolution marks the end of adolescence (Blos 1976). Blos's four cornerstones of character formation are described below.

The challenges detailed

Crucial to the psychoanalyst's portrayal of adolescent character is a basic understanding of object relations theory. This approach, broadly defined, rests on the assumption that in our relationships we react according to the internal representations we hold of people important to us in the past as well as to the person actually before us now. Greenberg and Mitchell put it succinctly:

> People react to and interact with not only an actual other but also an internal other, a psychic representation of a person which in itself has the power to influence both the individual's affective states and his overt behavioral reactions.
>
> (Greenberg and Mitchell 1983: 10)

Thus, our responses to those before us now may have only the vaguest of associations with present-tense external reality. Rather, interactions may be governed equally by internal representations of past important others who, in turn, define the present limits of our autonomous functioning.

Within psychoanalysis, a number of object relations theorists have made their contributions by exploring the implications of this last statement (for example, Fairburn, Guntrip, Jacobson, Kernberg, Klein, Kohut, Mahler). Blos's writings on the restructuring of internal representations during adolescence draw particularly upon the work of Margaret Mahler. Though Mahler's work is based on development in early life, Blos finds great parallels in the processes by which adolescents must deal with issues of self-differentiation. Blos's second individuation process will be discussed more fully than remaining challenges, for it is this issue which has stimulated the greatest theoretical and empirical interest among those attempting to understand the normative adolescent experience. The past 15 years have seen a burgeoning of both theoretical and empirical efforts to elucidate intrapsychic and interpersonal ramifications of this differentiation process.

The second individuation process

In groundbreaking work of the 1960s, Margaret Mahler conducted extensive observations of healthy mother–infant and mother–toddler dyads in a naturalistic setting to delineate the process by which the child differentiates itself from its primary caretaker and becomes an autonomous person. Separation and individuation refer to two tracks in the sequence by which the infant moves from an undifferentiated experience of self to a toddler with a sense of separateness from yet relatedness to the physical world of reality. By separation, Mahler *et al.* (1975: 4) allude to the child's 'emergence from a symbiotic fusion with the mother', while individuation denotes 'those achievements marking the child's assumption of his own individual characteristics'. In short, Mahler and her colleagues have attempted to chart 'the psychological birth of the human infant'.

Mahler follows these developmental tracks through a sequence of specific stages. One's resolution to these phases determines the health or pathology of character during the course of later life. Successful navigation of these stages is to Mahler what resolution of the Oedipal crisis was to Freud in setting the foundation for adult character structure. The hyphenated term 'separation–individuation' refers specifically to four subphases of development experienced during infancy and toddlerhood; separation–individuation subphases follow neonatal stages of autism and symbiosis.

At the beginning of life, according to Mahler, the newborn is unable to differentiate itself from its surroundings. There are not internal representations of the external world, for there is little awareness of external objects. Maintaining physiological homeostasis is the main task for the infant in this *autistic* phase of life, and it is only the gradual awareness of a caretaker (the mother, in Mahler's observations) which propels the child into the next stage of *symbiosis* at about three to four weeks of age. Now there is dim recognition of mother, but she is perceived only as an extension of the infant's self. In the observations of Mahler *et al.* 'the infant behaves and functions as though he and his mother were an omnipotent system – a dual unity within one common boundary' (1975: 44). It is from this base that the four subphases of separation–individuation proceed, encompassing a growing intra-psychic differentiation between self and other.

Recent research on infant development has challenged Mahler's descriptions of autistic and symbiotic stage capacities by demonstrating that infants are born with perceptual and cognitive capacities too sophisticated to suggest their inability to differentiate self from other (Horner 1985; Stern 1985). This research casts doubt on the whole existence of a symbiotic phase and the raison d'être for the stages of separation–individuation that lie ahead. Pine (1990, 1992), however, has responded with the proposition that infants experience *moments* of merger or non-differentiation which have an affective significance sufficiently strong to account for the merger wishes observed in later life. While young infants may not spend all of their time in states of merger, such experiences, along with caretaker response, will affect the subsequent course of separation–individuation subphases that lie ahead.

Beginning awareness of mother's existence as a separate person heralds the first subphase of the separation–individuation process, according to Mahler. She uses the term *hatching* to capture development during this time of *differentiation*, when the 5- to 10-month-old infant achieves the physical and intrapsychic capacities to check out holdings of the external world. Tentative explorations begin as infant slides from lap to floor and becomes a veteran of the not-too-far-from-mother's-feet environment. With increased locomotion, a new subphase ensues; *practicing* makes its developmental entrance between about 10 and 15 months and marks an interval of increased exploration, escalating into an exhilarating 'love affair with the world'. As long as mother remains available, a 'home base' for emotional 'refueling' through the day's new ventures, all is well. It is not until about 15 to 22 months in the *rapprochement* subphase that mother is experienced as a separate person, a self in her own right. Such recognition brings a sense of great loss to the toddler and calls for new strategies (seemingly regressive) in response. Attempts at 'wooing' mother, at re-engaging her in external activity as a hoped for filler to an intrapsychic vacuum, lie at the heart of the *rapprochement crisis*. The realization ultimately dawns, however, that there is no return to the self-object fusion of earlier times. The toddler's conflict between the need for maternal incorporation on the one hand and separation and individuation on the other is at its height. Father plays a vital role here in supporting the child against the backward symbiotic pull. It is not until the final, open-ended subphase of *libidinal object constancy* during the third year that life becomes less painful. Two accomplishments occur at this time: '(1) the achievement of a definite, in certain aspects lifelong, individuality, and (2) the attainment of a certain degree of object constancy' (Mahler *et al.* 1975: 109). Object constancy implies the child's intrapsychic incorporation of both the 'good and bad' parts of the maternal image to allow it some physical distance from the mother of reality. Such accomplishment sets the foundation for an intrapsychic structure that will be the basis of identity, at least until adolescence. While Mahler notes that clinical outcome to the infant *rapprochement* crisis will be mediated by developmental crises of adolescence, she does not comment specifically on the implications of optimal infant separation–individuation subphase resolutions for adolescents (Mahler *et al.* 1975). Blos was quick to appreciate the applications of Mahler's work to the intrapsychic restructuring occurring during adolescence:

I propose to view adolescence in its totality as the second individuation process, the first one having been completed toward the end
of the third year of life with the attainment of object constancy.
Both periods have in common a heightened vulnerability of personality organization. Both periods have in common the urgency
for changes in psychic structure in consonance with the maturational forward surge. Last but not least, both periods – should
they miscarry – are followed by a specific deviant development
(psychopathology) that embodies the respective failures of
individuation.

(Blos 1967: 163)

He likens the infant's 'hatching from the symbiotic membrane'
described by Mahler to the adolescent process of 'shedding family
dependencies', that loosening of ties with the internalized parent which
have sustained the child though phallic and latency periods. Adolescent
disengagement from this internalized parental representation allows the
establishment of new, extra-familial romantic attachments. Where such
adolescent intrapsychic restructuring does not occur, the young person,
at best, may merely substitute the original infantile attachment with a
new love object, leaving the *quality* of the attachment unaltered.

Blos (1967) notes further accomplishments contingent upon successful resolution to the second individuation process:

• the acquisition of stable and firm self and object boundaries
• the loss of some rigidity and power by the Oedipal superego
• greater constancy of mood and self-esteem, resulting from less
  dependence on external sources of support

Up until adolescence, the child has been able to make legitimate
demands upon the parental ego, which has often served as an extension
of its own less developed structure. Maturation of the child's own ego
goes hand in hand with disengagement from the internal representations of caretakers: 'disengagement from the infantile object is always
paralleled by ego maturation' (Blos 1967: 165). It is through ego
maturation that a firm sense of self, different from that of parents, not
overwhelmed by internalized superego demands and more capable of
self-support, emerges to mark the end of the second individuation
process:

Individuation implies that the growing person takes increasing
responsibility for what he does and what he is, rather than deposit-

ing this responsibility onto the shoulders of those under whose influence and tutelage he has grown up.

(Blos 1967: 168)

As Anna Freud has indicated, a mother's (or primary caretaker's) job is to be there to be left. Only in this way are adolescents able to disengage from parental internalizations and seek their own vocational and romantic fortunes in the world beyond the family doorstep.

Central to successful resolution of adolescent individuation is regression. It is only through the young person's ability to renew contact with infantile drives that the psychic restructuring of adolescence can occur:

> Just as Hamlet who longs for the comforts of sleep but fears the dreams that sleep might bring, so the adolescent longs for the comforts of drive gratification but fears the reinvolvements in infantile object relations. Paradoxically, only through regression, drive and ego regression, can the adolescent task be fulfilled.
>
> (Blos 1967: 171)

In the words of one wall poster I observed recently in a university bookshop, 'The best way out is always through'. Though not drawing any direct comparisons with the intrapsychic conflicts and regressive behavior of Mahler's *rapprochement* toddlers, Blos finds parallels between adolescent and toddler regressive functions to be striking. In Blos's view of the years of post-infancy, it is only during adolescence that regression can serve a normative developmental function.

Common adolescent regressive behaviors are phenomena such as a return to 'action' rather than 'verbal' language (for example, passivity in response to situations best addressed by verbal expression of need), idolization of pop stars and famous characters (reminiscent of the young child's idealization of parents), emotional states similar to merger (such as with abstractions like Theodore Dreiser's Right, Justice, Truth, Mercy, or with religious and political groups), and constant frenetic activity to fill the sense of internal object loss. Blos hastens to add that it takes a relatively intact ego to survive the test of non-defensive regression during adolescence. Where ego organization has been deficient through infant separation–individuation subphases, such deficiencies are laid bare with the removal of parental props during adolescence: 'The degree of early ego inadequacy often does not become apparent until adolescence, when regression fails to serve progressive development, precludes individuation, and closes the door to drive and ego maturation' (Blos 1967: 175). It is the peer group that, under optimal conditions, supplies support during the loss of childhood psychic structure. Just as the *rapprochement* child tries to re-engage mother or caretaker in its activities to cope with the pain of object loss, so too the adolescent seeks solace from peers while relinquishing intrapsychic object ties. Mourning accompanies the loss of childhood's self.

Blos illustrates, with clinical example, the second individuation process in need of outside assistance for resolution. Let us, however, move from the clinical to the commonplace and view, by way of example, a more normative adolescent experience in terms of Blos's first character challenge:

> To pass from the romantic to the commonplace, imagine if you will the father of an adolescent boy settling into his chair in front of the television set after a grueling day with the conviction that he has earned his preprandial drink and a half hour's peace. His son, with whom he has been on surprisingly good terms for several days, slouches into the room and in response to his father's greeting mutters something that might equally well be understood as either 'Hello' or 'Hell, no!' Ten minutes or so go by in silence, until, in response to the news commentator's remarks on the energy crisis, the son begins to mutter angrily. The father, thinking the boy's vocalizations are an invitation to conversation, says something viciously provocative such as, 'It looks as if we'll be facing some pretty tough problems in the next few years.' In response the boy launches into a condemnation of his father's entire generation. As he warms to the task, he becomes more pointed and specific, reminding his father that if he were only willing to walk or bicycle the seven or eight miles to work instead of driving that gas-guzzling Volkswagen, the energy shortage would soon be resolved. But no! The hedonistic, materialistic, and self-indulgent orientation displayed by his father and all his contemporaries is robbing the boy's generation of any hope of physical warmth, mobility, and perhaps even survival.
>
> To emphasize his disgust with the situation, the boy announces he is going to find his mother. If dinner isn't ready, he plans to raise hell. If it is ready, he won't eat. His father once more is left feeling that whenever he interacts with his son, he misses some crucial point that would explain the whole interchange.
>
> (Coppolillo 1984: 125–126)

The saga continues as the son returns within several hours to greet his father cheerfully and request use of the family car to drive his girl across town for pizza. To the father's suggestion of a stroll to the nearby pizza parlor to save gas for posterity, he receives an emphatic, 'No! That just won't do! The pizza across town is just what he has a taste for at the moment. All other considerations are unimportant' (Coppolillo 1984: 126). The father concludes that adolescence is indeed a period of 'normal psychosis' (and the son that his father merely wishes to deprive him of use of the family car).

In considering the above scenario, the young man's argumentative efforts with his father over the energy crisis appear as possible intrapsychic distancing techniques designed to combat fears of infantile re-engulfment. In attacking the lifestyle of the parental generation, the youth presses an ideological stand of 'his own' – a stand that is quickly abandoned, however, when inconvenient. The queen's well-known line to Hamlet, 'The lady doth protest too much, methinks', illustrates how forceful opposition to an innocuous reality may be fighting an other than external battle. Additionally, regression to infantile demands for immediate drive satisfaction (in both the Freudian and automotive senses here), coupled with rapid mood swings, are common to adolescence, indicating the fluidity of self and object representations: 'The unavailability of the accustomed and dependable internal stabilizers of childhood seems to be responsible for many of the typical and transient personality characteristics of this age' (Blos 1983: 582). Only when this labile young man is firm in his own sense of self will such fluidity disappear, along with the need to push anything other than his own genuinely felt (ego-syntonic) ideological concerns.

Before leaving Blos's second individuation challenge, brief mention must be made of resolutions which are less than optimal. Certainly, the tragic lives of many great artists and writers have been traced to both severe infant and adolescent separation and individuation difficulties. In chilling visual form, Norwegian painter Edvard Munch has dramatically communicated the separation anxiety plaguing his own existence in his well-known painting 'The Scream'. Terrified, despairing eyes and an open mouth forming an unbridled scream are primitive features of the artist's central character, who appears against the background of a sky ablaze. Munch's multiple and severe early losses resulted in his own incomplete adolescent separation and individuation processes; this theme of profound separation anxiety is reflected in many of his works (Masterson 1986). The life of Jean-Paul Sartre was also dulled by separation and individuation arrest (Masterson 1986). In his autobiography, *Words*, Sartre says of his own life, 'I had no true self' (1964: 75). 'My mother and I were the same age and we never left each other's side. She used to call me her attendant knight and her little man; I told her everything' (1964: 148).

Among means of avoiding the adolescent individuation challenge are efforts at distancing from parents in ways other than through intrapsychic separation. Blos (1967) notes that attempts by adolescents to create physical or ideological space from their families do little to address the underlying intrapsychic task. Such abortive resolutions are reminiscent of Erikson's negative identity:

> By forcing a physical, geographical, moral, and ideational distance from the family or locale of childhood, this type of adolescent renders an internal separation dispensable. . . . The incapacity to separate from internal objects except by detachment, rejection, and debasement is subjectively experienced as a sense of alienation.
>
> (Blos 1967: 167–168)

It is noteworthy that Blos here also makes use of the term *separation* in association with the second individuation process, though he does not detail either the separation or individuation tracks outlined by Mahler.

Reworking and mastering childhood trauma

Blos suggests that even those exposed to the kindest of childhood fates have innumerable opportunities for emotional injury. Furthermore, childhood trauma is a relative term; its impact depends both on the magnitude of the danger itself as well as the child's own vulnerability to such assault (Blos 1962). Mastering childhood trauma is a lifelong task. One often sets up life situations which, in effect, recreate the original injury and thereby provide opportunities for mastery and resolution. Adolescence, because of its role in the consolidation of character, is a time when 'a considerable portion of this task is being accomplished' (Blos 1962: 132). At the close of adolescence, infantile traumas are not removed but rather (optimally) integrated into the ego and experienced as life tasks. In cases of optimal character formation the individual is able to find satisfying ways to cope with what was originally an unmanageable childhood ordeal. Each effort at mastery of residual trauma results in heightened self-esteem. Reworking childhood's Oedipus complex is one specific example of this more generic adolescent task.

Blos (1968) draws upon Freud's writings to conclude that childhood trauma can have both positive and negative effects on character formation. Individuals may attempt to reactivate trauma, remembering and reliving it for integration into character as described above, or they may avoid the entire process, 'a reaction that leads to the reactive character formation via avoidances, phobias, compulsions, and inhibitions' (Blos 1968: 255). Adolescents who choose this latter option do not allow themselves the opportunity to come to terms with trauma, but rather remain under its directive in defensive maneuvers during the years that follow.

Because of the anxiety generated by residual trauma, there is often an urgency, a strong push toward expression in character: 'Due to its origin character always contains a compulsive quality; it lies beyond choice and contemplation, is self-evident and compelling: "Here I stand, I cannot do otherwise" (Luther)' (Blos 1968: 255). The lives of many highly creative individuals such as Martin Luther have been presented as psychoanalytic evidence of attempts to remold childhood trauma into a mature ego organization at the close of adolescence.

Ego continuity

The third precondition for optimal character formation is that of ego continuity. Blos regards this phenomenon as critical to character formation: '[A]dolescent development can be carried forward only if the adolescent ego succeeds in establishing a historical continuity in its realm. If this is prevented, a partial restructuring of adolescence remains incomplete' (Blos 1968: 256–257). Particularly apparent in situations where a child must accept a distorted reality to survive, lack of ego continuity results from a denial of one's own experience.

Ego continuity during adolescence serves a purpose beyond that of conflict resolution; rather, it has an integrative and growth-stimulating function as the internalized parental representation is no longer needed and cast by the wayside. Ego maturation gives rise to a 'sense of whole-ness and inviolability' during adolescence. It is only during late adolescence that the capacity to form one's own view of the past, present and future emerges (Blos 1976). Character formation at the close of adolescence is dependent upon the framework provided by ego continuity.

Sexual identity

The formation of character also involves establishment of a sexual identity, a sense of masculinity or femininity with irreversible boundaries. Sexual identity differs from gender identity, which is formed in early life. In traditional psychoanalytic form, Blos views adolescence as a necessary regressive return for completion of phallic stage Oedipal issues in order to establish, ultimately, a sexual identity. Just as Blos stressed the necessity of an adolescent return to pre-Oedipal periods for restructuring intrapsychic parental bonds, he indicates that mature heterosexual interest can emerge only upon a return and final resolution to conflicts of childhood's Oedipal years:

> I venture to say that not until adolescence has the developmental moment arrived for the oedipal drama to be completed and the realization of mature object relations to be initiated. This step must be taken in adolescence or it never will, certainly not without circumstantial good fortunes and therapeutic intervention – in any case, not without much suffering which not every human adult is capable to endure.
>
> (Blos 1989: 17)

With ego consolidation through the time of latency, however, the adolescent experiences such renewed Oedipal strivings at a different level. The Oedipus complex revived during adolescence is not identical to the childhood conflict:

> From my work with adolescents – male and female – I have gained the impression that the decline of the Oedipus complex at the end of the phallic phase represents a suspension of a conflictual constellation rather than a definitive resolution, because we can ascertain its continuation on the adolescent level. In other words, the resolution of the Oedipus complex is completed – not just repeated – during adolescence.
>
> (Blos 1979: 476–477)

Resolution during adolescence involves addressing both positive and negative Oedipal components (sexual love for both the opposite and same sex parent, respectively).

Character formation through adolescence

Whereas Freud saw adolescence as one general stage of psychosexual development, Blos felt the need for further detail here also. In tracing the formation of character through the adolescent passage, Blos (1962, 1971) describes four phases of development during which the challenges are addressed. Each phase forms part of an orderly sequence which has its own time and place of ascendence; phases are not linked to specific chronological ages but rather to the intrapsychic issues they address. While Blos does not attend to all life-cycle phases in charting the evolution of identity, he does detail phases preceding and following adolescence; they too encapsulate important times in the building and consolidation of character.

The period of *latency*, which precedes adolescence, provides a time in which the ego and superego gain growing control over the instincts. While the early Freudians saw latency as a time of sexual quiescence, Blos acknowledges that sexual interests and activities remain alive and well during this phase (as do many neo-Freudian psychoanalysts). In sum, the key function of latency is to provide a time for consolidation after the upheaval of the Oedipus complex.

Pre-adolescence heralds an increase in both sexual and aggressive drives with a concomitant decrease in ego control; stimuli which trigger impulse arousal often seem to have little direct relationship to the drive itself. Those working with young adolescents are aware how quickly any experience can become the source of sexual excitement:

> There are 'certain' words and conversations unhappily impossible to eradicate in schools. Boys pure in mind and heart, almost children, are fond of talking in school among themselves of things, pictures, and images of which even soldiers would sometimes hesitate to speak.
>
> (Dostoevsky, cited in Blos 1962: 61–62)

Direct gratification of instinctual impulse ordinarily meets strong superego resistance. Solution, for the mediating ego, rests with defenses such as repression, reaction formation and displacement. Compulsive interests and activities also function to contain pre-adolescent anxiety within manageable limits.

Early adolescence is distinguished by pubertal maturation alongside the young person's genuine beginnings of separation from early object ties. Additionally, sexual energy previously attached to the Oedipal triangle now begins to seek extrafamilial outlet. Superego codes are diminished as the old internalized ties with parents loosen, and the ego is left to fumble in its regulatory function. Same-sex friendships of early adolescence are idealized; that is, young people search for friends who possess qualities that they do not have. In this way desired characteristics can be obtained vicariously. One's ego ideal is often represented by such a friend. Not surprisingly, these early adolescent relationships are generally doomed to sudden demise. Not only are the demands placed on such friendships too burdensome to bear for long, but homosexual fears may also arise and bring abrupt closure.

It is only during the emergence of *adolescence proper* that one's interests turn to the heterosexual arena. Now there is no return to old Oedipal and pre-Oedipal object ties, and such finality shakes intrapsychic organization to the core. Life, according to Blos, is generally in turmoil, yet at the same time new doors to development begin to open. The consolidation of heterosexual love involves the ability to shift from the early adolescent overvaluation of the self (as evidenced by the self-serving function of the same-sex chum) to a genuine interest in the identity of another. Before this can happen, however, one must experience the intrapsychic vacuum between 'old' and 'new' loves, the time of transitory nothingness. Coping mechanisms often involve states of heightened affect or frenzied activity, ways to 'feel alive' and thus fill the intrapsychic void with an overdose of reality. In this way, boundaries of the self are protected from feared dissolution, accompanied frequently by poor judgment. Resolutions to both positive and negative Oedipal strivings are gradual and extend into adolescence's final phase.

Late adolescence sees a continued interest in the search for heterosexual love. Additionally, 'the individual registers gains in purposeful action, social integration, predictability, constancy of emotions, and stability of self-esteem' (Blos 1962: 128). Late adolescence is primarily a time of consolidation – a stabilizing of sexual identity into an irreversible pattern, establishing firm representations of self and others, and developing a greater sense of autonomy. Character has thus been formed.

Blos terms the final transition phase from adolescence to adulthood *postadolescence*. It is marked by further structural integration: 'In terms of ego development and drive organization, the psychic structure has acquired by the end of late adolescence a fixity which allows the postadolescent to turn to the problem of harmonizing the component parts of the personality' (Blos 1962: 149). The work of postadolescence is to find outlets in a social reality through which sexual drive and 'life tasks' (those resolutions to early trauma) can be expressed. With the decline of instinctual conflict, the ego is free to attend to this job.

A healthy character structure

What then is optimal psychic functioning at the close of adolescence? Blos (1983) has suggested that it involves the capacity to tolerate some degree of anxiety and depression, inevitable concomitants of the human condition. While the beginnings of adolescence go hand in hand with pubertal change, no such physiological delimiters mark its end:

In summary fashion, I might say that puberty is an act of nature and adolescence is an act of man. This statement emphasizes the fact that neither the completion of physical growth, nor the attainment of sexual functioning, nor the social role of economic self-support are, by and in themselves, reliable indices for the termination of the adolescent process.

(Blos 1979: 405–406)

What *is* a reliable index of character formation is the degree of coordination and integration among ego functions; adolescent closure occurs when character challenges become integrated and function in unison to mark an ensuing phase of greater autonomy and stability. Blos (1979: 410) notes this arrival 'when ego autonomy, in alliance with the ego ideal, challenges partially but effectively the dominance of the superego'. There is also a gradual change in the nature of relationships, both public and private, which are chosen with more discrimination and as a reflection of the individual's own needs and desires. Thus, if all goes well for our erstwhile pizza-driven, conservation-minded citizen of an earlier section, we might look several years hence to find a young man, very much in love with his marital and business partner, seated at Sunday dinner with his parents and engaged in a lively exchange of ideas on how the young couple's established fast-food packaging business might make use of recycled paper. Blos does conclude with a final warning, however, that '[e]ven if the consolidation of late adolescence has done its work in good faith, the framework of any personality structure can only stand up well over time if relatively benign circumstances continue to prevail' (1979: 411).

Criticism of Blos's identity construct

In a critical general analysis of psychodynamic literature on adolescent development, Adelson and Doehrman have noted the enormous gap between psychodynamic potential and its actual contribution to an understanding of this age period:

It is hard to imagine a satisfying theory of adolescence without the strongest contribution from psychodynamic theory. No other approach can offer, potentially, a comparable depth and range of observation; no other approach is as well suited – again, potentially – to pull together evidence drawn from other sources. Yet it is even harder to imagine that happening today, given the sad state of the art. It is at the moment a fossilized doctrine, resisting innovation in method, unshakably parochial in outlook.

(Adelson and Doehrman 1980: 115)

In the years since this statement was made, some theoretical progress has occurred, particularly in ego psychoanalytic psychology and object relations arenas, but many phenomena remain unexamined.

Resting on limited clinical recordings, Blos's construct evokes criticism applicable to much of the psychodynamically oriented literature. Not only are empirical foundations shaky, but normative developmental principles are inferred from observations of those appearing in clinical settings. Furthermore, Blos fails to deliver. In his discussion of regression, many specific questions regarding systems affected by and circumstances associated with a return to earlier stages remain unanswered (Adelson and Doehrman 1980). Such lack of attention to detail also appears in Blos's discussion of the second individuation process. While we are certainly 'now eager to trace the steps of individuation during adolescence', such steps are not subsequently delineated (Blos 1967: 166). A further instance of Blos's lack of precision has been raised by Richmond and Sklansky (1984) in pointing out his different usages of the term *character*. At times, Blos views character as that which regulates the adolescent process, while at others, character refers to the period's end product. These writers feel that Blos has been unable to find an organizing principle to account for development during adolescence.

An additional problem arises when we turn to empirical literature related to adolescent character challenges in the next section. Studies support another of Adelson and Doehrman's (1980: 112) general observations regarding psychodynamic theory: 'The realm of theory and the realm of empirical inquiry exist separately and fail to recognize or support each other.' There is frequent failure of empirically based research to support a number of Blos's theoretical postulates. While adolescence does, indeed, seem to encompass a second individuation process, research suggests that it is a phenomenon generally addressed in later, rather than middle, phases as indicated by the psychoanalyst. Rather than being a state of siege when Oedipal anxieties come to the fore, normative adolescence seems rather a time of steady, non-tumultuous maturation. 'Researchers who investigate normal adolescents continue to find evidence that development during adolescence is slow, gradual, and unremarkable' (Josselson 1980: 189). Indeed, results of Masterson and Costello (1980) and Offer (1991) show adolescent turmoil to be an indicator of psychopathology rather than normality.

Many gaps between Blosian theory and research on the normative adolescent experience need filling.

Criticism has also been leveled at Blos's utilization of the infant individuation concept itself. Both Pine (1985) and Schafer (1973) caution against the application of separation–individuation subphases to times of the lifespan other than infancy. During adolescence, for example, there is no primitive merging of self and object as in infancy, and these analysts find it misleading to refer to later developmental processes with identical terms. Schafer (1973: 43) has criticized what he sees as Blos's confusion between 'individuation' and 'giving up infantile objects': '*Psychologically*, only an already highly individuated person is capable of giving up his infantile relations to others.' More recently, Blass and Blatt (1996) have pointed out that symbiosis, the foundation upon which the adolescent separation–individuation process rests, needs further refinement when considered as a form of relatedness beyond infancy. Blass and Blatt point to the absence of a theoretical framework that can adequately account for the coexistence of a state of undifferentiation experienced beyond infancy with that of an independent identity. Caution is clearly necessary in defining the meaning of separation and individuation processes, particularly when referring to different stages of the life cycle beyond infancy.

A further voice of protest has come from feminist writers such as Gilligan (1982a) and Kaplan and Klein (1985), who argue against conceptualization of women's development as that of 'shedding of family dependencies, the loosening of infantile object ties in order to become a member of society at large' (Blos 1967: 163). However, Blos does not equate adolescent individuation with severing emotional bonds with parents. Rather, he describes a separation from infantile objects that in fact allows for a more mature form of relationship with parents as well as significant others. It is change in the quality of *how* one is both related and autonomous as a result of differentiation from internalized object ties that is the hallmark of the separation–individuation process of adolescence (Kroger 1992; Marcia 1993). Despite such criticism, infant developmental processes of separation and individuation continue to generate theoretical and research interest in their modified application to intrapsychic restructuring during adolescence.

Elaborations on the second individuation process of adolescence

There has been no single effort paralleling that of Mahler to delineate phases and subphases of the adolescent separation and individuation processes. While Blos has drawn general attention to parallels between the infant task of self-object differentiation and the differentiation between self and internalized object representations by adolescents, later writers have attempted to delineate some aspects of the adolescent process more fully. While similarities between the *processes* of infant and adolescent differentiation may exist, it must be remembered that the intrapsychic *organizations* during these two phases of the lifespan are quite different.

In extending Blos's conceptualization of adolescence as a second individuation process, several contributions from object relations theory have provided guides as to how Mahler's phases and subphases of infant differentiation might be applied to the adolescent experience (for example, Brandt 1977; Esman 1980; Isay 1980; Josselson 1980, 1988). These speculations have generally rested on theoretical and clinical observation, however, rather than empirically based data. Through several longitudinal investigations with late adolescents functioning in a university context, colleagues and I have been attempting to shed some light on subphases of adolescent intrapsychic reorganization which may parallel subphases of self-object differentiation during infancy (Kroger 1985; Kroger 1995; Kroger and Green 1994; Kroger and Haslett 1988). Comments will be drawn from this work to propose mechanisms by which late adolescents undergo the second individuation challenge. It is recognized that such efforts provide only a start to understanding the normative differentiation experience and that frequent and intensive interviews with diverse groups of adolescents over time are necessary to delineate the course of life's second individuation process.

I propose that parallels to Mahler's stage of normal symbiosis and separation–individuation subphases (differentiation, practicing, *rapprochement* and libidinal object constancy) occur in normative adolescent development. Similarities to infantile autism can be found among those adolescents who have failed, by varying degrees, to internalize a parental representation from earlier years. Empirical indicators for these suggestions have come via studies of ego identity status – a psychosocial measure providing clues as to underlying intrapsychic organization.

Marcia's psychosocial identity statuses (described in the previous chapter) may reflect various stages in the underlying differentiation between self and object representations. Identity achievements are characterized by an intrapsychic organization in which self and object representations are clearly distinct. Support for this proposal has come from various studies indicating an association of greater individuation (in terms of ego development, locus of control, field independence, use of mature defenses; object representation, a clear 'I' position and relationships with others) with the identity achievement position (Berzonsky and Adams 1999; Brickfield 1989; Chapman and Nicholls 1976; Cramer 1995; Ginsburg and Orlofsky 1981; Johnson *et al.* 2003; Josselson 1982, 1987; Kroger 1990; Orlofsky *et al.* 1973; Papini *et al.* 1989; Perosa *et al.* 1996, 2002; Shulkin 1990).

Moratoriums, differentiating from internalized parental representations, have shown parallels to infants in subphases of differentiation, practicing and *rapprochement*. In work by Josselson (1982), Orlofsky and Frank (1986) and Kroger (1990), early memories of moratorium subjects found them wishing to explore the world, with or without others (reminiscent of infant differentiation and practicing). Observations of moratoriums vying for power but ambivalent once it was held are reminiscent of behaviors during the infant *rapprochement* crisis (Donovan, cited in Marcia 1976b; Podd *et al.* 1970). On a measure of self-differentiation, moratoriums have scored as more fused with and simultaneously more cut off from significant others than other identity statuses (Johnson *et al.* 2003). Moratoriums have also shown more emotional reactivity than other identity groupings (Johnson *et al.* 2003). The authors interpret these findings as indicative of wishes to individuate from parents while simultaneously wishing to remain fused with their internalized parental representations.

The foreclosure status would seem to reflect an intrapsychic organization having parallels with the symbiotic phase of infancy. Research with foreclosure adolescents has shown little differentiation between their self and internalized parental representations (Josselson 1982, 1987; Kroger 1985, 1995; Kroger and Haslett 1988; Papini *et al.* 1989; Shulkin 1990). Foreclosures have also shown more emotional overinvolvement with others, including triangulation and overidentitfication with parents (Johnson *et al.* 2003; Perosa *et al.* 1996, 2002). Foreclosures' perceived lack of parental support, fear of parental opposition and a history of giving in to parental demands also reflect little differentiation between self and internalized other (Perosa *et al.* 2002).

Diffusions have, on the whole, had little opportunity for internalizing parents with concomitant difficulty in developing a cohesive sense of self (Jordan 1970, 1971; Josselson 1987); a fused and highly undifferentiated family system providing little support for developing a unique identity has characterized diffusions' child-rearing environments (Perosa *et al.* 2002). Particularly noteworthy for the identity diffusions also have been high scores on an emotional cut-off scale from the Differentiation of Self Inventory (Johnson *et al.* 2003). Emotional distancing characterizes the relationships diffusions hold both with family and peers.

From longitudinal work of Kroger and Haslett (1988), those late adolescents remaining foreclosed over a two-year interval were very likely to evidence a non-secure attachment profile. Moratoriums, at the conclusion of the study, were about equally divided between secure and non-secure attachment styles, while achievements were highly likely to be secure in their attachment style, evidencing greater intra-psychic self–other differentiation. More recent longitudinal work by Kroger (1995) has differentiated between 'firm' and 'developmental' foreclosures. Late adolescents who remained foreclosed over the course of their university study evidenced significantly higher nurturance seeking needs at the outset (and conclusion) of the study than those initial foreclosures who later proceeded to moratorium and achievement positions.

A pictorial scheme for adolescents, in the process of differentiating themselves from the internalized parent, appears in Figure 3.1.

In this scheme, the diffusion position has not been described, for diffusion (in the Eriksonian sense of having no central 'core') would not reflect a normative resolution to the second individuation process. Subphase representations should serve as a useful base for describing social reaction to best facilitate the adolescent individuation process. Just as the caretaker must adjust his or her response to infant action through each developmental subphase for optimal ego structuraliza-tion, so too must social reaction resonate with adolescent need in each second individuation subphase to provide a context for optimal development.

Measuring the adolescent separation–individuation process

There have been a number of instruments developed over the past two decades for the measurement of the adolescent separation–individuation process. Among these instruments are the following: Separation–Individuation Inventory (Bartolomucci and Taylor 1991); Separation–Individuation Theme Scale (Coonerty 1989); Separation–Individuation Process Inventory (Christenson and Wilson 1985); Adolescent Separation Anxiety Test (Hansburg 1980a, 1980b); Psychological Separation Inventory (Hoffman 1984); Separation–Individuation Test of Adolescence (Levine *et al.* 1986); Individuation Scale (Maslach *et al.* 1985); Adolescent Individuation Measure (Sabatelli and Williams 1993).

I am physically different from mother, but I carry her image inside me; without mother, I do not exist.

Foreclosure – fusion of self with internalized other

I may exist in my own right, but I must check to see if that is all right with mother.

Moratorium – differentiation

I exist in my own right, and I must show this to mother by being totally in control.

Moratorium – practising

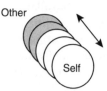

If I exist in my own right, then I am totally alone; I do and do not want to exist in this way.

Moratorium – rapprochement

I exist in my own right, and so does mother; it is all right to exist in this way.

Achievement – self–other constancy

Figure 3.1 Subphases of adolescent separation–individuation

The last decade has witnessed refinements to some of these measures. For example, McClanahan and Holmbeck (1992), Levine and Saintonge (1993), Kroger and Green (1994), Levine (1994) and Holmbeck and McClanahan (1994) have suggested refinements to Levine's Separation–Individuation Test of Adolescence and Dolan *et al.* (1992) and Lapsley *et al.* (2001) have made refinements to Christenson and Wilson's Separation–Individuation Inventory. In addition, a new measure, Parental Separation Anxiety (Hock *et al.* 2001), has also been developed to assess parents' feelings about separation from their adolescent offspring.

Space limitations prohibit a full discussion of all of these measures. However, I will provide details on two of the above instruments most commonly used in contemporary adolescent research. Levine's (Levine *et al.* 1986, Levine 1994) Separation–Individuation Test of Adolescence (SITA) is currently a 103-item, self-report inventory that presents a series of statements reflecting attitudes about relationships with parents, teachers and peers. Items are presented in Likert Scale format on a five-point scale, ranging from 'strongly agree or is always true of me' to 'strongly disagree or is never true of me'. The SITA's nine scales are derived from elements of the early separation–individuation process described by Mahler *et al.* 1975. These scales are Separation Anxiety (significant others experienced as abandoning), Engulfment Anxiety (close relationships feared as envelopement), Nurturance Seeking (strong caretaker attachment), Peer Enmeshment (strivings for intense peer intimacy), Teacher Enmeshment (strivings for intense attachments to teachers), Practicing-Mirroring (narcissistic strivings), Rejection Expectancy (significant others perceived as callous and hostile) and Healthy Separation (balance of dependence and independence strivings). The SITA was developed through a three-step validation procedure with attention to theoretical-substantive validity and internal structural validation. Cronbach's alphas for the nine scales have ranged from 0.64 to 0.88 for both clinical and non-clinical samples.

Hoffman's (1984) Psychological Separation Inventory is another commonly used instrument that assesses dimensions of the adolescent separation–individuation process. The instrument is comprised of four subscales with a total of 138 items. The functional independence (FI) subscale assess the adolescent's ability to manage personal and practical affairs without requesting parental involvement. The emotional independence subscale (EI) assesses the adolescent's freedom from excessive reliance on parental approval, closeness and emotional support. The conflictual independence (CI) subscale measures the adolescent's freedom from excessive anger, guilt, resentment and mistrust of each parent. Finally, the attitudinal independence (AI) subscale assesses the extent to which the adolescent expresses attitudes and values that are distinct from those of parents. It must be noted that Hoffman's measure assesses only dimensions of differentiation from parents and does not assess qualities of connection. Hoffman reported Chronbach alphas ranging from 0.84 to 0.92 on the four subscales and a correlations of 0.49 to 0.96 for individual scales over a two-week interval. Subsequent work has examined scales with respect to a number of indexes of late adolescent coping to support the construct validity of this measure.

Historical backdrop to Blos's separation–individuation challenge

Blos's early directorship of the Experimental School, run by Anna Freud and Dorothy Burlingham, and his contact with Freud and psychoanalytic circles in Vienna laid the foundations for Blos's interest in adolescents (Esman 1997). Blos's emigration to New York brought him into contact with the work of Margaret Mahler and inspired his consideration of adolescence as a second separation–individuation process, albeit with important distinctions from the first infant process. While Blos retained his ties to classic psychoanalytic foundations, his work, nevertheless, served as a bridge to some object relations approaches and later elaborations of the second separation–individuation process during adolescence.

From classic psychoanalysis, it is the drives that govern motivation and behavior. Relationships or interpersonal interactions were important to Freud, but only insofar as they satisfied instinctual needs (the drives). By sharp contrast, an object relations approach focuses on people and environmental influences to explain motivation. Many object relations models focus on the process of identification to examine the forces of environmental influences on the development of the ego. Furthermore, while classic psychoanalysis focused on conflict among id, ego and superego structures, object relations writers focused on the early structuralization of the ego itself (Greenberg and Mitchell 1983). Blos assessed adolescents' changes in object relations through discussions of separation anxiety as well as the mourning of earlier internalized ties to parents, considerably extending Freud's notion of signal anxiety (McCarthy 1995). By considering adolescence as a second separation–individuation process, Blos has inspired many later theorists and researchers to delve more deeply into the structural reorganizations of the ego and forms of optimal character formation upon entry into adult life via the second separation–individuation process.

Research findings on adolescent separation–individuation

The second separation–individuation challenge entails both intra-psychic and interpersonal changes. The past 15 years have witnessed a growing body of empirical investigations into the adolescent intrapsychic separation–individuation process in relation to interpersonal relationships involving family and peers, social adjustment, career decision making and psychopathology. More recent researches into the relationship between adolescent separation–individuation and ethnicity and cultural context will be overviewed in the section on current directions in adolescent separation–individuation research.

Ultimately, the relationships with parents themselves provide a crucial gauge of success in the intrapsychic restructuring of early object ties on the part of adolescents. The GAP Report (Group for the Advancement of Psychiatry 1968) indicated that, among other accomplishments, it is when one can return to parents in a new and equal relationship that adolescent individuation is complete. The coexistence of individuality and connectedness in adolescent relationships with their families appears crucial to optimal adolescent separation–individuation. The quality of such relationships provides some measure of intrapsychic developmental progress for the adolescent. Quintana and Lapsley (1990) found a positive relationship between attachment to parents and differentiation from them, while Rice (1991) found continuity in attachment to parents over time coupled with increases in independence from them in a sample of late adolescent college students. Benson *et al.* (1992: 189) reported that 'the secure base provided by attachments to mothers and fathers acts as a protective factor against a floundering inability to make commitments', while results from Blustein *et al.* (1991) showed that attachment to and independence from at least the same-sex parent is predictive of progress in career commitment. In a meta-analysis of adolescent attachment relations with parents, Rice (1990) called for further longitudinal studies to examine the importance of attachment relations for adolescent development. Individuation appears most likely within the context of a family structure capable of supporting and encouraging such maturation (Adams and Jones 1983; Enright *et al.* 1980; Grotevant and Cooper 1986; Pinquart and Silbereisen 2002; Silverberg and Steinberg 1987).

Interestingly, research by Perosa *et al.* (1996) shows, however, that family variables account for only about 21 per cent of the variance in the actual identity formation process described by Erikson (1968). While the intrapsychic separation–individuation process appears to be a vital step toward identity formation (character formation for Blos), other factors are also important. Ultimately, personality and/or dispositional factors such as ego resilience, self-esteem, openness to new experience, introspectiveness and willingness to explore also play an extremely important role in character formation.

Several researchers have examined specific family interactions in relation to adolescent separation–individuation. Bjornsen (2000) investigated Blos's (1985) suggestion that an important part of the second separation–individuation process is receiving a family 'blessing'. In his investigation of fathers and sons, Blos defined a blessing as the father's acknowledgment and acceptance of the son's adult status and, most importantly, the son's adult masculinity. Some form of blessing is needed before 'childhood can be brought to a natural termination' (Blos 1985: 12). Bjornsen examined the possible role of the blessing to the adolescent separation–individuation process for both genders in a sample of college students. He found that 71.5 per cent of the 281 late adolescents sampled had received some form of blessing from a parent, and they had described the event as meaningful. Additionally, of those who had not received a blessing, about half wished that they had. Adolescents of this investigation wrote powerful and sensitive accounts of the blessing they received or wished they had received. The study did not provide details of whether or not gender of the parent was important in providing a blessing. The role of the father in adolescent separation–individuation has also been specifically explored, since many studies have indicated fathers to be less involved with their adolescent offspring than mothers (see Shulman and Klein 1993 for a review). The availability rather than immediate presence of the father appeared crucial to optimal adolescent differentiation (Shulman and Klein 1993). Indeed, fathers more than mothers conveyed the feeling that they could rely on their adolescents' competence and considered them as independent individuals. Where fathers are absent through divorce, it appears that 'big brothers' can aid male adolescents from single-parent families with the second separation–individuation process (Saintonge *et al.* 1998).

Peer relations have also been extensively examined in studies of adolescent separation–individuation. Perceptions of social support have been positively related to healthy separation–individuation during adolescence and negatively related to dependency denial and engulfment (McClanahan and Holmbeck 1992). Quintana and Kerr (1993) found that participation in relationships which supported autonomy, mirroring and nurturance needs was associated with freedom from depression among college students and that, conversely, engulfment anxiety separation anxiety and denial of dependency were associated with depressive complaints. Individuated late adolescents are disinclined to stereotype others (Humphreys and Davidson 1997).

Mazor *et al.* (1993) have also explored intrapsychic and interpersonal aspects of adolescent separation–individuation in a cross-sectional study of kibbutz children and adolescents in Israel. They found that their older subjects construed self and self–other relationships from a more differentiated perspective than younger ones and that the fear of engulfment was higher in early adolescence and subsequent age groups than in late childhood. Furthermore, in mid- and late-adolescence, there appeared ambivalence between fears of merging and separateness in relationships with others. Studies of adolescent intimacy have found reasonably consistent results across several methods of assessing separation–individuation resolution. High intimacy has been associated with a firm sense of identity and intrapsychic separateness from early object ties. Additionally, those adolescents forming either enmeshed or superficial (stereotypic) peer relationships have not differed in type of disorder rating for separation–individuation capacity (Levitz-Jones and Orlofsky 1985; Millis 1984). Similar results have also come from a study of intimacy among young adult women (Bellew-Smith and Korn 1986).

One 'peer' issue that has been examined in several recent studies is the role of the imaginary audience and personal fable in adolescent separation–individuation. Lapsley and others have been exploring functions that the imaginary audience and personal fable phenomena may serve during the adolescent separation–individuation process (Goossens *et al.* 2002; Lapsley 1992; Lapsley and Rice 1988; Vartanian 1997). Lapsley's research suggests that adolescents' use of imaginary audiences and personal fables are best conceptualized as defensive and restitutive mechanisms that facilitate resilience and coping during the second individuation process. Although Lapsley's initial research on these mechanisms has not been entirely replicated or confirmed (Goossens *et al.* 2002), a greater understanding of adolescent coping mechanisms for weathering the second separation–individuation process promises to be a productive line of future research activity. Goossens *et al.* (2002) have suggested that such research concentrate on the exact role of the invulnerability/ omnipotence complex as well as developmental changes in this complex as adolescent separation–individuation proceeds. Using multiple measures of the imaginary audience and personal fable, Vartanian (1997) adds that some resolution of measurement issues surrounding these two constructs is also needed.

The ability to tolerate aloneness also allows insight into intrapsychic developments during adolescence. Coleman's early (1974) work focused on feelings associated with solitude. The following sentence completion responses extracted from that research indicate increasing tolerance of solitude with age:

Eleven-year-old girl: WHEN THERE IS NO ONE ELSE AROUND you are lonely as if the world was empty.
Eleven-year-old boy: IF A PERSON IS ALONE he gets nervous.
Eighteen-year-old girl: IF A PERSON IS ALONE they have time to think about life.
Seventeen-year-old boy: IF A PERSON IS ALONE he chooses his own path.

(Coleman 1974: 37–38)

Responses of the younger subjects may be interpreted as reflecting separation anxiety when external objects are not available to support an intrapsychic structure as yet undifferentiated from early object ties; older adolescents appear more comfortable with using aloneness in the service of their own individuation efforts. More recently, Larson (1997) has also examined emergence of the ability to tolerate solitude in adolescence as a feature of the second separation–individuation process. With age, solitude had a positive effect on emotional state. Adolescents (but not pre-adolescents) who spent intermediate periods of time alone were better adjusted than those spending small or large amounts of time alone.

Psychological adjustment has also been investigated in relation to adolescent separation–individuation. Perhaps one of the most encompassing investigations has come from Boles (1999), who developed a model of the relationship between adolescent individuation, parental representation and psychological adjustment. The empirically derived model shows that quality of parental representations facilitates the adolescent separation–individuation process, which in turn facilitates psychological adjustment in late adolescence. Additionally, an adolescent's stage in the separation–individuation process mediates the influence that the quality of parental representations have on psychosocial adjustment in late adolescence.

Research on adolescent separation–individuation has consistently pointed to more optimal psychosocial adjustment for those who successfully navigate this intrapsychic passage (Holmbeck and Leake 1999; Holmbeck and Wandrei 1993; Lapsley and Edgerton 2002; Rice *et al.* 1990). Rice *et al.* (1990) found that the adolescent's affective response to separation–individuation is strongly related to college adjustment. Students who reported positive separation feelings (non-anxious and unresentful reactions to a variety of separation experiences) also reported being well adjusted to university life, while those with negative, angry or resentful responses to separation had more difficulty managing adjustment to college. More recently, Lapsley and Edgerton (2002) have found college adjustment to be positively associated with secure attachment and optimal separation–individuation. Furthermore, adolescent separation–individuation, family relations, and personality variables have been found to be better predictors of psychosocial adjustment than cognitive or home-leaving status (Holmbeck and Wandrei 1993).

Home-leaving strategies have also provided clues to the development of intrapsychic separation and individuation processes during late adolescence. Secure emotional attachment (reflecting engagement in the second individuation challenge) has been associated with an easier leave-taking during late adolescence, while conflicted attachment has been linked with problematic departure (Henton *et al.* 1980; Kraemer 1982; Sullivan and Sullivan 1980). Moore and Hotch (1981, 1982, 1983) have found that the best indicators of successful intrapsychic separation from parents are economic independence, personal control and separate residence. Emotional dissociation has been the most negative indicator of successful intrapsychic separation. Anderson and Fleming have suggested the following:

> [W]hile it is important, as others have found, . . . for adolescents to maintain a positive, supportive relationship with parents, their own identity and psychosocial adjustment needs require that this be outweighed by feelings of physical separateness and personal control over their own lives.
>
> (Anderson and Fleming 1986: 457)

Adjustment to demands of the world at large appears intricately interwoven with resolution to the second individuation challenge.

The relationship between separation–individuation difficulties, eating disorders, and depression among adolescent women have also been explored in work over the past 15 years (Armstrong and Roth 1989; Friedlander and Siegel 1990; Marsden *et al.* 2002; Milne and Lancaster 2001; Rhodes and Kroger 1992; Smolak and Levine 1993). This body of work points to similar intrapsychic and familial factors that contribute to the etiology and maintenance of eating disorders for women and to the serious consequences for those who may fail to attain a sense of psychological separateness. Marsden *et al.* (2002) illustrates that perceived parental control may be a mediating factor between separation–individuation and eating disorders. Milne and Lancaster (2001) have used path analysis to show that adolescent women's concerns with maternal control predict separation–individuation difficulties, which predict interpersonal concerns, which in turn predict symptoms of depression.

Current directions in adolescent separation–individuation research

Perhaps one of the most interesting questions at present is whether or not the adolescent separation–individuation process is a phenomenon found in a diversity of cultural contexts. Many collectivist cultures, for example, may not encourage the development of individuation during adolescence. A number of empirical investigations of adolescent separation–individuation have now begun to appear both across and within varied cultural or ethnic contexts (e.g. Choi 2002; Gnaulati and Heine 2001; Kalsner and Pistole 2003; Scharf 2001). All of these studies demonstrate variations in patterns of adolescent separation–individuation by ethnic group and/or cultural context. Scharf (2001), for example, has explored variations of separation–individuation and attachment patterns among adolescents within four Israeli contexts: those living in a city; those from a kibbutz familial setting; those from a kibbutz communal setting; a transitional group raised in a communal setting as young children but who then moved into familial sleeping arrangement prior to age 6 years. The group who had lived in a communal setting (sleeping away from parents as young children) in the kibbutz evidenced less competent coping as adolescents in situations that evoked separation anxiety as well as a higher incidence of non-autonomous attachment representations. Much remains to be explored regarding child-rearing ecologies and their relationship optimal adjustment during adolescence and adulthood.

A recent innovation to understanding the relationship between family dynamics and adolescent separation–individuation has come via attempts to explore parental separation anxiety associated with the adolescent's increasing independence and eventual home-leaving. Bartle-Haring *et al.* (2002) and Hock *et al.* (2001) developed a means of assessing a parents' ease with this process and have begun validating the measure. The newly constructed Parents of Adolescents Separation Anxiety Scale (PASAS) is a 35-item instrument designed to assess parental emotions associated with adolescent separation–individuation. Factor analyses supported the formation of two subscales: Anxiety about adolescent distancing and Comfort with secure base role. Adolescents of parents who had higher anxiety scale scores on the measure reported lower quality of attachment to both mothers and fathers. Additionally, longitudinal work with the instrument has found that mothers' sense of providing a secure base for their college adolescents is associated with their adolescents' identity achievement, while fathers' anxiety about distancing was associated with their daughters' foreclosure ratings increasing over time and their sons' foreclosure scores decreasing. A focus on both parents' and adolescents' feelings about the second separation–individuation process is a very promising future direction for future research.

Finally, the role of adolescent separation–individuation in relation to career development has attracted a number of recent studies. Most have focused on the role of adolescent separation–individuation in relation to parental attachment and career maturity (e.g. Lee and Hughey 2001; O'Brien 1996; Santos and Coimbra 2000; Tokar *et al.* 2003). Some complex relationships among these variables have been found. Through the use of structural equations modeling, Tokar *et al.*, for example, noted the joint influence of adolescent separation–individuation and attachment security on career development to be greater than either of these two factors alone, while Lee and Hughey (2001) found parent attachment to play a greater role in career maturity than separation–individuation. Santos and Coimbra also found those with low levels of intrapsychic separation from parents to be at both ends of the spectrum for two types of career indecision that were assessed: generalized and developmental indecision. What can be concluded from these studies is that some links do exist between between adolescent separation–individuation, parental attachment and career decision making, though these links may be mediated by variables such as vocational self-concept crystallization.

Implications for social response

Though Blos does not discuss in depth the role of the social context in facilitating adolescent resolution to the four character challenges, parents, teachers, counselors, psychotherapists and others working closely with young people may all play critical parts in facilitating movement through the second individuation process. Other adolescent character challenges are also affected by reactions from these socialization agents, as well as from the general structure of society itself. In passing from the family to a place in the larger social order, that order must be ready to receive:

> [N]o adolescent, at any station of his journey, can develop optimally without societal structures standing ready to receive him, offering him that authentic credibility with which he can identify or polarize. . . . the psychic structure of the individual is critically affected, for better or worse, by the structure of society. . . . what I try to emphasize here is the fact that the successful course of

adolescence depends intrinsically on the degree of intactness and cohesion which societal institutions obtain.

(Blos 1971: 975)

Blos continues by noting that character formation may at times be helped not by efforts at individual remediation but rather by the rehabilitation of those very social institutions in which the adolescent is expected to find some suitable niche. Disaffected youth, though often instigators of social revolution, are seldom its cause. A society, through its institutions, must remain sensitive and responsive to youth's insights (often deadly accurate) into problems of the social structure (Blos 1979).

In comments on the earlier onset of puberty, Blos cautions against the simplistic conclusion that family and school must respond to the earlier arousal of sexual drive: 'We have ample evidence to demonstrate that an acceptance of the young adolescent as a self-directing, sexually active "young person" interferes severely with the preparatory functions of this stage' (Blos 1971: 970). He continues to argue that it is critical to prolong rather than abbreviate childhood in order to allow time for intrapsychic restructuring to occur. A young person pressing toward earlier sexual activity may do so at the expense of a firmly established sexual identity in adult life.

Blos cautions that parents and social institutions must also recognize the role they may play in adolescents' struggles for freedom from infantile dependencies. Where intrapsychic change is difficult, declarations of independence are often projected outward, in exaggerated form, onto institutions (for example, universities) which have provided youth with temporary accommodation through the adolescent passage. It is important for adults to recognize their potential for association with an internalized parental image rather than their existence merely as external agents of reality in evoking adolescent response.

In terms of the second individuation challenge, it is informative to move beyond Blos to recent efforts at subphase delineation, for each stage presents a time of special need which must be recognized and addressed to provide optimal conditions for development. Mahler's observations of what constitutes 'ordinary devoted mothering' through each subphase of infancy is helpful in understanding ways to facilitate the second individuation process. Assuming the adolescent has enjoyed the security provided by significant overlap between self and parental representation since the end of pre-Oedipal stages, the removal of that overlap is now possible. As Mahler has observed for infants, a stage of normal symbiosis is absolutely critical in order for separation–individuation subphases to proceed.

In normative adolescent development, the differentiation process begins of its own accord. It can be facilitated by adults who, despite youths' withdrawal from the closeness of earlier latency relationships, do not react in retaliation but rather with understanding of new needs for distance and independent action. Respect for adolescents as individuals in their own rights rather than as extensions of one's self are crucial adult attitudes for aiding the second individuation process. As in all adolescent separation–individuation subphases, use of transitional objects may also assist adolescents' efforts in relinquishing infantile object ties (Kroger 1998).

Counseling or psychotherapeutic intervention may be necessary when delayed or premature differentiation from the internalized parental representation takes place. Inhibited differentiation is likely to be responsible for what Erikson and Marcia describe as a foreclosed identity. Here, many of the adolescent's actions will be aimed at receiving parental approval, thereby gaining narcissistic gratification and self-esteem. With such youths it is the therapeutic aim to promote differentiation in a manner age appropriate yet paralleling the way in which a 'good enough' mother assists her infant through the differentiation process. Following establishment of a caring relationship, therapeutic response might take the form of gentle, developmental 'nudges' coupled with explorations of the youth's guilt and fear over abandoning the internalized parent (Feldberg 1983). Additionally over time, therapeutic work must involve the adolescent's de-idealization of the internalized love object as well as working through the mourning process (Blos 1979).

Premature differentiation in adolescence is characterized by separation which cannot keep pace with individuation. Such misalignment may stem from fear of engulfment by the internalized parent. As a result, there is insufficient ego strength to support the push towards expression of autonomous action; poor decisions, which may result in serious injury or situations having long-term consequences, are often the result. Here, it is the therapeutic aim to harness differentiation by setting firm limits and assisting the family to do likewise. Interpretation and confrontation may also be used to work through anxieties and so bring adolescent separation and individuation tracks into closer alignment (Feldberg 1983).

Adolescent parallels to the practicing subphase of infancy bring continued efforts to test an intrapsychic structure permitting more autonomous functioning. As the practicing toddler is assisted in further exploration by new locomotor abilities, so too may adolescents acquire the skill (and driver's license) necessary for motorized movement further into the world beyond where buses and family outings go. It is still vital, however, that significant others offer the adolescent a solid 'refueling' base from which new explorations can be launched. Parental support and encouragement for such exploratory effort during adolescence parallels the importance Mahler *et al.* (1975) place on maternal reaction to the infant in all separation–individuation subphases. A balance between support and limit setting would seem to provide the optimal conditions for resolution to demands of this practicing subphase of adolescence.

Adolescent *rapprochement* is marked by swings between efforts at distancing and renewed efforts for closeness, as youths seek to return internalized self and object overlap to earlier levels of organization. The ability of adults to maintain their own ground in the face of adolescent regressive and progressive development is a difficult but necessary stance. A caregiver's vulnerability to adolescent assault (in defense against the latter's infantile regressive pulls) does not enable one to remain emotionally available as youths' intrapsychic moorings become unfastened.

Libidinal object constancy represents the infant resolution to separation–individuation subphases; for the adolescent, this stage involves a consolidation of structural reorganization. Brandt nicely states features of this final phase:

> The identity crisis of adolescence is thus caused not only because it is hard for the adolescent to find himself, but because in the process he must find himself alone. Kramer (1958) . . . sees the 'experience of identity as finding oneself painfully separated from one's accustomed environment, alone, and forced to rely on one's own resources. The experience of separation from the first love object, mother, and the sensation of aloneness is one of the factors in the creation of a sense of identity.' Without this separation no true autonomy or independence of the ego or superego is possible, and hence no real sense of identity can be achieved.
>
> (Brandt 1977: 517–518)

This final phase, the aim of normative parenting, counseling, and psychotherapeutic effort, would see adolescents able to meet in a relationship of 'I' and 'Thou', alone and separate but able to hold genuine interest in the identity of an other.

Recent researches into the adolescent separation–individuation process also point to clinical or counseling implications for those working with youth. Lapsley and Edgerton (2002) suggest the potential counseling or clinical use of PATHSTEP, an instrument designed to detect separation–individuation difficulties. Items from the instrument may be used as initial probes in making sense of a client's difficulties (e.g. 'Does the sense of who you are tend to get lost when you are in a close relationship?'). The authors also point to the importance of conflictual independence in normal adolescent separation–individuation. Clients with conflictual dependency problems would be at lower risk for adjustment difficulties than those with problems of self-differentiation. Holmbeck and Wandrei's (1993) research on college adjustment among first-year students suggests that adjustment may be less related to their cognitive perceptions of home-leaving and more related to object relational functioning. Therapeutic assistance that is directed solely to the cognitive domain for such students may be less successful than that assisting developments in the second separation–individuation process. Therapists working with students from collectivist cultural backgrounds in western settings may be most effective by helping such youth to examine the personal importance of their collectivistic senses of self and strengthening their sense of ownership of collectivist attitudes (Choi 2002).

Summary

Character formation as outlined by Blos involves the resolution of at least four challenges in order for identity to develop and stabilize at the close of adolescence. Challenges addressed through a sequence of phases are the second individuation process, reworking and mastering childhood trauma, developing a sense of ego continuity and forming a sexual identity. Object relations theorists have proposed more detailed accounts of mechanisms that may operate during the second separation–individuation process, and a growing body of research is exploring this phenomenon in different cultural contexts. It is vital that individuals and social institutions involved with youth appreciate their potential associations with adolescents' internalized representations of infantile love objects which must be restructured by adolescents if optimal resolution to character formation is to occur.

Further reading

Boles, S. A. (1999) 'A model of parent representations, second individuation, and psychological adjustment in late adolescence', *Journal of Clinical Psychology* 55: 497–512.

Kroger, J. (1998) 'Adolescence as a second separation-individuation process', in

E. E. Skoe and A. L. von der Lippe (eds) *Personality Development in adolescence*, London: Routledge.

Lapsley, D. K., Aalsma, M. C. and Varshney, N. M. (2001) 'A factor analytic and psychometric examination of pathology of separation–individuation', *Journal of Clinical Psychology* 57: 915–932.

Scharf, M. (2001) 'A "natural experiment" in child rearing ecologies and adolescents' attachment and separation representations', *Child Development* 72: 236–251.

4 Identity through a cognitive-developmental lens

Kohlberg's contributions

> All this simply bewilders me, mother. People may differ about matters
> of opinion, or even about religion; but how can they differ about right
> and wrong? Right is right; and wrong is wrong; and if a man cannot
> distinguish them properly, he is either a fool or a rascal: that's all.
>
> (Stephen, in George Bernard Shaw's *Major Barbara*, 1907)

Young Stephen's bewilderment in response to varying opinions of the
'one true morality' reflects not only his conception of matters moral but
also the very structure of his identity itself. Set in an upper-class drawing room at the turn of the century, *Major Barbara* opens as late adolescent Stephen discusses with his mother, Lady Britomart, the financial
futures of her three children. It seems that the siblings' only assurance
of future monetary security rests in financial support from the
estranged husband and father, Undershaft, a manufacturer of muni-
tions which destroy human life. Elder daughter Barbara, a major in the
Salvation Army, is at this point in her career 'saving' starving souls in
the exchange of bread for salvation. Upon reunion with her father at
the close of Act I, Barbara and Undershaft agree to sample the other's
understanding of morality (each with hope of converting the other).
Through Acts II and III, assorted lovers and Salvation Army shelter
'converts' all add their own constructs of morality to the family debate,
as Barbara undergoes transition to a new level of moral reasoning. The
dialogue and interpretations of justice by each of the play's central
characters reflect their markedly different constructions of morality,
which in turn point to underlying differences in the very structure of
their own identities. Characters from *Major Barbara* neatly exemplify
stages in the evolution of moral understanding within Kohlberg's
cognitive-developmental framework and will later be revisited to
introduce the theorist's stage sequence.

Questions about universal justice and the development of one's sense of ethics led Lawrence Kohlberg into a career devoted to the study of moral reasoning. Drawing upon Piaget's investigations of children's moral philosophies, Kohlberg not only helped legitimate moral enquiry as a field of scientific study but also extended the observation of moral development from childhood into the adolescent and adult years of life. Unlike many other cognitive theorists addressing the growth of knowledge, Kohlberg was not content merely to chart developmental change but continued to explore, in very practical terms, the implications his views held for social response, particularly in the field of education. 'Educating for a just society' has been the focus of several attempts by Kohlberg to work with adolescents in communities aimed at enhancing participants' levels of moral decision making.

Unlike some other theorists discussed in this volume, Kohlberg does not address directly the question of identity. Rather, he views the development of moral reasoning as one subdomain of ego functioning, which in turn is an aspect of identity. A study of Kohlberg's work does allow one to make inferences about identity, however, as moral reasoning processes are tapped. It also allows the foundation upon which Kegan (reviewed in Chapter 6) bases his efforts to delineate the structural evolution of the self over the course of the lifespan.

Kohlberg the person

Born in 1927 in New York, Kohlberg spent his late adolescent years in various laboring jobs. He traced his future career path to a decision he made after high school to help smuggle Jewish refugees through the British blockade into Palestine. Kohlberg then spent three years in the merchant marines, followed by time as an engineer on a navy iceboat purchased by the Jewish defense force. This boat, full of refugees, was captured on its way to Palestine and Kohlberg, along with the rest of the crew and passengers, was held in a camp in Cyprus. Eventually Kohlberg and several others escaped and lived on a kibbutz in Palestine until it was safe to return to the United States (Power 1991). From these experiences, Kohlberg began struggling with the question of how one could justify disobeying the law and legitimate authorities. Later, this question became the central issue that Kohlberg posed to research participants (Rest *et al.* 1988).

Plagued also with moral questions about violence, Kohlberg decided to enrol at the University of Chicago and take time for serious ethical reflection through the study of philosophy; at the same time, he completed his BA in a record one year (Rest *et al.* 1988). As an undergraduate, Kohlberg was torn between a career in law, with the opportunity it provided to work towards social justice, and one in clinical psychology, where help could be offered at a more individual level of intervention. After summer work as an attendant in a psychiatric hospital, Kohlberg decided to embark on graduate studies in clinical psychology through the University of Chicago. A further crucial career turning point came one day during his internship. A paranoid patient in his office was agitated, shouting that the chief psychiatrist of the institution was persecuting her. At this point the chief psychiatrist entered, having overheard the cries, and prescribed electric shock treatment. Kohlberg protested that this action would only confirm the woman's sense of injustice. While his protests were to no avail, they did provide the impetus for a redirection of his studies to research on social justice and the development of moral reasoning.

Kohlberg's PhD revolutionized theories of moral development. In a climate fixated on the role of the Freudian superego for determining concepts of justice, the young researcher's proposal of evolutionary stages in development offered a creative alternative avenue of enquiry into this dimension of human behavior. In contrast to his BA, Kohlberg's PhD was awarded after nine long years of research. His only comment was that it is not always possible to predict human behavior. Appointments at Yale, the Institute for Advanced Study, University of Chicago, and Harvard University's Graduate School of Education followed. It was at the latter institution that Kohlberg spent most of his academic career, establishing the Center for Moral Education. There he attracted a number of scholars from around the world and undertook longitudinal studies of the development of moral reasoning alongside the evaluation of educational programs designed to enhance moral understanding. He furthermore encouraged active discussions with critics who disagreed with his views in a climate of mutual respect (Walsh 1999). A great tragedy occurred in 1971, however, when Kohlberg contracted a parasitic infection while doing cross-cultural work in Central America. Over the ensuing years, enormous physical pain and fatigue became his constant companions. Nevertheless, Kohlberg persisted with his many enthusiasms as best he could. Ultimately, though, Kohlberg made the decision to end his own life in 1987 at the age of 59 years. In so doing, he left family members and a wide circle of friends, colleagues and students of all ages remembering him for his great generosity, enthusiasm, inspiration and engaging intellect (Walsh 1999). Kohlberg also left a legacy of over one hundred publications to future generations of researchers for continued exploration of the work he began.

Kohlberg's view of identity

In contrast to more underlying or holistic notions of identity described by Loevinger and Kegan in the next two chapters, Kohlberg conceptualizes moral reasoning as only one subdomain of ego functioning evolving alongside others (for example, cognition) in the course of identity development. If one examines relationships between such subdomains of ego development, there often appears a 'necessary but not sufficient' conditional link between them. Thus, a certain stage of cognition appears to be a necessary but not sufficient condition for a certain stage of moral reasoning. Additionally, in Kohlberg's view, subdomains of ego functioning develop in relation to different types of environments. Thus, Piaget addresses the development of cognition in relation to the natural or physical world, while Selman explores the impact of cognitive change on the meaning of social relationships; Kohlberg examines the development of moral reasoning in relation to the social world, while Snarey explores the development of moral reasoning in relation to the natural or physical environment (Snarey *et al.* 1983). Though Kohlberg is not a theorist of ego development, many of his notions do allow inferences about identity and provide the foundations for a structural view of the self quite different from those of Erikson or Blos, described in preceding chapters.

Kohlberg proposes that the development of moral reasoning evolves through a series of stages, each capturing a mode of reasoning about justice that is *qualitatively* different from preceding and succeeding stages. No longer was it necessary to think about people having *quantitatively* different superego controls shaped by their cultures or socializing agents; rather, Kohlberg pointed the way towards an understanding of morality based on differing constructions or meanings of justice by individuals. Furthermore, each stage appears to occur in a universal, hierarchical and invariant sequence; progressively more complex and comprehensive structures of moral reasoning emerge through the course of development.

> [My view] implies that moral development may be defined in terms of the qualitative reorganization of the individual's pattern of thought rather than the learning of new content. Each new reorganization integrates within a broader perspective the insights that were achieved at lower stages.
>
> (Colby *et al.* 1983: 1)

In contrast to views of development that stress age-related tasks (for example, Erikson), Kohlberg's theory implies that age may not be an accurate indicator of one's ethical reasoning stage (at least during the adolescent and adult years). Some age-related trends in Kohlberg's scheme do appear, however.

Before detailing Kohlberg's developmental scheme, it must be noted that it is to moral reasoning rather than moral behavior or moral feeling that his research efforts have been addressed: 'I have always tried to be clear that my stages are stages of justice reasoning, not of emotion, aspirations, or actions' (Kohlberg 1984: 224). The complex relationships among these different aspects of morality have been the focus of a host of studies to be discussed in a later section. At this point, I turn to a cognitive-developmental framework for describing moral reasoning, a structural indicator of identity.

Moral reasoning development

By extensively questioning an initial sample of 84 boys aged 10, 13 and 16 years of age about nine hypothetical dilemmas, Kohlberg (1958) attempted to identify the type of reasoning used most frequently by each individual. In so doing, he proposed six hierarchical stages in the development of moral reasoning and continued, with colleagues, to reassess his initial subjects at three- to four-year intervals over the course of 20 years. Results from this longitudinal research have supported the general idea of a developmental hierarchy indicated by his initial scheme (Colby *et al.* 1983).

Kohlberg describes an hierarchical and invariant stage sequence of moral reasoning that is comprised of six stages falling into three levels of judgment which reflect the increasing internalization of rules and principles (Kohlberg 1958). Remnants of Piaget's moral realism to moral relativism transition can be seen in the progression from the first to second stages of judgment in Kohlberg's scheme. It is not until the final level of post-conventional moral reasoning that individuals become capable of making moral decisions that are truly their own, unconstrained by self-interest, fear of punishment, the need for another's approval, or the letter of the law. From Kohlberg's recent longitudinal work, it is sobering that only about 15 per cent of adults at 36 years of age appear to be functioning predominantly at this highest level of reasoning (Colby *et al.* 1983). Indeed, the highest stage (stage 6) within this post-conventional level was dropped from analysis in the 20-year follow-up, as none of the interviewees were using this mode of reasoning. Let us now return to Shaw's *Major Barbara* to detail Kohlberg's six stages and the types of reasoning used within each.

Level 1: Pre-conventional

At this general level, one responds to cultural labels of good or bad, right or wrong, but interprets such labels in the interests of the self. The physical or hedonistic consequences of an action for the self are the prime considerations in moral decision making, alongside rigid adherence to authority. This level is comprised of two stages.

Stage 1: Heteronomous morality

At this lowest stage of moral reasoning, that which is right or just is that which is in one's own self-interest. Obedience to authority is valued to avoid punishment and achieve self-gratification; the physical consequences of an action to one's own interests determine its 'rightness' or 'wrongness'. This stage is characteristic of reasoning used by children between about 4 and 10 years of age. None of Shaw's late adolescent or adult characters appear to be functioning at this stage.

Stage 2: Individualism, instrumental purpose and exchange

Here, the respondent holds a one-way concern about another person; another's value is determined by the way in which she can meet the respondent's needs. Still reasoning from a perspective of self-interest, an individual at this stage acknowledges the value of others but does so in a hedonistic way. The needs of another are considered only insofar as they will benefit the stage 2 respondent. 'You scratch my back and I'll scratch yours' rather than a desire for loyalty is the prime motivator here.

At the West Ham shelter of the Salvation Army, a recent 'convert' down on her luck named Rummy Mitchens enters into conversation with a fellow compatriot, Price. Shaw captures the rationale of Rummy's self-interest, characteristic of the stage 2 reasoner, as she offers the Army her soul for salvation in exchange for the bread of survival. Price chides Rummy for her ethical stance:

Price: Oh Rummy, Rummy! Respectable married woman, Rummy, gittin' rescued by the Salvation Army by pretendin' to be a bad un. Same old game!

Rummy: What am I to do? I can't starve. Them Salvation Army lasses is dear good girls; but the better you are, the worse they likes to think you were before they rescued you. . . . And where

would they get the money to rescue us if we was to let on
we're no worse than other people? You know what ladies and
gentlemen are.

(Shaw 1966: 30)

Rummy considers another primarily as an agent for meeting her own
needs, indicative of stage 2 reasoning.

Level 2: Conventional

At this general level, maintaining the expectations of family, social
group, or nation as valuable for their own sake, regardless of consequences, is perceived as the 'true morality'. There is a desire here to
avoid any disruption to the smooth functioning of social norms,
either in the small group or larger legal system. There appears also a
need to support and justify these social orders for their own sake.
This level usually dominates pre-adolescent, adolescent and adult
thought. Two stages are again present within this general level of
moral reasoning.

Stage 3: Mutual interpersonal expectations, relationships and interpersonal conformity

A concern about conformity to opinions of others and group norms
are the motives which drive this stage of moral judgment; the desire to
be a 'good boy' or 'nice girl' and to please others characterizes this
mode of thought. There is conformity to stereotyped notions of what
is 'natural'.

The stage 3 orientation of Shaw's Lady Britomart in an exchange of
moral views with husband, Undershaft, is the source of much comedy
in Act III. Bound by conformity to social convention and family
tradition, Lady Britomart appeals to her husband's sense of familial
obligation to make son Stephen his heir:

*Lady Britomart:*Andrew: this is not a question of our likings and dislik-
ings: it is a question of duty. It is your duty to make Stephen
your successor.
*Undershaft:*Just as much as it is your duty to submit to your husband.
Come, Biddy! these tricks of the governing class are of no
use with me. I am one of the governing class myself . . . I
have the power in this matter; and I am not to be humbugged
into using it for your purposes.

(Shaw 1966: 64)

Indeed, Undershaft's power lies in his disembeddedness from the group-oriented, duty-bound, other-pleasing moral logic of his wife.

Stage 4: Social system and conscience

This 'law and order orientation' views right behavior as that which upholds a social system's laws or rules, which are viewed as fixed. Doing one's duty to maintain the social order for its own sake and avoiding a breakdown in the system regardless of consequences is the motivating force behind this stage of reasoning. Here, one often hears cries of 'What would happen if everyone did it?' as a rationale for moral response.

Son Stephen in Shaw's *Major Barbara* is an exemplar of stage 4 morality. His thoughts, cited at the beginning of this chapter, portray a view of morality as black and white, just and unjust. Why 'right is right and wrong is wrong' is the issue which must be addressed to pinpoint Stephen's stage of moral understanding, however. Hints are provided in a statement the young man makes to his father:

Stephen (springing up again): I am sorry, sir, that you force me to forget the respect due to you as my father. I am an Englishman and I will not hear the Government of my country insulted.

(Shaw 1966: 67)

In Stephen, his mother's stage 3 familial duty logic is transcended by a stage 4 need to uphold the government of his nation. Stephen's desire to defend and uphold national rules and values for their own sake arises on several occasions and evidences his law-and-order orientation.

Level 3: Post-conventional or principled

At this level, the reasoner is able to define moral values in a manner quite apart from social group conventions or the prevailing legal system. While one may still identify with such systems, they are now considered relative to other possible orders. Morality here is internalized; at this level, one may still be concerned with relationship to the community or one's views of morality may be more individualistic in nature. Two stages are also present within this level.

During the course of *Major Barbara*, Barbara herself undergoes transition from a conventional to a post-conventional level of moral reasoning. Her previous commitment to uphold the heavenly order becomes subsumed under her new commitment to a self-determined code of ethics:

> *Barbara:* I have got rid of the bribe of bread. I have got rid of the bribe of heaven . . . When I die, let him [God] be in my debt, not I in his; and let me forgive him as becomes a woman of my rank.
>
> (Shaw 1966: 89)

Barbara's newfound sense of moral identity comes through her disembeddedness from a context governed by others' rules to a recognition that she now can make them.

Stage 5: Social contract or utility and individual rights

At this stage, one is aware that group values are relative; community norms are now viewed as potentially changeable if warranted. There is a desire to adhere to community rules, but such rules have been critically evaluated by its members prior to commitment. There appears at this stage an emphasis on social order, but on a legal system which is maintained not for its own sake (as in stage 4) but rather in relation to the changing needs of the community. Rules governing the social order are modifiable by mutual consensus. This orientation was present among writers of the United States constitution.

Stage 6: Universal ethical principles

At this stage that which is right is determined by one's own conscience in accordance with self-chosen ethical principles. Such principles involve an abstract notion of justice and may transcend the written law, if that law is in violation of ethical codes which uphold equality in human rights and a respect for human dignity. At stage 6, a concern for the equality and dignity of each human being is the primary motivating force in the conceptualization of what is just. In relation to the moral issue of obedience to authority and punishment, these six stages might be summarized with logics as follows:

1 Obey rules to avoid punishment.
2 Conform to obtain rewards, have favors returned, and so on.
3 Conform to avoid disapproval, dislike by others.
4 Conform to avoid censure by legitimate authorities and resultant gain.

5   Conform to maintain the respect of the impartial spectator judging in terms of community welfare.
6   Conform to avoid self-condemnation
(adapted from Kohlberg and Gilligan 1971).

It is important to note here, however, that whether or not one conforms to authority is not that which determines stage placement; only a probing of the logic giving rise to the initial response can illuminate the underlying structure of moral reasoning. Individuals might equally indicate lack of obedience to authority yet present rationales revealing vast differences in underlying stages of moral reasoning.

From Kohlberg's 20-year longitudinal assessment of moral reasoning development, the great majority of respondents scored at only one stage or at most two adjacent stages over the nine moral dilemmas. Only 9 per cent of subjects evidenced a third stage of reasoning in their responses (Colby *et al.* 1983). Furthermore, about 67 per cent of all responses fell within the subject's modal stage, and 32 per cent (almost all) of the remaining responses fell within an adjacent stage. Subjects neither skipped stages nor reverted to the use of a previous stage. These findings are generally consistent with results from earlier administrations and point to a notion of 'structured wholeness' or an underlying logic of moral response to each stage of reasoning. Such findings also support the notion of an invariant stage sequence in the evolution of ideological structure.

Change in one's stage of moral reasoning has been strongly linked to the Piagetian processes of assimilation, accommodation and equilibrium. Furthermore, an individual's mixture of stage responses appears to be a necessary forerunner of change (Turiel 1969, 1974). Kohlberg (1973) and Turiel (1969) have construed moral reasoning development as failure in the process of assimilation. An individual will initially attempt to incorporate a new logic of morality into an existing schema or cognitive structure. When such efforts fail, it becomes necessary to accommodate, to change existing cognitive structures so that a new level of understanding can emerge. When children have been exposed to reasoning one stage beyond their current level of functioning, they often appear capable of perceiving the contrast between the two stages. This awareness, in turn, leads to a state of disequilibrium in cognitive functioning (Turiel 1969). The development of moral reasoning is an ongoing process of re-establishing cognitive equilibrium; such development seems possible only when an individual has already begun to evidence the reasoning of two adjacent stages. Transition to a new stage is not abrupt, but rather a slow gradual process indicated by the increasing frequency of responses at the higher of two adjacent stages. There are, however, vast individual differences in the rate of change and the highest stage an individual reaches during the years after childhood.

Listen now to Major Barbara describe this state of disequilibrium in her transition to a new stage of moral reasoning and its impact on her sense of personal identity:

Barbara: Today I feel – oh! how can I put it into words?. . . . I stood on the rock I thought eternal; and without a word of warning it reeled and crumbled under me. I was safe with an infinite wisdom watching me, an army marching to Salvation with me; and in a moment, at a stroke of your pen in a check book, I stood alone; and the heavens were empty . . .

*Undershaft:*Well, you have made for yourself something that you call a morality or a religion or what not. It doesn't fit the facts. Well, scrap it. Scrap it and get one that does fit. . . . Don't persist in that [old] folly. If your old religion broke down yesterday, get a newer and better one for tomorrow.

(Shaw 1966: 80)

For Barbara, the transition phase was not quite as rapid as her extracted statement might indicate, but her words, nevertheless, do portray the experience of transition as she seeks (and eventually finds) a new equilibrium.

Continuing to refine moral reasoning's six stages until the time of his death, Kohlberg has at times suggested the occurrence of additional stages. Kohlberg and Turiel (1971) have indicated the possibility of a 'premoral' stage 0, which precedes stage 1 and is indicated by responses in which the individual neither understands rules nor judges good or bad in terms of some higher authority. Additionally, Kohlberg (1973) proposed stage four and a half in an attempt to account for the pattern in early longitudinal data whereby one-fifth of subjects who obtained a stage 4 or stage 5 modal score during high school seemingly regressed to stage 2 by the second year of university study. Most subjects had returned to stages 4 or 5 by the age of 25. Stage four and a half was intended to reflect a transitional state in the movement from conventional to principled moral reasoning, rather than a 'real' structural regression in level of response. Kohlberg (1973, 1984) has also postulated a seventh stage of reasoning, in which the question 'Why be moral in a universe filled with injustice and suffering?' is addressed. Transition to stage 7 involves a shift from the universal humanistic orientation of stage 6 to a cosmic perspective. Kohlberg continued speculation on the metaphysical features that might characterize a seventh stage throughout his career. Efforts to rescore Kohlberg's longitudinal data with a new Standard Issue Scoring manual have been made. This scoring system allows the assignment of a more exact dilemma score tapping qualitatively different structures rather than more superficial content differences. This new system has continued to identify the original six stages of moral reasoning, though a downward revision of initial principled reasoning scores has occurred. Furthermore, virtually all regression anomalies in earlier data accompanying the transition from stage 4 to stage 5 have disappeared with the more refined scoring system along with responses characterizing stage 6 (Colby *et al.* 1987).

During the early, middle and late adolescent years, in which stage of moral development might we expect to find most youths reasoning and responding? From Kohlberg's Standard Issues Scoring system used in his 20-year longitudinal research, stage 5 scores did not rise beyond 15 per cent of total sample scores even as late as age 36; the percentage of those reaching at least the 4/5 transition during mid-adulthood was only 16 per cent. Even under the original scoring system only about 30 per cent of subjects used stage 5 reasoning at the age of 16 (Kohlberg and Kramer 1969). It appears from the work of Kohlberg and his associates that conventional reasoning is the predominant mode of adolescent thought on issues of justice; this level also predominates during the young adult years that follow (Colby *et al.* 1983).

An optimal level of moral reasoning

In preceding chapters it has been possible to address the question of what constitutes a healthy identity or character structure. For structural theorists such as Kohlberg, however, this question is inappropriate. A focus on the health or pathology of identity must give way here to the concept of development, the stage at which an individual is currently functioning in his or her own evolution. Although Kohlberg believes it is possible and justifiably good to advance one's stage of moral reasoning to a more mature form, the question of health versus illness is not an issue.

Research by Turiel (1966) has indicated that it appears possible to advance one's moral reasoning one stage beyond the present stage of functioning. It has also become apparent that children and adolescents actually prefer a more advanced over a less advanced stage of reasoning (Rest *et al.* 1969). Given that stage advancement is possible, what might Kohlberg regard as the goal for adolescent development within this moral subdomain of ego functioning? Time has brought changes to his views on this issue.

Kohlberg (1980b) traced the development of his own thinking on the aim of educating adolescents for a just society. His first public lecture on the topic was given in 1968 (shortly after the death of Martin Luther King) and called for the promotion of a stage 6 level of morality in which education should aim to cultivate respect for human dignity and universal principles of justice and equity. However, the 1960s it seemed 'were no more safe for stage 6 exemplars than was Socrates' Athens' (Kohlberg 1980b: 456). A 1976 bicentennial lecture brought revision to Kohlberg's vision, in which he now called for schools to make the world safe for stage 5 morality (that social contract orientation which still purports the rights of individuals):

> Empirical research between 1968 and 1976 did not confirm my theoretical statements about a sixth and highest stage. ... My longitudinal subjects, still adolescents in 1968, had come to adulthood by 1976, but none had reached the sixth stage. Perhaps all the sixth stage persons of the 1960s had been wiped out, perhaps they had regressed, or maybe it was all my imagination in the first place.
>
> (Kohlberg 1980b: 457)

However, at that time he recognized stage 5 morality to be in some danger also, possessed by only a minority. (Indeed, a United States majority votes down the Bill of Rights presented each year as an unlabeled proposition in the Gallup poll.) Principled moral reasoners seemed to be falling by the wayside. By 1980, Kohlberg was advocating a further retrenchment to a view that stage 4 was the most appropriate goal of civic education. With the 'me generation' of the late 1970s United States and its stage 2 narcissistic morality, Kohlberg's hope was that adolescents might come at least to function in a rule-governed school environment which would prepare the way for their participation as future citizens in upholding a larger social order. His hope also was an exposure to and eventual appreciation of fifth stage principles of constitutional democracy. Thus, Kohlberg's initial vision of a population's moral logic based on principles of universal justice and equality at the close of adolescence has been replaced by the hope that most adolescents can at least become capable of adhering to legal norms which govern their societies, with a possible glimpse of the social democratic mode of thought.

Measuring moral reasoning

A number of measures currently exist to tap various dimensions of moral reasoning and action, such as level of moral judgment, ethic of care, moral motivation, moral sensitivity, moral character and prosocial behavior. For purposes of this section, however, two measures that stem directly from Kohlberg's work and are designed to assess one's level of moral reasoning will be reviewed here: Kohlberg's Moral Judgment Interview (MJI; Kohlberg 1969, 1984) and Rest's Defining Issues Test (DIT; Rest 1979).

Kohlberg's (1969, 1984) Moral Judgment Interview is a semi-structured interview presenting the respondent with nine hypothetical dilemmas involving conflicts of justice. These dilemmas raise conflicts between preserving life or upholding the law, between consideration of extenuating circumstances or punishment, between adhering to authority or upholding a contract. The dilemmas also raise questions such as the way in which a community distributes its desirable assets, enters into contracts or agreements, or deals with its offenders. Rather than accepting an individual's 'yes' or 'no' response to the rightness or wrongness of a hypothetical action, the interviewer probes the respondent's rationale behind responses in order to gauge the structure underlying a subject's moral reasoning. Human life is valued at each stage; however, the way in which it is valued differs. Examples of two of Kohlberg's dilemmas follow:

> In a country in Europe, a poor man named Valjean could find no work, nor could his sister and brother. Without money, he stole food and medicine that they needed. He was captured and sentenced to prison for six years. After a couple of years, he escaped from the prison and went to live in another part of the country under a new name. He saved money and slowly built up a big factory. He gave his workers the highest wages and used most of his profits to build a hospital for people who couldn't afford good medical care. Twenty years had passed when a tailor recognized the factory owner as being Valjean, the escaped convict whom the police had been looking for back in his hometown. Should the tailor report Valjean to the police? Why or why not?
>
> (Kohlberg 1984: 649)

In this dilemma, the question arises of how a community should deal with its offenders, particularly given the circumstances of Valjean's initial reasons for incarceration as well as his later social contributions.

Joe is a fourteen-year-old boy who wanted to go to camp very much. His father promised him he could go if he saved up the money for it himself. So Joe worked hard at his paper route and saved up the forty dollars it cost to go to camp, and a little more besides. But just before camp was going to start, his father changed his mind. Some of his friends decided to go on a special fishing trip, and Joe's father was short of the money it would cost. So he told Joe to give him the money he had saved from the paper route. Joe didn't want to give up going to camp, so he thinks of refusing to give his father the money. Should Joe refuse to give his father the money? Why or why not?

(Kohlberg 1984: 643)

In this dilemma, the value of a social contract (a promise) is in conflict with the value of obeying an authority figure. In all dilemmas, additional probing questions are asked to clarify the logic behind each response: for example, does a good citizen or son have certain duties to perform? Should a lawbreaker be punished if acting out of conscience? Should a promise be kept?

Both a global stage score as well as a weighted average score may be derived from the MJI. The MJI has demonstrated acceptable levels of interrater reliability (88–100 per cent within 1/2 stage, and 75–88 per cent exact agreement). Test–retest reliability has generally ranged from 90–100 per cent agreement, and alternate form and internal consistency reliability have also been demonstrated (Colby and Kohlberg 1987). Kohlberg and Colby (1987) also provide support for both construct and predictive validity of the MJI.

Rest's (1979) Defining Issues Test (DIT) is an objective measure of moral judgment development, based on Kohlberg's stages of moral reasoning. It is the most commonly used measure for assessing moral reasoning stage (Thoma 1994). However, it assumes a somewhat different model of moral reasoning than that of Kohlberg (1984). Rather than attempting to map a respondent's responses directly onto a developmental continuum, the DIT adds a qualitative dimension to the assessment process. Thus, the DIT describes moral judgment according to the degree to which a respondent prioritizes a particular stage of logic in relation to others. The DIT consists of six stories that raise issues of competing social claims. Twelve statements representing various stages of moral reasoning follow each dilemma. Respondents are asked to rate the importance of each statement and to select the four most important issues that each statement addresses. A resulting P or N2 score indicates an overall index of moral development as a continuous rather than stage score. Rest and his colleagues have demonstrated satisfactory construct and predictive validity (Rest, *et al.* 1999). A new edition (DIT2; Rest *et al.* 1999) updates dilemmas and response items and shortens the original DIT measure.

Historical backdrop to Kohlberg's moral reasoning model

Some 26 years before Kohlberg completed his dissertation, Piaget (1932) had suggested that there were just two moralities of justice. Through extensive observations and interviews with children of 'what's fair', Piaget had suggested that shifts in the quality of moral reasoning accompany changes in the stages of cognitive development. A child functioning at the pre-operational level of thought before about 7 years of age evidences a logic of *moral realism*, whereby the rightness of an act is judged in terms of its consequences rather than the intentions of the actor. Piaget often asked questions such as 'Who is naughtier: John who opens a door and accidentally breaks fifteen cups that were behind the door and that he did not see, or Henry, who tries to sneak some jam out of the cupboard while his mother is out, climbs on a chair, and, in the process, breaks one cup?' A child in the stage of moral realism will reply, 'John, because he broke more cups.' The intentions of the actors are not considered here; only the results of actions matter. At this stage of moral realism rules are also immutable and God given, or at least handed down by some all-knowing authority. Witness the consternation of any 6-year-old moving to a new school, where the rules of a game may be at considerable variance from those in the preceding locale. The principle of imminent justice haunts the moral realist, as punishment is believed to be forthcoming immediately upon transgression.

Through a transition phase accompanying the shift to concrete operational thought, the young adolescent begins to shift to a stage of *moral relativism*. Appearing more consistently with the acquisition of formal thought during adolescence, the reasoning of the moral relativist not only considers the intentions of the actor but also appreciates that rules are arbitrary and subject to change upon group consensus. At this stage, Henry becomes the culprit of the earlier dilemma, for his 'less-than-honorable' intentions are weighed against the unintentioned results of John's door-opening behavior. Rules and authority now are also subject to question. The cynical irony of Murphy's law that 'no good deed goes unpunished' can now be appreciated, with the moral relativist's growing awareness that punishment is not inevitable and often escapable.

Upon this Piagetian base, Kohlberg proceeded to develop his evolutionary ideas. He describes the emergence of his research interests as follows:

> As a graduate student planning a study of moral development, [I] knew superego formation was pretty well completed by age 6. As an enthusiastic reader of Piaget, however, [I] knew that the development of autonomous morality was not completed until the advanced age of 12 or 13. To allow for the laggards, [I] decided to include children as old as 16 in a study of the development of moral autonomy. When [I] actually looked at [my] interviews, it dawned on [me] that children had a long way to go beyond Piaget's autonomous stage to reach moral maturity. Accordingly, [I] constructed a six-stage scheme of moral development, a schema in which superego morality was only stage 1 and what Piaget termed autonomous morality was only stage 2.
>
> (Kohlberg and Kramer 1969: 93)

Now, over 30 years since Kohlberg proposed his developmental model of moral reasoning, many criticisms have seen developments to Kohlberg's original ideas and means of assessing moral reasoning. Kohlberg's innovative, qualitative interviews used to evaluate level of moral reasoning were revised and refined to ensure validity and reliability. This development came in response to both cognitive-developmental and neo-behaviorist critiques concerned with use of 'scientific methods'. Further debates have ensued through the last three decades, raising concerns about gender bias, cultural relativism and more recently social circumstances and the nature of moral dilemmas in interaction with individual development.

Criticism of Kohlberg's construct

In the decade following Kohlberg's (1969) publication, two primary foci of criticism arose: one raised questions of methodology and the second conceptual problems and use of the theory. Often described as intuitive rather than empirical, Kohlberg's original scoring system endured much criticism (Kurtines and Greif 1974; Rubin and Trotter 1977). Imprecise instructions coupled with non-standard administration procedures and lack of reliability (consistency over time) were all problems raised with Kohlberg's early work, arising at a time when many were revising complex scaling procedures and concerned with approaches regarded as 'unscientific'. This outcry from critics has been responsible for the more clearly defined Standard Issue Scoring currently in use. Further methodological criticisms through the 1970s and 1980s questioned the validity of moral stages based on dilemmas far removed from the 'real-life' experiences of most individuals. Criticisms also came regarding the use of male characters as central agents of dilemmas for testing female subjects, and cultural bias in the value conflicts addressed by dilemmas, particularly in those societies where human life is not sacrosanct (Gilligan 1982a; Kurtines and Greif 1974; Simpson 1974). Some of these early criticisms have sparked new lines of enquiry, described below.

Among early conceptual critics were Gilligan (1982a), Sullivan (1977), Simpson (1974) and Harré (1987); each addressed different aspects of the assumptions underlying Kohlberg's scheme. Perhaps one of the more popularized critics has been Carol Gilligan, with her plea that women's voices need to be heard in the creation of theories addressing personality development. Gilligan has suggested that morality really involves two different types of orientations: one a justice and equality perspective (addressed by Piaget and Kohlberg), and the second an ethic of care and responsibility toward others. Both perspectives are used in the moral decision-making process by both men and women. However, men are far more likely to give responses based on the justice perspective that emphasizes separation and autonomy, while women's responses are more characterized by care and concern for others.

Gilligan herself proposed a three-level alternative to Kohlberg's scheme in which emphases on the needs of the self (level 1) give way to a focus on the needs of others (level 2), finally to be balanced at level 3 with a concern for the needs of both self and others (Gilligan 1982a). These levels were based on a study of women in the actual process of making an abortion decision, rather than on responses to hypothetical story dilemmas. At level 1, women in Gilligan's sample considered the possibility of abortion in terms of self-interest alone. Factors such as not having to be lonely and the excitement and novelty of having a baby were weighed against giving up personal freedoms and enduring possible financial hardship; whatever issues were considered, self-interest was the prime motivator. At level 2, issues were reconsidered solely in terms of one's responsibility to others. The ramifications of an abortion to the unborn child, partner, other relations and friends were considered at the exclusion of one's own needs and interests. At level 3, these two earlier ways of reasoning were brought into balance and the abortion decision was based on consideration of one's own circumstances as well as the impact of the abortion on others. As with

Kohlberg's moral dilemmas, it was the reasoning process rather than the decision itself that gave evidence to an underlying stage of development.

Reviews by Walker (1984, 1991, 1995a), addressing the question of possible male sex bias in Kohlberg's original theory, evidence few studies supporting such a claim. Gilligan (1985) argued that her thesis does not suggest sex differences in the ways men and women will respond in Kohlberg's stage scheme but rather stresses the need to *hear* another moral orientation (care) in understanding the development of moral logic. In reply, Kohlberg (1984) does not feel that Gilligan's own data adequately supports her claim for a different voice. Gilligan has indicated that she believes that her sequence complements that of Kohlberg's rather than that it should be considered an alternative model (Gilligan and Attanucci 1988).

Although Kohlberg and Gilligan have plotted developmental sequences that parallel each other in many ways, Gilligan does not share Kohlberg's view that development is driven primarily by cognitive and biological maturation for both sexes. Rather, Gilligan (1989) believes that the development of moral reasoning for girls lies in response to a social crisis – that of finding their own voices in contexts which will hear them. Brown and Gilligan (1992) argue that in order to live in contemporary culture, girls at the precipice of adolescence often lose their vitality, their resilience, their sense of themselves and their character in order to enter adolescence and meet the social expectations for women in their contexts. Gilligan and her colleagues have advocated greater use of a relational model for identifying self and the moral voices of care and justice, particularly for girls on the verge of adolescence (Brown *et al.* 1991). Gilligan has pursued her work through the 1990s, studying women and challenging the prevailing culture in psychology by examining girls' and women's conceptions of self, the meaning of relationships, an understanding of morality, knowing, and love (Brown and Gilligan 1992; Gilligan *et al.* 1990; Gilligan *et al.* 1991). Though differing in their views, Gilligan and Kohlberg remained friends to the time of Kohlberg's death (Gilligan 1998).

Sullivan (1977) argued that Kohlberg's theory is a style of thinking rooted in socio-historical circumstance and not capable of portraying a universal and timeless experience, while Simpson (1974) argued that Kohlberg's stages are not culturally universal. Sullivan was particularly critical of Kohlberg's conception of stage 6 reasoning as a parochial rather than universally accurate model of a moral being; the stage is abstract and formal and ignores the moral significance of one's ties to the community. Taking a different tack on a similar theme, Simpson argued that an insufficiently large number of cultures had been studied for the claim of universality to be made. Furthermore, the lack of post-conventional reasoning found in all the cultures Kohlberg studied also undermined such claims. Kohlberg (1984) disputed the latter argument with supportive evidence from a variety of cultural settings. In numerous samples from both western and non-western cultures, stage 5 reasoning has been reasonably well represented. In a major review of the issue of cultural diversity on claims of universality, Boyes and Walker (1988) found that Kohlberg's developmental stage model does hold universally and that the theory does reflect much of what is morally relevant in different cultural settings. However, evidence also indicates that the theory misses or misconstrues some important moral concepts from several different cultures (for example, the concept of harmony in Confucian morality).

Criticism through the 1990s has come primarily from contextual, narrative and post-modern approaches to the study of moral development. Contextual critics have focused on issues of inconsistency in moral judgment across various types of moral dilemmas as well as type of moral reasoning involved in real-life dilemmas. One phenomenon that has become apparent through the past decade is that people often fail to use their highest available stage of moral development when reasoning about moral issues of everyday life. For example, Carpendale, Krebs and associates have noted that in reasoning about dilemmas set in a business context (Carpendale and Krebs 1992, 1995) or involving drinking and driving (Denton and Krebs 1990), people fail to reason at levels reflected in their own responses to traditional Kohlberg moral dilemmas. Most typically, participants reason at much lower stages on such real-life dilemmas than they do on abstract dilemmas under test conditions.

Kohlberg (Colby and Kohlberg 1987) differentiated between moral competence and performance, arguing that performance in actual situations may not match reasoning (competence) demonstrated in interview situations. Krebs *et al.* (1997) have countered that the Kohlbergian model of morality does not give a good account of how people actually make moral decisions in their everyday lives. They propose that a model of moral judgment and behavior derived from evolutionary theory may provide a better account of real-life moral decisions than the Kohlbergian model. This new model suggests that people faced with real-life dilemmas weigh the outcomes and consequences both to themselves and others in ways that uphold co-operative systems, as well as enhancing one's perceived self-worth. The adaptive social consequences are that one is perceived as a moral person and treated as such. However, Carpendale (2000) has proposed an alternative explanation for the discrepancy between moral reasoning given in various situational contexts. He argues that the explanation lies in the nature of what consistency actually means, and a discussion of Carpendale's views and their implications continues in the following section on moral reasoning research.

Kohlberg's (1981) contention of structured wholeness in stages of moral reasoning has also come under fire when various features of dilemmas have been examined (i.e. dilemma characteristics, methods of responding and type of audience). Teo *et al.* (1995) have found that transpersonal dilemmas (involving conflicts in formal roles, social institutions and functions) pull for higher scores than do personal dilemmas (involving conflicts in personal relations) among those reasoning at the conventional level. At the same time, preconventional reasoners score higher on moral judgments involving nonauthoritative issues (those dilemmas that do not elicit acceptance through authority and institutions) than authoritative ones. Again, Carpendale's (2000) explanation suggests that such results do not violate the principle of structured wholeness central to a structural model of understanding. Thus, questions of context and the relationship between reasoning and action have dominated criticism of Kohlberg's developmental scheme since the early 1990s.

However, contextual, narrative and post-modern critics have also voiced their views that no objective moral criterion exists to rank order responses to moral conflicts. They also argue that rationality is devoid of emotion and moral sensitivity, and that what is unique to individual narratives is underestimated in the approach that Kohlberg employs to understand moral reasoning development. Harré (1987: 220) illustrates how a culture may contain a 'multiplicity of interacting, overlapping and complementary moral orders' and that different social contexts hold different systems for defining appropriate moral response. Harré believes Kohlberg's stage structures simply define different moral orders, none any better or more complex than any other. Thus, to Harré, the audience to whom moral judgments are directed defines the moral order; there is no developmental stage sequence which defines moral response. More recently, Day and Tappen (1996) are among those furthering a narrative approach that understands morality as a paradigm of social construction. Here, language constitutes meaning, and their narrative view assumes that moral thoughts, feelings and actions are linguistically mediated and thus socio-culturally situated. Morality is again contextually situated, Day and Tappen contend, and moral reasoning must be understood in multidimensional terms. In addition to contextual influences, morality must also be understood in terms of the prejudices, assumptions and moral commitments of researchers that, in turn, influence their understandings of others' moral stories, narrative researchers maintain. Others (e.g. Lourenço 1996) have countered that narrative approaches may lead to nihilism in terms of moral choices and opportunism in psychological and social relationships.

Research findings on the development of moral reasoning

Kohlberg's enormous contributions to an understanding of the development of moral reasoning have generated myriad studies addressing various aspects of the process. The 1970s and early 1980s saw researchers attempting to validate Kohlberg's model by examining its universal (cross-cultural) and developmental properties. Researchers also focused on the relationship of moral reasoning to intellectual development and various personality factors. With Kohlberg's increasing interest in the educational dimensions of his scheme, the 1980s also saw increasing interest in practical applications of Kohlberg's model as well as a more active concern with the relationship between moral reasoning and moral behavior. Attention in the 1990s and early years of 2000 has turned to consider broader issues in the understanding of moral reasoning, as researchers continue to focus on practical applications alongside some of the basic theoretical assumptions that Kohlberg had made.

Kohlberg (1969) claimed his stages to be culturally universal and added further fuel to the fire from critics by advocating that lack of exposure to role-taking opportunities stifles moral development for those growing up in pre-literate and semi-literate cultures. Even with more recent cross-cultural studies which have overcome some methodological problems inherent in early work, Kohlberg's highest stages have been consistently missing or infrequent in settings which do not encourage discussion or debate of moral issues (Edwards 1986; Snarey 1985; Snarey and Keljo 1991). Snarey (1985) identified major empirical assumptions underlying Kohlberg's claims. He found striking cross-cultural empirical support for the invariance of stage sequence and the existence of the full range of stages. Major cautions regarding the range and general applicability of stages across cultures were also noted, however, based on a review of some 45 studies of moral reasoning conducted in various cultural settings. From longitudinal and cross-sectional data obtained in 27 countries, stages 1 to 4 were virtually universal; stage 5, though rare in all populations, was evident in two-thirds of subcultures which included adults in the sample. However, evidence for post-conventional reasoning was found only in urban cultural groups or middle-class populations and was absent from folk cultures. Snarey argues that Kohlberg's stage scheme and scoring system may misinterpret the presence of higher stages of reasoning in some cultural groups. More recently, Verhoef and Michel (1997) point out that while a number of Kohlberg's findings have been verified in an African context, the cultural relevance of many of the dilemmas has been problematic. Recent cross-sectional work in European contexts has, however, generally supported Kohlberg's claim of cross-national applicability and universality of sequencing (e.g. Czyzowska and Niemczynski 1996).

As noted in the previous section, there has been an increasing concern in more recent researches about situational influences on an individual's response to moral dilemmas as well as individual variation in stage responses to the types of dilemmas used in the assessment of moral reasoning. Such variations would seem to contract one of the fundamental principles of Kohlberg's theory: the principle of structured wholeness. That principle implies that '[c]ultural factors may speed up, slow down, or stop development, but they do not change its sequence' (Colby and Kohlberg 1987: 6) and is fundamental to structural developmental models. From a series of studies on the role of contextual factors in moral reasoning development, Carpendale (2000) has offered an explanation for contextual inconsistencies that does not violate this principle of structured wholeness.

Carpendale (2000) notes that both Piaget and Kohlberg argue that moral development is not simply a matter of 'stamping in' cultural expectations. Kohlberg cited Piaget's 'structure of the whole' criterion, however, as implying consistency in moral reasoning stage across different contents and contexts. However, Piaget's understanding of structure was somewhat different. Piaget's position was that structures develop through the internalization of actions, that actions are content specific, and thus that one should expect individuals to develop at different rates according to different domains. Piaget had noted that 'a formal structure . . . will not be acquired all at once, irrespective of its content, but will need to be reacquired as many times as there are different contents to which it is applied' (Piaget 1952: 204). This tenet of Piagetian theory pertains directly to the issue of inconsistency that people often exhibit in various moral reasoning contexts. Moral reasoning may best be understood as a process of coordinating perspectives across various issues rather than the application of a moral principle. A modification of Kohlberg's theory to view the development of moral reasoning as a process of coordinating perspectives rather than the application of a principle or rule would bring Kohlberg's criteria for a structural stage more in line with Piaget's views, as well as providing an explanation of contextual inconsistencies in an ongoing developmental process.

A number of cross-sectional and longitudinal studies have addressed Kohlberg's claim of an irreversible and invariant stage sequence in the development of moral reasoning; virtually all have found an increase in more advanced stages of reasoning associated with increasing age – to a point. With few exceptions, all have also indicated a lack of any major regression over time (e.g. Armon and Dawson 1997; Colby and Kohlberg 1987; Edwards 1986; Snarey 1985; Walker 1989). From Kohlberg's own work, moral judgments become more advanced with increasing age for pre-adolescents and adolescents in industrialized western nations, regardless of social class or sex (Kohlberg 1958, 1969). In his 20-year longitudinal follow-up, the use of stages 1 and 2 decreased markedly from age 10, while stage 5 did not appear until the age of 20 and was not a stage attained by more than about 10 per cent of the sample beyond that point in time (Colby *et al.* 1983). Furthermore, no cross-sectional or longitudinal studies have found any stages to be 'missing' within the sample's age range. Strong evidence exists for the claim to an irreversible and invariant stage sequence, particularly with the Standard Issue Scoring procedure (Walker 1989).

Research based on the work of Piaget, Erikson, Loevinger and Kohlberg suggests interrelationships between the processes of cognitive functioning, identity formation, ego development and moral reasoning. Numerous results have pointed to a link between the use of formal operational thought and more advanced stages of moral reasoning (for example, Carroll and Rest 1982; Walker 1980). What has also emerged from such work is the finding that cognitive level appears as a necessary but not sufficient condition for one's mode of moral reasoning. In other words, one must generally attain formal operational thought to be able to reason at post-conventional levels. However, attaining formal operations does not necessarily ensure that one will use post-conventional reasoning in making moral decisions.

Measures of identity status based on Erikson's framework and ego development using Loevinger's model have also shown strong links with stage of moral reasoning. Podd (1972) presented evidence from work with late adolescent males to show a strong relationship between identity status and moral logic; identity achieved subjects used post-conventional reasoning, while pre-conventional and transitional moral reasoning were used most frequently by diffusions. Numerically, more subjects classed as foreclosed were using conventional modes of moral logic, though such results did not differ statistically from other identity statuses. Work by Hult (1979) and Rowe and Marcia (1980) have produced similar results. Skoe and Diessner (1994) have used Skoe's (1993) newly developed, care-based measure of moral reasoning to find a strong relationship between moral reasoning, ego identity status and Kohlberg's Moral Judgment interview. More recent work has also pointed to a significant relationship between ego development and moral reasoning as assessed by the Ethic of Care Interview but not between ego development and Rest's Defining Issues Test (Skoe and von der Lippe 2002).

One conclusion from Skoe's research is that an ethic of care plays a role in identity development for men and women, but that the care ethic may be more important to women than men in terms of identity development: '[G]ender differences in psychosocial development are more subtle and complex than simple main effects in response to standardized dilemmas' (Skoe and Diessner 1994: 285). From Loevinger's stage sequence in the development of the ego, longitudinal research has indicated links between current stage of ego development and that of moral reasoning. However, ego stage in early adolescence has not been able to predict later stage of moral reasoning (Gfellner 1986a; Kitchener *et al.* 1984).

The relationship between moral reasoning and moral behavior has been an ongoing and complex issue of debate and has raised some interesting questions. In earlier work, Blasi (1980) indicated that there does seem to be a fairly strong correlation between stage of moral reasoning and type of moral action. The question of what constitutes a virtuous moral act, however, has generated much debate and obviously is crucial to define before addressing any relationship between the two variables. According to Kohlberg, the definition of a moral act must include the actor's conception of right action and judgment of responsibility to perform the act. In other words, one who acts morally, 'practices what she preaches'. Considerable evidence from the literature does support the closeness of association between judgment and action; as one develops toward higher modes of moral logic, one's actions become more 'moral' (in reflecting a concern for basic human rights) and are more likely to take place. For example, both Nelson *et al.* (1990) and Gregg *et al.* (1994) found the moral reasoning of adolescent delinquents to be significantly lower relative to that of non-delinquents with age, socioeconomic status and verbal intelligence controlled. One very thorough investigation by Haan (1974) arose from the naturalistic setting provided by the Berkeley Free Speech Movement. Questioning subjects as to their activities during the demonstrations as well as administering Kohlberg's moral dilemmas, those individuals within each of Kohlberg's three moral decision-making levels evidenced very distinctive behaviors. More than half of all subjects reasoning at the lowest and highest levels participated in sit-ins and were often arrested; by contrast only 11 per cent of subjects at the conventional level took part in the sit-ins. In a re-analysis of this data using the Standard Issue Scoring system, however, a monotonic pattern emerged; that is, as stage of moral reasoning increased, a higher proportion of individuals sat in (Candee and Kohlberg 1987). In general, studies of moral judgment and action have indicated reasonably consistently a moderate relationship between moral reasoning and moral action (Kutnick 1986). However, it has been suggested that cognitive distortion is a major factor moderating this relationship (Krebs *et al.* 1995; Walker 1995b). Recent research has centered on the relationships among moral understanding, motivation, moral character and identity, and this broader focus represents a powerful future research direction for the field.

Current directions in moral development research

Darley (1993) suggested a return to basic questions of what issues people consider to be moral issues (or what domains do we regard as being domains of morality), what are the sources of moral imperatives and how are internal representations of moral rules coded in an array of different cultural settings. Darley argues that Kohlberg's legacy can be best respected by considering the conditions that arise from the moral problem or question at hand rather than automatically assuming an analysis of moral reasoning provides the correct approach. Along these lines, recent work has returned to basic questions in attempting to understand the relationship between moral reasoning and moral behavior. Efforts began in the early 1990s, with qualitative research into how people acquire their moral goals, how goals change and grow over the years, and how people sustain a focus on their goals. Broader issues of moral character and identity are being considered in attempts to link moral understandings with moral action (e.g. Bergman 2002; Lapsley and Lasky 2001).

Bergman (2002) reviews major proposals for linking moral judgment with moral behavior in an attempt to answer the question 'Why be moral?' He calls attention to a developmental dimension, 'character', or the integration of morality into one's sense of self. Character includes not only the place of morality in individual identity, but also the individual's use of psychological strategies to protect the self from internal contradictions; one strives to maintain internal consistency around one's moral beliefs. Moral reasoning does not inevitably result in moral action; rather, moral reasoning, in interaction with individual differences in character, personal responsibility and motivation produces action. The answer to 'Why be moral?' may thus be 'Because that is who I am, and I can do no other than be the person I am committed to being'. Colby (2002) points out from her research that people can exhibit strong moral character or integrity without being at Kohlberg's highest stages of moral reasoning.

Moral orientation has been an issue of great debate since Gilligan's (1982a) work, although in recent years its focus has prompted some important new research directions. Gilligan made two claims:

1   There are two gender-related orientations to morality (an ethic of justice and an ethic of care).
2   The dominant theories of human development (especially Kohlberg's) are biased against women.

As Walker (1995b) points out, the second claim has not been substantiated, while the first claim has inspired some more interesting issues. Garmon *et al.* (1996), Krebs and Vermeulen (1994) and Skoe and von der Lippe (2002) are among a number of researchers to point to variations by gender in response to care-oriented versus justice-oriented moral dilemmas. At least one investigation has even separated judicial (the application of rules) from legislative reasoning (the justification of rules) in moral dilemma interviews (Langford 1997). Important issues remaining to be explored pertain to the developmental origins of these varied orientations as well as their roles in the development of moral identity and morality's centrality in self-definition.

Implications for social response

Kohlberg himself devoted enormous energy to researching the implications of his moral reasoning stage scheme for social response: 'My own interest in morality and moral education arose in part as a response to the Holocaust, an event so enormous that it often fails to provoke a sense of injustice in many societies' (Kohlberg 1981: 407). The field of education has been the greatest beneficiary of Kohlberg's efforts at application. Following Kohlberg's death in 1987, his 'just community' approach to moral education did not long endure (Walsh 1999). However, many of the principles involved in Kohlberg's approach to moral education are carried forward in programs endorsed by many secondary schools today. This section will provide an historical overview of Kohlberg's writings on moral education, concluding with current efforts to facilitate greater moral commitments among adolescents in schools.

Kohlberg (1980a) outlined what he believes to be basic requirements for an approach to moral education. Such intervention must meet the following prerequisites:

> (a) of being based on the psychological and sociological facts of moral development, (b) of involving educational methods of stimulating moral change, which have demonstrated long-range efficacy, (c) of being based on a philosophically defensible concept of morality, and (d) of being in accord with a constitutional system guaranteeing freedom of belief.
>
> (Kohlberg 1980a: 17)

Kohlberg's care in stating the foundations for his proposed educational interventions were intended to bring to light what he regarded as two very dangerous and destructive avenues to moral education operative in the majority of United States schools – the 'hidden curriculum' and the 'bag of virtues' approaches.

The 'hidden curriculum' approach refers to the unconscious shaping of children's moral attitudes by teachers and schools unaware of their roles in moral education – without explicitly stating, discussing and formulating their educational purposes and practices: 'The *hidden curriculum* refers to the implicit values governing rewards, discipline, grading, and teacher–student interaction in the school' (Kohlberg and Wasserman 1980: 559). Kohlberg cites a conversation with his young son to illustrate the subtle yet powerful impact of the hidden curriculum:

> For example, my second-grade son one day told me that he did not want to be one of the bad boys in school, and when asked 'who are the bad boys?' he replied 'the ones who don't put their books back where they belong.' His teacher would probably be surprised to know that her trivial classroom management concerns defined for children what she and her school thought were basic moral values, and that as a result she was unconsciously miseducating them morally.
>
> (Kohlberg 1980a: 18)

Even the hidden curriculum of Neill's liberal Summerhill does not escape Kohlberg's attack; at Summerhill, unquestioning loyalty to the school, to the collective, is the unstated yet determining force guiding the school's socialization of students.

The second 'bag of virtues' tack is an explicit moral education. Here the school clearly dictates values it regards as 'right', and the institution proceeds to instill such beliefs in its young and captive audiences. For example, children attending such schools are commonly taught that the practice of certain 'virtues' will bring happiness, good fortune and good repute forevermore. The problem with such 'character building' programs is that reality does not abide by such rules. Kohlberg (1981) points to the fate dealt virtuous Charlie Brown, captured in the theme song of his show, 'You're a Good Man, Charlie Brown'. Charlie Brown, it seems, has a character of innumerable virtues – humility, nobility, cheerfulness, bravery, courtesy and honor, with a heart of gold to boot. In short, here is the embodiment of all noble qualities one could imagine wrapped up in one small, boy-shaped package – if only Charlie Brown weren't so 'wishy-washy'! Kohlberg argues that a 'bag of virtues' approach to moral education, in which aims are taught as virtues and vices through the praise and blame of others, produces youngsters like Charlie Brown – a wishy-washy mix of all things to all people with no sense of an autonomous self. Kohlberg defines his alternative goals of moral education as follows:

> Following Dewey and Piaget, I shall argue that the goal of moral education is the stimulation of the 'natural' development of the individual child's own moral judgment and capacities, thus allowing him to use his own moral judgment to control his behavior. The attractiveness of defining the goal of moral education as the stimulation of development rather than as the teaching of fixed rules stems from the fact that it involves aiding the child to take the next step in a direction toward which he is already tending, rather than imposing an alien pattern upon him.
>
> (Kohlberg 1980a: 72)

The ultimate aim of Kohlberg's moral education, that of advancement to higher stages of moral reasoning, is the only type of moral education which does not violate a young person's moral freedom; it is the only approach respecting individual autonomy and rejecting indoctrination. Implicit in this educational goal is the principle and promotion of a self-determined identity. To the question of parental rights in objecting to the teaching of values other than their own, Kohlberg replies: 'Respect for the parents' rights [in this case] is not respect for the child's autonomy, a more legitimate concern' (Kohlberg 1980a: 74).

With the foundations of Blatt's (1969) and Turiel's (1966) work, it has become clear that advancement to a higher stage of moral reasoning is possible to induce. This process, however, involves not simply a matter of adding more information but rather providing conditions that will facilitate a qualitative reorganization of moral reasoning structure. The first 'Kohlbergian' moral education program consisted of introducing hypothetical moral dilemmas into the classroom for discussion (Higgins 1991). Activities such as debates and challenging discussions with teachers, parents and peers as well as role-taking activities all become potential sources of disequilibrium and possible catalysts for movement to a more advanced mode of reasoning. It is only through such destabilization that new and higher stages of orientations to justice can occur. More recently, Narvaez (1998) also concludes that moral and social education programs must match the moral reasoning level of a text with the student's level of moral reasoning; children and teenagers may understand moral texts in ways quite differently than teachers intend, based on their own levels of development.

From the research of Kohlberg and associates (Colby *et al.* 1977), several concrete steps appear necessary to facilitate moral reasoning development in such programs of moral education. The first involves that of developmental match. Teachers or counselors must begin by carefully listening to the moral judgments and ideas actually being expressed by individual youths under their supervision. An accurate assessment of a young person's current stage of moral logic is critical to further intervention. Once a student's present stage of moral reasoning has been discerned, teachers then present arguments drawing from the *next* higher stage of reasoning. An atmosphere of openness and exchange is essential to this change process. Through such activities as moral discussions, classroom debates and opportunities for role play, one is exposed to ideas and situations that pose contradictions to one's present mode of cognitive functioning, creating a state of disequilibrium and dissatisfaction with the old structure.

Such programs for moral education have been implemented in a number of educational environments. Blatt and Kohlberg (1975) reported results of teacher-led discussions about moral dilemmas in four classrooms of early and mid-adolescents over the course of one semester. Students' moral stages were assessed and the teacher then began systematically introducing dilemmas and supporting arguments at a stage one step beyond that of lowest functioning students. As such arguments became comprehensible to these students, the process was repeated so that all class members were exposed to reasoning one stage beyond that used initially. At the term's end, significant changes in stage of moral reasoning had occurred; one-quarter to one-half of those in these classrooms increased their mode of moral reasoning by one stage, while essentially no change had occurred for control classes, who received no such teacher-induced intervention. Furthermore, change for the experimental group was maintained over a period of at least one year. Work by Colby *et al.* (1977) obtained similar results with larger samples of adolescents. Regardless of an adolescent's social class, intelligence, social and verbal skills, over 40 studies of such educational interventions have demonstrated effectiveness in advancing the development of moral reasoning for participants (Leming 1986). Change has been demonstrated to hold up over at least a one-year interval and moral discussions led by students have shown to be as effective as teacher-led discussions in promoting stage advancement (Higgins 1991).

However, self-destructive actions such as drug usage in the day-to-day lives of many adolescents caused Kohlberg to shift to a broader and potentially more forceful vision of moral education in the late 1970s and 1980s. The moral atmospheres of social institutions and their impact on moral development became the focus of writings on moral education. Institutional climates may stimulate or retard moral growth (Jennings and Kohlberg 1983; Higgins 1991). Rules, norms and justice structures within educational or other community institutions have their own stage of morality (as judged by a majority of participants). Furthermore, such moral atmospheres are capable of advancing over time. A 'just community' alternative high school program was found to develop to a higher stage as judged by community participants (Leming 1986). Social role-taking opportunities provided by such organizations as well as the level of justice within that setting are directly related to one's stage of moral reasoning; a higher stage of institutional justice appears to be a condition for an individual's development to a more advanced understanding of justice (Leming 1986).

Thus, community settings responsible for the welfare of adolescents may do much to facilitate the development of moral identity by themselves operating according to principles inherent in advanced levels of moral decision making. Ultimately, Kohlberg extended his 'just community' interests beyond the school and began to use real-life dilemmas in prison settings (Hickey and Scharf 1980). Here too efforts to advance moral reasoning and create a more just and concerned community have been demonstrated.

Through the 1990s, researches have continued to use Kohlberg's model of moral reasoning and some of the principles involved in the just community to consider means of best facilitating informed moral commitments and choices on significant controversial issues. Many educators have advocated continued practice of principles involved in Kohlberg's Cluster school approach, particularly to address problems of racial justice and self-governance (Blum 1999; Langford 1994). However, an absence of any dialogue about significant controversial issues in many high-school classrooms was found in a number of investigations summarized by Rossi (1996) through the 1980s. Researchers over the past decade have been exploring ways to provide adolescents with further experiences that may generate greater moral commitment. For example, community service experiences (such as serving food to the homeless in a soup kitchen), coupled with opportunities to engage in peer discussion and critical reflection on the issues that arise, have been found to facilitate increased compassion and broader conceptions of justice among high school students (Youniss and Yates 1997). Yates and Youniss (1996) have also found that student essays, collected over a three-month period of community service, reflect increases in 'transcendent reasoning' with greater understandings of justice and responsibility and concern with social and political processes. Such effects have also been found to continue into adulthood (Youniss *et al.* 1997). Oser (1996), however, warns of the need to try to ensure emotional conviction and genuine concern (moral motivation) among participants in any program aiming to facilitate just community principles for youth.

Summary

Kohlberg has viewed the development of moral reasoning as qualitative change, occurring in a universal, hierarchical and invariant sequence of six stages by which one resolves moral conflict. Although Kohlberg does not directly address the formation of identity, he views the development of moral reasoning as one aspect of ego functioning. Kohlberg's stages, strongly related to indexes of cognitive development, identity formation, ego development and moral behavior, reflect the increasing internalization of rules and principles. Kohlberg's 20-year longitudinal study indicates that conventional reasoning dominates adolescent and adult modes of moral decision making. It is possible to induce stage advancement by exposing adolescents to role models, debates and discussions, or institutional climates reflecting a mode of reasoning one step higher than their present stage of functioning. Since Kohlberg's death, research into moral reasoning has continued and expanded to consider its relation to contextual influences, moral motivation, behavior and identity.

Further reading

Carpendale, J. I. M. (2000) 'Kohlberg and Piaget on stages and moral reasoning', *Developmental Review* 20: 181–205.

Colby, A. and Kohlberg, L. (eds) (1987) *The Measurement of Moral Judgement*, vol. 1, New York: Cambridge University Press.

Smetana, J. G. and Turiel, E. (2003) 'Moral development during adolescence', in G. R. Adams and M. D. Berzonsky (eds) *Blackwell Handbook of Adolescence*, Oxford: Blackwell.

Walker, L. J. (1995a) 'Sexism in Kohlberg's moral psychology?', in W. M. Kurtines and J. L. Gewirtz (eds) *Moral Development: An Introduction*, Boston: Allyn and Bacon.

5 Ego development in adolescence

Loevinger's paradigm

> Since I cannot remain sane without the sense of 'I', I am driven to do
> almost anything to acquire this sense. Behind the intense passion for
> status and conformity is this very need . . . people are willing to risk their
> lives, to give up their love, to surrender their freedom, to sacrifice their
> own thoughts for the sake of being one of the herd, of conforming, and
> thus of acquiring a sense of identity, even though it is an illusory one.
>
> (Erich Fromm, *The Sane Society*, 1955)

Erich Fromm (1955) has pointed out that as human beings, we are the
only animals capable of saying 'I' and thus being aware of ourselves as
separate entities. He also adds that we are the only species finding our
own existence a problem, presenting an inescapable demand for attention. Looking at the development of the human race, Fromm sees that
the degree to which we are aware of ourselves as separate beings
depends upon the degree to which we have emerged from the clan. In
the medieval world, feudal lords and peasants were identified with their
social roles in a hierarchy. One was not a person who happened to be a
peasant; rather, one *was* his or her social station, thereby obtaining a
definition of 'I'. When, however, this social system broke down so that
'lords' and 'peasants' were no more, our forebears had a problem. A
response to self-definition other than through prescribed roles became
necessary, and the Renaissance brought great opportunities and newfound freedoms for individuals to create their own, unique personal
identities. Over the next few centuries, however, people gradually found
many different substitutes to solve the riddle of the 'I', for the act of
self-definition did require some effort. Indeed, by the early twentieth
century in the western world, totalitarian regimes were often welcomed.
The thought did occur to some observers that maybe human nature was
not really all that averse to tyranny – at least the problem of identity

was averted. Indeed, Fromm (1955: 63) sees self-definition through such identity substitutes as nationality, religion and social class to be 'the formulae which help a man [and woman] experience a sense of identity after the original clan identity has disappeared and before a truly individual sense of identity has been acquired'. While no longer maintaining feudal structures, we nevertheless find identifications with social roles to be convenient, and conformity to norms of the surrounding clan is often the means by which the riddle of the 'I' is bypassed. Jane Loevinger (1976) offers us a hierarchical vision of solutions to the problem of 'I' in her model of ego development. Like Fromm, she finds conformity to be the most common means by which late adolescents and adults deal with the problem of identity; unlike Fromm, she bases this conclusion on data supplied by thousands of respondents.

In contrast to some other identity theorists described in this volume, Loevinger's model has arisen from an empirical base of evidence. Whereas other writers on self, ego and identity have initially looked to theory for guidance in their construction of a paradigm, Loevinger's model has been derived from statistical analysis of empirical data; paradigm revision for Loevinger has occurred in response to anomalies in the data themselves. While some have argued that Loevinger has not constructed an explanatory theory of identity development, she has been one of the few social scientists studying identity or related phenomena to generate her model from a solid empirical base.

Also in contrast to Blos and Kohlberg described in previous chapters, Loevinger postulates an ego more holistic in form. Ego, to this social scientist, assumes a meaning markedly different from that understood by psychoanalytic ego psychologists and some cognitive-developmental theorists. Rather than *having* a collection of functions such as reality testing and impulse control, the ego to Loevinger *is* the 'master trait of personality', the frame around which the tent-like canvas of personality is stretched, the basis of identity. Furthermore, the ego, according to Loevinger, is a structure that develops over time, not necessarily bound by tasks related to chronological age. Though adolescents and adults will frequently find their solutions to the meaning of the 'I' from that framework of conformity suggested by Fromm, Loevinger's work indicates the existence and possible attainment of other more mature and autonomous ego structures during late adolescence and adulthood.

Loevinger the person

Loevinger was born in 1918 in Minnesota, the third of five children (Loevinger 2002). As a late adolescent, Loevinger left high school in her last year to enrol at the University of Minnesota, where she was drawn to coursework in psychometrics. She obtained her MS degree in this area when she was 20. At this time, just prior to the Second World War, Loevinger was strongly discouraged by others from pursuing a career. As a Jew with radical political sympathies, she found her first job offer with a child welfare institute withdrawn when this background became known. Loevinger also applied for an assistantship in her alma mater's Psychology Department, but her dismal employment prospects as a Jewish woman in academic life were pointed out by the department's head, who did not evidence any personal prejudice but advised that she marry a psychologist and thereby resolve her professional aspirations. Loevinger (2002) conveys these circumstances to give a perspective on the times and social context from which her career began.

Loevinger proceeded to enroll for a PhD at University of California, Berkeley. There, she described herself as 'born again', and she worked with Erik Erikson, Else Frenkel-Brunswik, Nevitt Sanford, Jean Walker Macfarlane and fellow graduate students Daniel Levinson and Donald Campbell (Loevinger 2002). She also met and married her husband, a physical scientist. During the Second World War, her husband and a number of other young scientists left Berkeley to establish a national laboratory in New Mexico, working in nuclear physics to advance the Allied war effort. Loevinger remained in Berkeley to work on her PhD thesis but joined her husband following its completion.

Loevinger's interests turned next to the problems of mothers with young children and women in general, following her own experience of motherhood. After the war, she and her husband proceeded to St. Louis, Missouri. Here, Loevinger obtained support from the National Institute of Mental Health to fund the construction of an objective test of mothers' attitudes toward child rearing. While she did not have a position at Washington University, she worked with a gifted group of its graduate students on this project. Eventually, she obtained an appointment at this university's Psychology Department, and it is from this context that Loevinger's research and writings on ego development have emerged. Now professor emeritus, Loevinger still maintains active writing and research interests.

The nature of the ego

On the nature of the ego, Loevinger has been reluctant to offer a precise and concise definition. When pressed to do so, she has preferred to point to stages she has delineated in the development of the ego, saying the ego is that entity which undergoes qualitative change as one moves through the developmental sequence (Loevinger 1979a). Loevinger finds no term really appropriate to capture the breadth of functions falling under the 'ego' rubric.

> The concepts of ego and ego development remain useful, the former to cover, among other things, the person's striving for meaning and self-consistency, which is the cornerstone of all psychotherapy, and the latter to cover aspects of character formation, interpersonal relations, and self-conception, which ought to be part of diagnosis.
>
> (Loevinger 1979a: 4–5)

In an early work, Loevinger (1976) elaborates the ego's screening property, which works to exclude observations and information that do not fit its frame of reference. We selectively perceive (or misperceive) 'reality' to meet the structure of our own ego stages, thereby keeping anxiety at bay.

> Let me put the theory into my words: What Sullivan calls the 'self system' acts as a kind of filter, template, or frame of reference for one's perception and conception of the interpersonal world. Any observations not consonant with one's current frame of reference cause anxiety; therefore, to avoid or attenuate the anxiety, such perceptions are either distorted so as to fit the pre-existing system or they are 'selectively inattended to', in Sullivan's phrase.
>
> (Loevinger 1976: 49)

This quality of selectivity is what gives one's stage of ego maturation remarkable stability during late adolescent and adult life.

Loevinger (1994: 5) indicates that the term *ego development* was selected to denote the many factors involved in personality development, such as motives, moral judgment, cognitive complexity, ways of perceiving oneself and others: '[p]erhaps the word *outlook* captures something of the core idea'. She rarely uses the term *ego*, preferring instead to avoid confusion with the psychoanalytic concept and to focus on the broad meaning of her own conceptualization of ego development. Loevinger differentiates ego development from the term *self* by reserving self to describe an internal, subjective experience accessible only to the individual while ego development denotes an aspect of the person that is more or less public and classifiable by an outside observer (Loevinger and Blasi 1991).

Where Kohlberg saw separate and distinct subdomains of functioning as contributing to ego development, Loevinger sees the ego as a more holistic entity that *is* these functions. While Kohlberg and his colleagues preferred to delineate and assess separate ego subdomains such as moral reasoning in the social sphere and natural (physical) worlds, Loevinger finds the ego to be an indivisible, unitary structure engaged simultaneously in the activities of impulsive control, interpersonal style, conscious preoccupation and cognitive functioning. The ego, to Loevinger, is that which gives one a general framework through which to view the world. Perhaps Loevinger's most succinct description of the ego's task is 'the search for coherent meanings in experience' (Loevinger and Wessler 1970: 8).

Somewhat easier for Loevinger is defining what the ego is not. The term *ego* has been interpreted in at least four different ways through the rise of psychoanalysis, and Loevinger (1976) finds only that meaning used by Erikson to be somewhat compatible with her own conception of the term. However, the developing ego Erikson describes occurs within normative age groupings (defined by different psychosocial tasks which must be met for development to proceed). Loevinger, on the other hand, finds enormous variability of ego stages within any single age group (particularly during late adolescence and adulthood). Furthermore, Erikson does not necessarily take the ego to be a unitary system of functions as does Loevinger (Snarey *et al.* 1983). Thus, Loevinger's concept of the ego – a unitary framework from which we generate meaning and coherence – is a notion differing markedly from most other uses of the term *ego* within psychoanalysis. In both early and later writings on the meaning of ego, she also explores the relationship of ego development to other physical, psychosexual, and intellectual development streams (Loevinger 1976, 1993b).

The ego and its development

Loevinger's (1997) model of ego development now poses nine stages of qualitatively different ways of organizing one's experiences of self and the external world. The low end of the continuum is marked by organizations in which one comes to understand the world through one's impulses (E2) and later through a self-protective stage (E3) which seeks to control the self and others in terms of what is best for one's own self-interests. The conformist stage (E4) is an organization marked by interpreting the world via the needs, expectations and opinions of others, while the self-aware level (E5) is able to describe an inner life and is aware of the thoughts and feelings of both self and others. The conscientious stage (E6) is noted by a strong feeling of responsibility for one's own thoughts, values and behavior as well as those of others. The individualistic stage (E7) is characterized by insight into psychological causation and a strong sense of individuality and personal identity. The autonomous stage (E8) is an organization that respects the needs for the autonomy of both self and others, without too strong a sense of responsibility for others. The last, integrated stage (E9) is very rare and is similar to Maslow's description of the self-actualizing person.

It is perhaps most clearly through the early diaries of Anaïs Nin that one is allowed to glimpse Loevinger's ego stages commonly seen in development during adolescence. Nin's diaries during her second decade move from concrete, vivid descriptions of her life as an 11-year-old Parisian immigrant to New York to those of a 17-year-old young woman with a complex and differentiated internal life. Nin's writings are used to illustrate those ego stages and transformations commonly occurring during adolescence.

Presocial stage

This stage characterizes the state of affairs for the newborn infant, as yet unable to discriminate self from not-self, as yet not having an ego (let alone impulse control). In differentiating the self from its surroundings, an infant comes gradually to achieve a sense of object constancy. Discovering the non-self is the main conscious preoccupation during this stage. One who remains unable to differentiate that which is self from that which it is not is said to be *autistic*. Loevinger's presocial stage of development is identical to that referred to by Mahler *et al.*'s (1975) description of the autistic self.

Symbiotic stage

This stage corresponds to Mahler *et al.*'s (1975) description of the symbiotic infant, in which the primary caretaker and infant are perceived by the latter as one entity. While able to discriminate the self from its surrounding environment, the infant cannot yet distinguish itself from the main caretaker. The infant here is ruled by impulse, is symbiotic in its form of relatedness and is consciously preoccupied with the self. It is during this symbiotic stage that language begins to develop, assisting the differentiation process. Loevinger (1976: 16) notes an interesting phenomenon: 'Partly for that reason [lack of language in life's earliest stages], the remnants of the Presocial and Symbiotic stages do not appear to be accessible by means of language in later life, as remnants of all later stages are.' Because ego stage is assessed by language on the SCT, these earliest two phases of development remain uncharted by Loevinger.

Impulsive stage (E2)

It is only from the threshold of the impulsive stage that it is possible to assess ego development by SCT items. The preschool child is governed by impulses and is fearful of retaliation; other people are strongly needed, but as objects of dependency, to be manipulated and exploited. (Additionally, others are viewed either as all-good or all-bad, with no mixture of extremes.) The present, with all the problems it insistently presents, is the focus of this stage's dealings with time. Past or future are not of any immediate value, for what they bring is not happening *now*. Bodily feelings, particularly the sexual and aggressive, are conscious preoccupations. Gradually, external constraints help to curb the child's impulses, later to come under the self's control. However, those at the impulsive level have no awareness of self as such and there is little distance from impulses themselves. (Impulses are most frequently described in the present tense, for example.) A child or adolescent who remains at this stage too long is often labeled incorrigible or uncontrollable.

Self-protective stage (E3)

This stage is marked by the child's first attempts to control her own impulses; there is now sufficient distance from the impulses to make possible their control. In learning to anticipate short-term rewards and punishments, the child's fragile and guarded efforts of impulse control become apparent, enabling greater autonomy from external agents. The self-protective stage receives its name from this very characteristic quality of vulnerability. Self-interest (or opportunism) remains the primary motivator, as rules are used in the service of one's own desires; it is getting caught that labels an act 'bad'. The self-protective child understands, however, that there are rules which have some function, a point lost on the impulsive child. For the self-protector, blame is conveniently externalized so that other people or circumstances rather than one's own actions are at fault and responsible for one's present predicament. Interpersonal relations, while not strongly dependent, are characterized by a wary, manipulative mode and control is the primary conscious preoccupation.

Conformist stage (E4)

The state of conformity, captured eloquently by Erich Fromm, marks a developmental milestone for the ego. Now, for the first time, there arises the ability to identify one's own welfare with that of a group (family or, later, peer group). At the same time, however, 'the self is not much different from others in the group, whatever one's group may be' (Loevinger and Blasi 1991). Such a step requires trust in one's self and the world; where trust is lacking, the world is viewed as a community of 'enemy agents', and foundations are thus laid for an opportunistic, exploitative, deceptive self-protective adolescent and adult ego state. For the conformist, rules are obeyed because they are approved by the group and not because punishment lurks on the horizon; the group's disapproval, in and of itself, is enough to regulate the conformist's behavior. Impulses are similarly controlled through desire for social acceptance. Such is the state of development for Eric Hoffer's 'true believer', who does not endure solitude easily and is attracted to mass movements: 'Though stranded on a desert island, he must still feel that he is under the eyes of the group. To be cast out from the group should be equivalent to being cut off from life' (Hoffer 1951: 61). People within the conformist's group are liked and trusted, though those of other groups are often mistrusted, stereotyped and flatly rejected. Living according to stereotyped roles prescribed by the group is the conformist's modus operandi. While he or she values cooperation rather than competition (the latter value characteristic of those in the preceding stage), others are evaluated by the conformist in terms of external appearances and material possessions rather than through highly differentiated internal feelings, characteristic of more mature ego stages. Inner life tends to be described by the conformist in rather bland, banal, concrete clichés, with social acceptability, reputation and status serving as primary preoccupations. The conformist stage normally emerges during early adolescence and may be retained through late adolescent and adult life.

Through a framework of conformity at the age of 11 years, Nin uses her diary to confess the secrets of her soul, a young soul seemingly eager to please while at the same time limited in the vocabulary to describe its inner life. Events are described in vivid although concrete terms and feeling states have a clear, albeit banal, ring:

> January 2 . . . I have made a resolution to keep my diary all year long. Nothing comforts me like being able to tell all my sorrows, my joys, my thoughts to a silent friend . . . Now let's talk seriously. In

February I will have a birthday, 12 years old. I am so old! It's high time for me to become a little woman. I have tried so often to do that, and then for the least thing I get angry, and I must start over again. I get back on my feet, but the road is slippery, be careful. Yes, I am a big girl and I must become perfect. Afterward it will be too late. Maman is calling me. I shall go, I don't want to slip down the path of disobedience.

(Nin 1978: 39–40)

Though normally assessing ego structure in a different manner, Loevinger would likely find such lines typical of the conformist adolescent. Here, an enormous developmental milestone has been achieved as the ego regulates itself via the norms for 'womanly behavior' determined by the prevailing reference group. That path of obedience to mother seems desirable for the approval it brings, rather than the punishment it avoids; such is the logic of the conformist individual, oriented to others and giving somewhat banal descriptors of inner life.

Self-aware stage (E5)

This stage is probably the easiest to study, for it is the modal state of adult ego development within the United States (Loevinger 1976). Notable features of the self-aware stage are an 'increase in self awareness and the appreciation of multiple possibilities in situations' (Loevinger 1976: 19). Vaguely defined feelings, often self-conscious, come to mind in descriptions of inner life by an ego functioning at the self-aware level. Now there is an awareness of the self as a self and a separation from total identification with the norms of the group (Loevinger and Blasi 1991).

Perception of alternatives and exceptions paves the way for the true conceptual complexity of the next stage. For example, at this [Self-Aware] level a person might say that people should not have children unless they are married, or unless they are old enough. At the next [Conscientious] stage, they are more likely to say unless they really want children, or unless the parents really love each other.

(Loevinger 1976: 19)

Awareness of individual differences begins to emerge at the self-aware level, in contrast to the stereotypic thinking of the conformist; at the more mature ego stages of development, a premium is placed on individual differences. At the self-awareness level, the self can be aware of itself, distinct from (though still related to) the group; multiplicity is the conscious preoccupation of this ego state.

Several years further into her second decade, Nin begins to evidence a more self-aware ego structure in descriptions of her own qualities and behaviors; as the age of 14 years approaches, greater ability to reflect on the complexity of her inner life is becoming apparent. There is a change of focus in her diary now from what she does to how she feels.

> February 17. My birthday is coming on the 21st. There are only a few days left until then, and as I see the beginning of another age for me drawing near, I reflect, I feel sad at times, and other times I am happy. I am sad when I think that time goes by so quickly and that I don't do anything. I feel happy sometimes when I think that this 14th birthday brings me a little closer to being a young lady, which is the theme of all the beautiful stories of adventure, real misfortunes, love. Because I hope that in growing up, I am going to find the young man of my dreams.
>
> (Nin 1978: 157)

As Loevinger states, 'Untying what-I-am from what-I-ought-to-be opens the way for beginning to differentiate one's real and ideal self' (Loevinger 1987: 228). Nearing the age of 14, Nin appears to be differentiating her feelings more clearly and describing inner life in somewhat more complex and varied terms, though her dreams may still be those of the surrounding clan rather than her own individually secured desires. Loevinger indicates that those at the self-aware level are still basically conformists with somewhat greater ability to differentiate emotions; this description would seem to reflect Nin's life framework as she approaches her fourteenth birthday.

Conscientious stage (E6)

At this stage, qualities such as the ability to generate long-term, self-evaluated goals are present, coupled with the ability for critical self-evaluation, a sense of responsibility, and an ability to describe individual differences in traits. Loevinger (1976) notes that only a few youngsters have attained this stage by early adolescence (13 or 14 years). In the conscientious stage, rules are internalized so that what is considered right or wrong depends upon one's personal evaluation of the circumstances. While the self-protector obeys rules to avoid punishment and the conformist does so to receive group approval, the conscientious individual evaluates rules and standards, long-term goals and ideals in accordance with her own ethical principles.

> A person at this stage is less likely than the Conformist to feel guilty for having broken a rule, but more likely to feel guilty if what he does hurts another person, even though it may conform to the rules. At this stage a person is his brother's keeper; he feels responsible for other people, at times to the extent of feeling obliged to shape another's life or to prevent him from making errors.
>
> (Loevinger 1976: 21)

In general, conscientious individuals see themselves as authors of their own destinies, intensive and responsible in their interpersonal relationships.

Additionally, a rich inner life of far greater conceptual complexity characterizes the ego at this conscientious stage of maturity. One's own behavior, as well as that of others, is viewed in terms of patterns having underlying motives, more vivid and realistic than such descriptions by those at less mature stages of ego development. Achievement tends to be measured against one's own standards rather than by recognition from the surrounding social environment (for the conformist) or competitive advantage (for the self-protector). Differentiated inner feelings are predominant conscious preoccupations at this stage of development.

By age 16, Nin's capacity for self-examination is even more evident. As she rereads pages of her earlier diary entries, she reflects on the changes she has experienced in herself and the oncoming transition she senses:

> June 13 . . . During the last two hours I have been busy rereading several of my diaries. . . . I have gone through so many impressions. . . . Around me, the natural and inevitable tragedy of life unfolds. My personality is developing, my handwriting is changing, my spelling is a little better, my ideas are becoming clear and precise. I am neither naive nor shy, and am less ignorant. At 16 I have changed so much that right now, when I analyze my feelings, I understand that the little eleven-year-old girl and *her* character exist only in the notebooks.
>
> This transformation, which is so normal, is like an abyss that makes me dizzy. It is a deep mystery of nature that takes my breath away. Even now, I may be on the threshold of another transformation, on the threshold of another being that will be added to or

will replace the one that I am about to leave behind, as one gets rid of an old worn coat. . . . Each of us is a book without an Epilogue, an unfinished book whose Author reserves the right to write the ending, since He wrote the beginning. . . .

(Nin 1978: 250–251)

This new self-conscious quality apparent in Nin's self-analysis is characteristic of what Loevinger finds at the conscientious stage of ego maturity. Actions are now described in psychological terms; absolute statements are replaced by comparatives and contingencies. Self-critical, the conscientious stage individual also has the self-respect evident in Nin's diary entry. A beginning sense of self-authorship is also apparent. By her eighteenth year, Nin struggles with the conflicting demands of a literary lifestyle and family responsibilities; such perceived polarities, however, must await further integration and possible transcendence during more mature ego stages.

Individualistic stage (E7)

An increased sense and appreciation of individuality and concern for emotional independence are hallmarks of this level (in contrast to excessive responsibility for others at the preceding stage of ego functioning). Close relations with others, however, are often viewed as incompatible with achievement strivings. An awareness of inner conflict dawns, but such conflict is frequently externalized (for example, if only God, spouse, children and so forth, were more accommodating, there would be no conflict between my career, marriage and motherhood roles). At the next higher autonomous stage, such internal conflict is accepted as a way of life, with increasing ability to tolerate paradox and ambiguity:

> To proceed beyond the conscientious stage a person must become more tolerant of himself and of others. This toleration grows out of the recognition of individual differences and of complexities of circumstances at the conscientious stage. The next step, not only to accept but to cherish individuality, marks the Autonomous Stage.

(Loevinger 1976: 22)

Conscious preoccupations at this stage lie with individuality, development, and roles.

Autonomous stage (E8)

The ability to cope with conflicting needs and responsibilities is the distinguishing feature of this stage of ego development. Loevinger (1976) indicates that the autonomous individual probably has no more conflict than those at less mature stages of ego maturation but acknowledges and deals with it rather than projecting it onto the environment or denying it. Greater tolerance for ambiguity and increased cognitive complexity mark the autonomous individual's frame of reference. 'He [the autonomous individual] is able to unite and integrate ideas that appear as incompatible alternatives to those at lower stages' (Loevinger 1976: 23). In terms of interpersonal relatedness, there is a respect for another's autonomy coupled with desire for interdependence. Conscious preoccupations are self-fulfillment and psychological causation. The autonomous stage of ego development is the highest found in most samples and probably in most populations (Loevinger and Blasi: 1991).

Integrated stage (E9)

The highest stage of ego development yet identified by Loevinger is defined by the ability to transcend conflicts of the autonomous stage. In addition to the qualities of cognitive complexity, more mutual interpersonal relations, and respect for autonomy which were all present in the preceding stage, there is now a new consolidation of identity and a savoring of individuality. Loevinger equates this stage of ego development to Maslow's description of the self-actualizing person. The integrated individual is difficult to study, in part because so few exist and in part due to limits in the ego maturity of the test interpreter: 'Moreover, the psychologist trying to study this stage must acknowledge his own limitations as a potential hindrance to comprehension. The higher the stage studied, the more it is likely to exceed his own and thus to stretch his capacity' (Loevinger 1976: 26). The integrated individual holds identity as the primary conscious preoccupation.

Studies using Loevinger's model have generally pointed to an ego developing through a hierarchical and invariant sequence of stages. While evidence for sequentiality is not conclusive, mean ego stages in both longitudinal and cross-sectional studies have generally increased with age (Loevinger 1979c; Loevinger *et al.* 1985). Like other developmental theories of identity formation, it is not possible to appreciate the most common ways of making the self and outer world cohere during adolescence without understanding preceding and succeeding possibilities. Unlike other theorists of identity, however, Loevinger has been silent regarding the mechanism(s) driving those qualitative ego stage reorganizations and the principles governing connections between stages.

Loevinger has based her model of ego development on results of many refinements to an instrument she developed, the Washington University Sentence Completion Test (SCT; Loevinger, 1976). The form for adolescents and adults is comprised of 36 incomplete sentence stems, which the individual is instructed to complete. This instrument will be described in some detail in the following section. However, it may be instructive at this point to see how adolescents with varying levels of ego development might respond to one of the SCT items. Table 5.1 illustrates the varied types of responses given by individuals at different stages of ego development to the same sentence completion item.

These responses indicate a sequence of shifts toward greater internalization of responsibility and increasingly complex differentiation of experiences. Results from some US surveys indicate that the conscientious-conformist (self-aware) stage is the most commonly occurring state of ego maturity in the general adult population. However, those

Table 5.1 SCT responses at different ego levels relevant to adolescence

Stem: When I am criticized . . .

Stage	Response	Comment
Self-protective	I get mad and don't talk to them.	Need to protect the self.
Conformist	I feel as if I'm not wanted.	Feelings of rejection by the group.
Self-aware	I generally sulk for a while.	Feeling conscious of the self.
Conscientious	I lose confidence in myself.	Evaluation of the self.
Individualistic	I reassess my thoughts or actions, and then act upon constructive criticism.	Taking responsibility for one's actions.
Autonomous	I often am angry at first. Then I think about it and decide if it is justified or not. I also think about who has given the criticism and their motives.	Indicates conceptual complexity with three possibilities considered.

Source: Adapted from Loevinger (1987: 230).

without tertiary (college) education are usually functioning at or below that level, while those with tertiary education are generally functioning at or beyond that level (Holt 1980; Loevinger *et al.* 1985).

The common observation of high conformity to peer pressure during early and middle adolescence fits well with what one might predict of behavior for those at the conformist stage of ego functioning; this observation is also in accord with results from validational studies for those at lower stages of ego development. Loevinger and Blasi (1991) do note that conceptual complexity is related to ego development. While some may argue that a measure of ego development stage is nothing more than a poor measure of intelligence, they suggest otherwise:

> [W]e have seen a few examples of people relatively low level, conformist or self-aware, among intellectually superior individuals. Almost a fourth of the distinguished men in Vaillant's ... Grant study, selected during their college years as men of exceptional potential, tested at the self-aware level in their mid-fifties. An unpublished Washington University study of educable retarded high school students found some of them also at that level.
>
> (Loevinger and Blasi 1991: 165)

An optimal level of ego development

Loevinger makes no claim that a higher stage of ego development is necessarily a healthier stage (Snarey *et al.* 1983). While Kohlberg demonstrates the premium he places on more advanced levels of moral reasoning through his programs of educational intervention, Loevinger has not embarked on any similar venture to attempt the raising of one's ego development stage. Furthermore, she does not attempt any philosophical justification of why a higher stage is better (as does Kohlberg). Loevinger, however, like Kohlberg and Kegan, does provide a means for assessing normative developmental patterns. Again, like those theorists covered in adjacent chapters, health versus illness is not at issue in Loevinger's model of ego functioning.

Loevinger (1976) takes great care to avoid any association of ego stage with good adjustment or positive mental health. She points out that an individual at almost any stage of ego functioning can be well or poorly adjusted. While a low (for example, impulsive) stage of ego functioning maintained long past its normative demise may make functioning in the larger social order marginal, it nevertheless can be done. Indeed, some adults at the self-protective (E3) stage of development may have very profitable and successful careers. Up until recent decades, academic psychology curricula placed great emphasis on a 'psychology of adjustment'. Gradually, writers such as Fromm, Jahoda, Maslow and Schachtel have questioned adjustment and conformity to social norms as the epitome of development. Individuals at Loevinger's higher stages of ego functioning may be very 'poorly adjusted', refusing to sacrifice their own values and goals to the dictates of the larger social order. With regard to the issue of psychotherapy, Loevinger (1976: 427) cautions the clinician to 'keep his patient's problems and adjustment conceptually distinct from ego level; a person of any ego level may become a patient, though there may be differences in the kind of pathology or presenting symptoms characteristic for different levels'. Early and mid-adolescents might be expected, normatively, to operate from a self-protective or conformist framework; whereas a greater range of ego stages can be observed during late adolescence, the conscientious-conformist (self-aware) position is modal. Any association between stage of ego functioning and good social adjustment or positive mental health should be avoided during any phase of the lifespan, according to Loevinger.

Measuring ego development

Loevinger and her associates (Loevinger 1998) developed the Washington University Sentence Completion Test (SCT) over a period of many years in order to measure ego development. Although the SCT was originally developed for use with girls and women, a scoring manual for boys and men has also been developed (Redmore *et al.* 1978). The SCT's current late adolescent and adult form (Form 81 for Men and Form 81 for Women) is comprised of 36 incomplete sentence stems, which the research participant is instructed to complete in any way that he or she wishes. Some typical test items are as follows: 'What gets me into trouble is . . .'; 'Being with other people . . .'; 'I feel sorry . . .'. Forms for men and women are closely comparable, with nouns or pronouns matching the gender of the participant.

Loevinger and her colleagues have developed an empirically derived scoring manual (Hy and Loevinger 1996; Loevinger and Wessler 1970; Loevinger *et al.* 1970) to provide guidance for rating each sentence completion item at one of the ego development stages. A single, total protocol response is then assigned to the SCT in one of two ways. A rating is assigned either on the basis of an item sum score, in which the response to each item is translated into an ordinal scale score and added to form a total score, or on the basis of what Loevinger has termed ogive scoring rules, based on the cumulative distribution of item ratings for a total protocol. The first and second pages of the SCT each contain 18 items and have been designed for use as abbreviated alternate forms (Loevinger 1985, 1998).

Reliability for this instrument has been assessed in terms of internal consistency (Cronbach's alpha = 0.91; Loevinger and Wessler 1970) and interrater reliability, which has also been high (Gfellner 1986; Loevinger and Wessler 1970). Construct validity has been evaluated in a number of reviews (Hauser 1976; Manners and Durkin 2001) and will be discussed further in the section on current directions in ego development research.

A new version of Loevinger's measure of ego development, the Sentence Completion Test for Children and Youth (SCT-Y; Westenberg *et al.* 1998c; Westenberg *et al.* 2001), has been developed to examine ego development in children and younger adolescents. Westenberg *et al.* (1998c) note that Loevinger's scoring manual and descriptions of ego stages were based primarily on individuals aged 16 years or older. Indeed, Loevinger's revised scoring manual for Form 81 (Hy and Loevinger 1996) contained no responses from children and few from adolescents. In their focus on lower stages of ego development in children and youth, Westenberg *et al.* (1998c) found a more positive 'spin' given to items indicative of impulsive, self-protective and conformist stages of ego development than Loevinger had noted in her samples of 16-year-olds. For example, Westenberg *et al.* found that the impulsive stage of development in childhood is not limited to responses of aggressive impulses, characteristic of older impulsive-stage individuals found by Loevinger. Rather than the manipulative and exploitative characteristics of self-protective adults, self-protective children and adolescents were more focused on self-sufficiency and instrumental but appreciative relationships with others. Initial reliability and construct validation for this instrument, administered in oral form, has been high (Westenberg *et al.* 1998c).

Historical backdrop to Loevinger's model of ego development

Loevinger had been concerned about psychology's lack of attention to women, and thus wished to focus her research attentions on women in order to address this gap (Loevinger 2002). Loevinger's fascination with the ego and its maturation arose in trying to make sense of puzzling results from a measure of mothers' attitudes towards problems of family life (Family Problem Scale; Loevinger 1998a). Test items were designed to assess women's attitudes to small-scale domestic concerns for the purpose of checking the explanatory power of various psychological theories; however, results were confusing. Examining how items clustered in factor analyses, Loevinger found the test seemed to be measuring how authoritarian a family was in its ideology (as construed by the mother). Although the measure provided no evidence supporting the influence, for example, of psychosexual stages in determining attitudes to family problems, it did point towards a more general way in which women organized their attitudes towards child rearing.

Loevinger and her associates then began looking for homogeneous clusters of items to indicate various personality patterns or traits. Items were revised and refined, but gradually Loevinger's research group came to realize that rather than clusters of personality traits, there was a continuum of attitudes with qualitatively, rather than quantitatively, different markers along a developmental sequence. At this point, Loevinger recognized that a broad term like *ego development* was needed to denote the moral development, cognitive complexity and interpersonal relations that her items were assessing. The next problem arose from the lack of an established instrument to validate Loevinger's new measure. Thus a projective sentence completion test was developed to focus upon these issues. This instrument, originally a four-stage measuring scale, was revised through several versions over time and scoring manuals were developed eventually to become the Washington University Sentence Completion Test. Over time, forms for men were also developed. Loevinger was strongly committed to developing a manual where criteria for stage placement were clearly recorded and available for future research purposes. Continued item and manual revision have led to the SCT's current Form 81 for Women and Form 81 for Men, which is used in research on ego development at the present time.

Loevinger's choice of the term ego development to describe her 'master trait of personality' met with great criticism from psychoanalytic circles, and she has expended much energy to differentiate her model of ego development from that used in classic psychoanalytic theory. Among other issues, Loevinger and Blasi (1991) point out that while psychoanalysis generally focuses on the period of infancy to describe the process of ego development, the SCT assesses development only after speech has begun. Loevinger's theory has also been regarded by some as either derived from psychoanalysis or a more recent version of it (e.g. Snarey *et al.* 1983). Loevinger (1993b) has vigorously rebuked both of these assertions. More recently, Blasi (1998) has also argued against consideration of Loevinger's model of ego development as lying within more contemporary cognitive-developmental models, for many of her assumptions and methods do not fit neatly within this tradition. Loevinger argues that her model of ego development, derived entirely from empirical data, is unique in its understanding and assessment of different organizations of life experiences that follow a hierarchical, developmental order over time (Loevinger 1993b).

Criticism of Loevinger's construct

In the first major independent review of Loevinger's ego development construct, Hauser (1976) raised several issues in need of clarification – issues which have been re-echoed by critics in the decades since that time. Of primary concern has been the lack of attention paid by Loevinger to mechanisms driving development through her stage sequence, giving rise to ego stages in the first place. Hauser voices such questions below:

> Two important theoretical questions implicit in such a model are the following: What is the mechanism of change? And, what principle is at the core of the 'qualitative levels of organization'? . . . In more deeply analyzing the model itself, it would be important to propose explicitly more abstract formal principles that govern both the 'vertical structure' (connection between stages) and 'horizontal structure' (organization within stages . . .).
>
> (Hauser 1976: 952)

Because an organizational principle has not been delineated, Hauser also questions the means by which affect and cognition are related within each of Loevinger's stages and how motivation influences development. At present, these theoretical and conceptual issues remain unresolved and have also sparked further protests from critics.

A second issue which has generated critical discussion is Loevinger's suggestion of an indivisible ego. Snarey *et al.* (1983) found it necessary to postulate an ego having various subdomains, each separately amenable to empirical study. When the ego has been approached in this way, *décalage* relationships between subdomains have appeared. (*Décalage* means 'uncoupling'. Thus, related contents may evidence somewhat different levels of structural development. For example, a certain stage of cognitive development appears as a necessary but not sufficient condition for a more advanced stage of moral reasoning.) Snarey *et al.* believe that Loevinger is unable to recognize and account for such differential developments in her ego development scheme. Loevinger counters the claim for *décalage* relationships among subdomains on mathematical grounds, indicating problems such as lack of the necessary precision in measuring instruments necessary to justify *décalage* notions. A further problem Loevinger finds in the divided ego construct is failure by researchers to specify interrelationships among all subdomains by providing age norms and matching of ego subsystems on rigorous empirical grounds. Most recently, Manners and Durkin (2001) have found little empirical evidence for Loevinger's claim to an indivisible ego as the 'master trait of personality', subsuming other developmental domains. This study will be discussed in some detail in the following section.

Loevinger's approach to the study of ego development lies in contrast to the approach taken by trait psychologists, and these differing orientations have been the subject of several recent interchanges between Loevinger and her critics (for example, Loevinger 1991, 1993a, 1993b; Costa and McCrae 1993). Loevinger's approach to personality suggests the development of the ego occurs through qualitatively different levels of reorganization. This orientation lies in contrast to a trait approach that views personality as comprised of basic traits which remain relatively stable over time. Loevinger (1993a) does not believe such a trait-factor approach can reveal important qualitative differences; for example, between the conformist and conscientious stages in individual ego development. The distinction between a person conscientiously following the authority of others or conscientiously living according to one's own conscience are blurred in a trait approach.

Further criticism has been leveled at Loevinger's SCT test scoring scheme, with alleged confusion between content and structure (Broughton and Zahaykevich 1988; Josselson 1980; Snarey *et al.* 1983). Broughton and Zahaykevich suggest that this fusion makes it difficult to assess the extent of class and cultural bias on the SCT. Josselson argues that beyond the conscientious stage, ego functioning seems to be defined by particular social values rather than any structural elements. She cites the 'cherishing of individuality' characteristic of higher ego stages as a feature having more to do with cultural values rather than maturational form. Noam (1992) furthers the argument by suggesting that complexity and maturity are fused in Loevinger's stage model of ego development. From his work with clinical populations, Noam argues that complexity often exists in stark contrast to integration; with clinical groups, scoring at a higher stage of ego development does not mean that integration has been attained. Both Snarey *et al.* (1983: 321) and Mitchell (1993) also question Loevinger's assumption that empirical evidence should constitute the highest law of the land. Snarey *et al.* conclude that Loevinger's ego development construct has been 'a trade-off between significant empirical gains and obvious philosophical shortcomings' (Snarey *et al.* 1983: 321), while Mitchell questions whether methods of study might sometimes lose touch with meaning in personality development.

Loevinger (1997) has responded to all of the above criticisms by saying that they are approximately correct, factually. However, the question is whether these criticisms are strengths or weaknesses of the method. She argues that the strength of her model of ego development, by contrast to other structural developmental measures, is that it is based solely on masses of data. The definitions of stages are derived from data. Stages are described both in terms of structure and content of subject responses, for example, for both vary with stage of ego development according to the data. Despite these issues, Loevinger's paradigm has become an increasingly popular pathway to assessing identity (ego development) in adolescence and adulthood. Three books devoted to research on ego development have been published since 1996 and attest to this trend (Hy and Loevinger 1996; Loevinger 1998b; Westenberg *et al.* 1998a).

Research findings on ego development

Loevinger's ego development measure has sparked enquiry into many issues such as refinements to the SCT, sex differences and developmental patterns of ego change during adolescence and adulthood, links with related personality variables, and attempts to promote ego growth in contexts ranging from families to school classrooms to prison settings. Several broader questions have also been examined over the past decade. One concerns the validity of ego development theory and its measurement. While Loevinger (1979c) and Hauser (1976) both published major critical reviews of the model, Manners and Durkin (2001) have undertaken a more recent empirical review that addresses the construct, predictive and discriminant validity of ego development theory as well as questions involving its measurement. From their review, these authors offer a number of conclusions. There is strong support for the construct validity of ego development theory in relation to external criteria from alternative measures. A number of these studies will be summarized later in this section. There is also substantial support for the validity of three central premises of Loevinger's model: that the ego is unitary in nature, that the ego represents an integration of diverse personality characteristics, and that there is sequentiality to the development of the ego stages. Ego development is also an entity distinct from verbal fluency, intelligence and social class.

From this same review, however, two dimensions of Loevinger's model were called into question (Manners and Durkin 2001). There was little support for Loevinger's contention that ego development is a master trait of personality, subsuming other developmental domains of character development, cognitive style, interpersonal style and conscious concerns. Furthermore, though moral and ego development were found to be strongly related, neither domain dominated the other. Independent work by Novy *et al.* (1994) reached a similar conclusion. The second dimension called into question by Manners and Durkin (2001) concerned Loevinger's claim for the irreversibility of ego stages. It appears that the phenomenon of regression in ego development does occur more frequently than might be expected by error alone.

A further recent review attempts to understand why ego development so frequently stabilizes by the end of adolescence at stages far below the maximum potential (Manners and Durkin 2000). Proposals are based on Loevinger's theoretical reflections on the ego development process, results from intervention studies, theory and research on the related model of moral stage development as well as general personality change in development. The authors conclude that stage stability is not an inherent characteristic of late adolescent and adult ego development, and ongoing development is possible during and beyond adolescence. Meeting and dealing with various types of internal or external life experiences are likely associated with gains in ego development during and beyond adolescence. These experiences are ones that would disequilibrate the current ego development structure, with accommodation responses associated with transition to a more complex stage. Many individual differences will influence the degree of exposure to disequilibrating life experiences and how such an event is resolved.

The question of gender differences in ego development has also been examined. Cohn (1991) conducted a meta-analytic study to assess the size and stability of gender differences in ego development throughout adolescent and adult development. His findings indicated that sex differences in ego development were moderately large among students 12 to 17 years of age, favoring females, but these differences declined among university aged students and disappeared among samples of older men and women. It thus appears that adolescent girls achieve milestones in ego development earlier than boys, but that this difference declines with age.

Investigations into developmental patterns of ego maturation during adolescence have been the primary focus of a number of studies into the formation of adolescent identity. Longitudinal studies of ego development during adolescence have been undertaken by Adams and Fitch

(1982), Allen *et al.* (1994), Dubow *et al.* (1987), Gfellner (1986a), Kitchener *et al.* (1984), Krettenauer *et al.* (2003), Loevinger *et al.* (1985), Novy (1993), Redmore and Loevinger (1979), Redmore (1983), Rogers (1998) and Westenberg and Gjerde (1999). Most, though not all, of these longitudinal designs have pointed to change in ego development stage over at least a one year span during adolescence. Most, though not all, have similarly indicated a generally steady progression in stage development during the course of adolescence. Upon closer examination of results from these studies, it appears that greatest gains in ego development emerge during the secondary school years, with greater stability occurring in late adolescence and young adulthood (Adams and Fitch 1982; Gfellner 1986a; Kitchener *et al.* 1984; Redmore and Loevinger 1979; Redmore 1983; Westenberg and Gjerde 1999). Longitudinal results have generally indicated an increase from the self-protective to the conformist stage from grades 8 to 12; patterns of movement from mid to late adolescence have not been consistent across longitudinal studies. In one of the few studies of ego development from early adolescence through early adulthood, Westenberg and Gjerde (1999) found an individual, on average, gained approximately 1.5 steps in ego development. However, there were large individual differences in the timing and extent of ego development. Some environments (such as those university contexts with a narrow curriculum focus) may be associated with regression in ego maturity (Adams and Fitch 1983; Loevinger *et al.* 1985; Kroger 1996).

Cohn (1998) has undertaken a meta-analytic assessment of age trends in ego development. While his data also included studies of ego development during adulthood, he has explored the following questions: (a) What makes people mature? (b) What experiences act as pacers for development? His research indicates that ego development stabilizes for most individuals by early adulthood. He also found that certain educational experiences which encourage perspective taking are associated with gains in ego development, though not beyond the self-aware stage. Cohn's results of age trends in ego development will be discussed further in the section on implications for social response.

Socio-economic status has predicted acceleration in ego development (Gfellner 1986b); students in higher socio-economic groups generally attained ego stages one to two years in advance of their counterparts from lower socio-economic backgrounds. Browning (1987) has also noted a statistically significant relationship between ego development and education, with greatest impact of parental educational level coming before age 18 years for the offspring. Finally, parental child-rearing styles have predicted ego development during adolescence and adulthood. Child-rearing styles characterized by acceptance, a non-authoritarian approach to punishment and identification of the child with the parent have been associated with higher levels of ego development some 22 years later in adulthood (Dubow *et al.* 1987). Fathers' displays of autonomy and relatedness toward their adolescents (such as providing challenging interactions within a broader context of autonomous relatedness) were predictive of greater gains in adolescent ego development over a two-year interval (Allen *et al.* 1994).

A number of studies have examined relationships between sex role identity and ego development (for example, Costos 1986, 1990; Nettles and Loevinger 1983; Prager and Bailey 1985; Schwarz and Robins 1987; Snarey *et al.* 1986). Perhaps the most consistent thread running through such findings is that ego stage seems positively related to androgynous role expectations but not to androgynous self-conceptions. Ego development may be related to some sex-role attitudes and to self-conceptions of agency and communion. However, an association between ego development and self-conception of masculinity and femininity has received minimal support.

Additional variables of identity status, moral reasoning and cognition have been related to Loevinger's ego development stages. Consistent findings have come from those studies examining the relationship between ego identity status and ego development. Achievement and moratorium subjects have scored significantly higher in ego development than foreclosure and diffusion subjects (Adams and Shea 1979; Berzonsky and Adams 1999: Ginsburg and Orlofsky 1981; Kroger and Green 2004). When identity has been assessed on a self-report high to low continuum, moderate positive correlations have been attained between ego identity and ego development stage (Adams and Fitch 1981). When identity status and ego development have been studied longitudinally over a one-year timespan in late adolescence, movement of subjects into higher stages of both identity constructs has been noted, though the relationship between identity status and ego development for individual subjects was not reported (Adams and Fitch 1982). In exploring the predictive relationship between ego identity (measured on a self-report high to low continuum) and ego stage over time, knowledge of either variable has been equally effective in predicting the other over a one-year time interval (Adams and Fitch 1981).

The relationship between moral reasoning and ego stage as well as cognition and ego stage have also been explored. Snarey (1998) conducted a narrative review of the ego development and moral reasoning literatures. He found clear evidence that ego development and moral reasoning development are empirically related across the lifespan;

however there was variation across studies. For example, Gfellner (1986b) found low positive correlations between ego stage and moral reasoning stage in early but not late adolescence in a cross-sectional investigation of the two variables; in a longitudinal investigation of these variables over a four-year interval from early to mid-adolescence, ego development and moral reasoning related at fixed points in time, but ego development stage in early adolescence did not predict subsequent moral reasoning stage (Gfellner 1986a). Kitchener *et al.* (1984) reported increases in use of principled moral reasoning over a two-year span during late adolescence and young adulthood; no change in ego stage was observed, however. Recent work has also examined links between ego development and the ethics of both care and justice reasoning; no consistent results have yet been obtained (Skoe and von der Lippe 2002; Rogers 1998).

The relationship between cognition and ego stage has been the focus of a small number of studies. Hurtig *et al.* (1985) reported relationships between ego development and measures of both physical-mathematical cognitive functioning as well as social-interpersonal cognitive functioning. Cognitive functions contribute significantly to ego functioning during mid-adolescence, but the type of cognitive function and its degree of impact depend upon the subject's sex; ego functioning was predicted by interpersonal reasoning for females and by physical-mathematical reasoning for males. The authors question the assumption of a necessary link between higher levels of cognitive structure and ego maturation unless there is an expansion of the concept of cognitive structure beyond that of formal operational thought. Significant relationships between different measures of intellectual development and ego stage have been observed by Alisho and Schilling (1984), Cramer (1999) and Ginsburg and Orlofsky (1981).

The relationship between ego stage and family interaction during adolescence has been the focus of several studies based on Loevinger's model. Adolescent ego development has been related to parental behavior (Allen *et al.* 1994; Hauser *et al.* 1984; Leaper *et al.* 1989; Novy *et al.* 1992; von der Lippe 2000; von der Lippe and Møller 2000). Adolescents who elaborated their ideas and increased their contributions to family discussions were at higher levels of ego development. Correlational findings suggested the possibility that some families enhance adolescent discourse through acceptance of and empathy with their adolescents, while families who promote a repressive atmosphere (through parental judging, devaluing, constraining) are associated with regressive and repetitive adolescent speech patterns. Parents' effective enabling and accepting behaviors were strongly related to higher stages of adolescent ego development in Hauser *et al.*'s (1984) work. From this study, however, it was not possible to discern whether a parent's behavior was reactive to rather than responsible for the adolescent's speech pattern. Using Hauser's *et al.*'s (1984) family communication coding system, von der Lippe and Møller (2000) found that adolescents' but not parents' ego level predicted family negotiation scores. Examining adolescents' perceptions of parenting styles, Gfellner (1986a) found higher ego stages of adolescents related to perceived parental loving and supporting, while perceived parental demanding was associated with lower stages of adolescent ego development. Results of studies addressing ego stage and family interaction style point towards a picture generally consistent with expectation that adolescents at higher stages of ego development behave in warmer, more responsive ways and come from families which support and enable, while adolescents at lower stages of ego development evidence more impulsive and acting-out behaviors and come from families in which parents are demanding and judgmental in interaction with their teenagers.

Current directions in ego development research

Manners and Durkin (2001) point to a number of ego development arenas in need of further study. Greater research attention is needed to understand variable rates of ego development across genders and contexts. Additionally, a deeper understanding of when and why people experience regression in ego development is needed. Further research is also needed into the predictive validity of ego development. One might, for example, explore stages of ego development in relation to behavioral outcomes such as parenting style, social behavior and leadership style. While Noam and his colleagues (Noam *et al.* 1991b) have begun examining associations between ego development and psychopathology among adolescents, it would also be useful to examine potential means of predicting those who will advance in ego development and those who will remain stable or regress over time.

Kroger (1996) has undertaken a narrative analysis of intra-individual, longitudinal studies of ego and identity development to understand further the role of regression in normative structural change during adolescence. From clinical interview material accompanying some of these studies, I have identified three types of regressions that appeared more frequently than could be anticipated by error alone: regressions of disequilibrium, rigidification and disorganization. Different triggers appeared to be associated with these different types of regressive movements. Research into triggers that may be associated with varied types of regression and potential mediators would appear a fruitful research direction for future longitudinal studies of intra-individual change in ego development during adolescence.

Cross-cultural applications of the SCT have recently been explored (Carlson and Westenberg 1998). The Washington University Sentence Completion Test has been translated into at least 11 languages to explore issues as varied as quality of conflict negotiation in families of adolescent girls to contextual differences across academic disciplines (Costa and Campos 1989) to the development of a children's version of the SCT (Westenberg *et al.* 1998a). While cross-cultural comparisons have rarely been the focus of studies involving the SCT in other contexts, its use in varied cultural contexts has certainly increased over time. Carlson and Westenberg (1998) review studies conducted with the SCT outside the United States and offer thoughts for methodological issues to consider. Future cross-national and cross-cultural work might productively explore cultural variations in patterns of ego development.

Recent studies utilizing the SCT have also been examining other dimensions of personality that may be associated with ego development stages. In a rare longitudinal study of ego development from ages 7 to 22 years, Krettenauer *et al.* (2003) examined how externalizing and internalizing behavioral problems in childhood predicted ego development at age 22 years. Both types of indicators were associated with ego development at age 22, even when SES and education level were controlled. Externalizing problems predicted ego stages below conformity, while internalizing problems were related to difficulties in attaining ego development stages beyond conformity. These results are consistent with a cross-sectional study of hospitalized adolescents, aged 12 to 16 years (Recklitis and Noam 1999). Recklitis and Noam (1999) found avoidance and ventilation to be associated with lower levels of ego development, while problem solving and interpersonal strategies were associated with fewer problems and higher levels of ego development. Cramer (1999) has found different constellations of IQ and defense mechanisms to predict stage of ego development in a normative sample of young adults.

Implications for social response

A number of implications for those working with adolescents in varied arenas arise from Loevinger's (1976, 1987) writings on ego development. While Loevinger herself has confined her work to refining her ego development measure, other researchers and clinicians have explored a number of applications of Loevinger's ego development model. These include the therapeutic implications of her ego development model, interventions to help facilitate ego development in varied settings, the relationship between ego development and mental health, and the relationship between client and therapist ego levels as well as supervisor and trainee ego levels in therapeutic outcomes. Perhaps the bulk of research addressing ego development applications for adolescents over the past decade has focused on attempts to facilitate ego development in clinical, judicial and educational spheres and on explorations of ego development and its relationship to optimal functioning.

Regarding intervention, it must be noted at the outset that, unlike Kohlberg, Loevinger (1976) questions the use of interventions to advance the present stage of ego functioning. While Kohlberg justifies, philosophically, his belief that 'higher is better' and aims to promote more mature forms of reasoning through educational means, Loevinger is cautious about the goal of raising ego development as an appropriate therapeutic or educational aim. Nevertheless, efforts have been undertaken to promote ego development among adolescents in a range of settings.

Swensen (1980) has described, from a theoretical base, what he believes to be the implications of Loevinger's model for the field of counseling; yet it has been only more recently that these ideas have been expanded and examined empirically. Swensen draws attention to the importance of both individual and environmental factors on client behavior. He proposed that those at less complex stages of ego development would likely be more subject to environmental influences, while those at higher stages would be more capable of either changing or transcending their environments. Swensen points out two transition periods in Loevinger's model important for counseling interventions that would have relevance for adolescents – the transition from behaving according to self-interest to regulating one's interests with those of others and the transition from this latter organization to the internalization of rules (like behaving in accordance with one's own inner standards) and at the same time experiencing greater mutuality in relationship. Swensen finds it necessary to recognize the impact of the environment before, during and after these transitions in the planning of therapeutic interventions.

For adolescents (and adults) below the conformist stage, the environment is having enormous influence on behavior and therapy should be directed toward changing environments or changing the reward/punishment system operating within the adolescent's environment. At the self-protective stage (where we might expect to find younger adolescents), Swensen suggests the utility of either behavior therapy with a cognitive orientation or Glaser's reality therapy. Both these approaches recognize the individual's capacity for some degree of self-control and would seem suited to that framework of the less mature self-protector ego structure:

> Behavior [of the self-protector] is calculated to gain the rewards the individual seeks from the environment without incurring punishment. A therapy that helps the person to gain the sought-after rewards without simultaneously provoking punishment or retaliation would be applicable.
>
> (Swenson 1980: 386)

For the adolescent (or adult) conformist whose actions are guided by the opinions and rules of a reference group, Swensen recommends Ellis's rational-emotive therapy to help differentiate rational from irrational beliefs. A conformist is likely to be grappling with conflicting role demands and unable to please everyone; this conflict is likely to cause much distress, for the conformist's ego structure thrives on the group's approval. Ellis's approach could assist the conformist to resolve conflicting demands from such role requirements, as well as point the way to a more self-aware orientation in the resolution of incompatible demands.

Adolescents (and adults) at the self-aware stage are in the process of shifting from external to more internal sources of behavioral standards and belief systems as well as developing greater authenticity in relationship. Ellis's approach, in Swensen's view, offers most to individuals at this stage of ego organization, for rational-emotive therapy aims at helping people to question many irrational beliefs derived from the status quo and focus on more personally satisfying values and beliefs. For example, Ellis (1962) encourages people to question the irrational belief that 'I must be liked by everyone in my group', the raison d'être for the conformist and an appropriate challenge for one at the self-aware stage.

For those at the conscientious, individualistic and autonomous stages, therapies shifting from environmental manipulation to greater personal focus on self-fulfillment and existential issues would be most appropriate, in Swensen's view. The client-centered therapy of Rogers might be particularly valuable for those (primarily late) adolescents and adults at the conscientious stage, with a newly emerging awareness of their own internal standards and more differentiated inner life. Client-centered therapy, in particular, encourages self-exploration and resolution of conflict on one's own terms, seemingly useful for the conscientious stage client. Humanistic and existential approaches, concerned with more philosophical issues, might be particularly appropriate to individualistic and autonomous stage clients, with their greater abilities to accept the individuality of other human beings and all the issues this capacity raises.

Swensen concludes by cautioning that adolescents at higher stages of ego functioning may, nevertheless, appear at university counseling centers with problems such as test anxiety, more characteristic of the lower stage self-protector; for such situations, a behavioral strategy that recognizes and aims to reduce the anxiety would be appropriate. However, even under such circumstances the client's ego stage must be recognized and addressed. Thus, an exam-anxious, self-aware student might best be helped by the counselor's presentation of a behavioral strategy as one that can assist people to gain greater control over impulses and reactions to stress. Eventually, the aim would be a therapy of 'self-help', which this self-aware student self-administers. In their study of treatment requests, Dill and Noam (1990) discovered that higher ego stage patients in an outpatient setting were more likely to request insight therapy, while lower ego stage individuals were more likely to request reality checks and behavioral intervention. However, further research into the relationship between client stage of ego development and the type of therapeutic orientation that will best meet the client's needs is greatly required.

There has been some research into interventions aimed to facilitate adolescent ego development in school, judicial and clinical settings. Manners and Durkin (2000) offer an extensive review of intervention programs aimed to facilitate ego development during adolescence and adulthood. Deliberate Psychological Education programs (e.g. Erickson 1990; Sprinthall 1994), aimed to stimulate ego development and moral reasoning in high school students, have been most effective in facilitating ego development when exercises were disequilibrating, cognitively and emotionally engaging and interpersonal in nature. Additionally, intervention programs have been most effective when providing personally salient experiences aimed to help promote ego development (e.g. training in responsibility and autonomy for trainee nurses in the context of a nursing training program, White 1985). Interestingly, most efforts to facilitate ego development have not aimed to assess the participant's level of functioning on entry to the program and to design a program accordingly – a step Kohlberg found vital to the facilitation of moral reasoning. A further finding across a number of intervention studies in the Manners and Durkin (2000) review was that those individuals at or below the self-aware stage either remained stable or advanced in ego stage, while those at the conscientious stage or above did not advance. This finding may result from the lack of disequilibrating experiences to 'stretch' or pace those individuals functioning at higher stages of ego development at the outset.

Several research groups have been examining the relationship between ego development and mental health, also discussing implications for intervention. Rierdan (1998) has pointed to the role that ego development may play as a predisposing or protective factor that interacts with life stressors to either lead to or avoid psychopathology. From Rierdan's work with depressed pubertal adolescent girls, there was no direct relationship between ego development and maladjustment. Rierdan questions whether preconformist levels of ego development represent a generic vulnerability to all forms of psychopathology or whether the various preconformist stages involve vulnerability to different pathologies. She also questions whether different levels of ego development may be associated with different forms of the same disorder. These and other questions must await future research.

Noam and his colleagues have found a strong relationship between ego development and symptom expression during adolescence and adulthood (Dill and Noam 1990; Noam 1992; Noam *et al.* 1991a). The Harvard/McLean Laboratory of Developmental Psychology and Developmental Psychopathology has been monitoring inpatient samples of over 1,200 children and adolescents suffering from affective, conduct, anxiety and attention-deficit disorders in addition to normative and outpatient samples (Noam 1992). Results of this work point toward a strong relationship between ego development and symptomatology, with adolescents at pre-conformist stages of ego development evidencing more externalizing behaviors (impulsivity, acting out, delinquency) and conformist adolescents consistently more prone to directing aggression against the self (feeling guilty and/or depressed). At higher, post-conformist stages of ego development, however, research linking ego development and internalizing symptomatology has been less conclusive. Some findings, however, do indicate that with increasing developmental complexity, psychopathology becomes more internalized.

Noam (1998) has furthered these ideas by suggesting that particular vulnerabilities, risks and symptom combinations may characterize each stage of ego development. He summarizes many complex associations emerging from his research by noting that higher stages of ego development are not necessarily more adaptive. From some of his researches, better adaptation is related to maturation in ego development, but other of his researches have shown that higher ego stages are related to more internalizing disorders (e.g. depression, suicidal ideation). Delay at early stages of ego development is a risk factor for externalizing disorders (e.g. acting out, aggression), however. Moving to more complex levels of ego development does not necessarily imply that earlier forms of making sense of the world are integrated into the new, more complex structure.

Further issues that have been addressed in ego development research are the relationship between client and therapist ego level as a factor in therapy as well as the optimal relationship between ego stages of supervisor and trainee. With regard to the first issue, there may be differential effectiveness among therapists at different stages of ego development. This suspicion has been supported by work with young offenders by the California Youth Authority (Palmer 1974). Young persons high in ego maturity have responded best to teams high in predicted efficiency (high ego level), while the relation has been reversed for those young offenders at lower stages of ego maturity. Loevinger and others have suggested that therapists have a 'pacer' function and that therapy may work best when the therapist functions at a stage of ego development just beyond that of the client. Carlozzi *et al.* (1982, 1983) have found therapists' counseling efficacy to be related to their higher stages of ego development. Several publications have examined the optimal relationship of ego stages between supervisor and counselor trainee, and Borders (1998) reviews the impact of counselor trainee ego stage and their perception of clients, acquisition of counseling skills and actual performance. The content of client descriptions varied markedly by trainees' stages of ego development, as did mode of trainee affect or cognition. Swensen (1980) has suggested that great difference in stages of ego development between client and therapist is likely to reduce effectiveness of supervision, and work by Borders (1989) has supported this proposition. Trainees may be assisted most by supervisors at their same stage of ego development or one stage beyond. (Supervisors should never be at a stage of ego maturity lower than their trainees.) Cebik (1985) proposes a model of matching trainees and supervisors so that the latter are in close proximity to trainees and thereby able to serve as pacers.

Summary

The ego, according to Loevinger, is that 'master trait of personality' which serves as an organizing framework for one's customary orientation to one's self and to the world. Ego development is but one of four lines of development (ego, physical, psychosexual, intellectual) which are conceptually distinct. In contrast to Kohlberg, however, Loevinger views the ego as a unitary entity, rather than being comprised of various subdomains having *décalage* relationships. Ego development proceeds through a series of stages, believed to be hierarchical and invariant in sequence, which mark a continuum of increasingly complex and differentiated means by which one perceives oneself, the world and one's relationships in it. Loevinger has developed a Sentence Completion Test comprised of 36 items, which enables people to project their organizing frameworks onto the instrument. Individuals are assessed according to ego stage through their responses; adults in the general US population have a modal level at the self-aware stage of ego development. Greatest gains in ego development occur during early and mid-adolescence, with girls generally reaching higher ego stages earlier than boys. No sex differences in stage of ego development have regularly appeared at maturity, however. Recognition of an adolescent's ego stage has important implications for counseling, psychotherapeutic and educational purposes.

Further reading

Hy, L. X. and Loevinger, J. (1996) *Measuring Ego Development*, 2nd edn, Mahwah, NJ: Lawrence Erlbaum Associates.

Loevinger, J. (ed.) (1998) *Technical Foundations for Measuring Ego Development: The Washington University Sentence Completion Test*, Mahwah, NJ: Lawrence Erlbaum Associates.

Loevinger, J. (1992) 'A century of character development', in S. Koch and D. E. Leary (eds) *Development*, Baltimore, MD: American Psychological Association.

Manners, J. and Durkin, K. (2001) 'A critical review of the validity of ego development theory and its measurement', *Journal of Personality Assessment* 77: 541–567.

Westenberg, P. M., Blasi, A. and Cohn, L. D. (1998) *Personality Development: Theoretical, Empirical, and Clinical Investigations of Loevinger's Conception of Ego Development*, Mahwah, NJ: Lawrence Erlbaum Associates.

6 Identity as meaning-making

Kegan's constructive-developmental approach

> Peter: I . . . I don't understand what . . . I don't think I . . . I DON'T
> UNDERSTAND! . . .
> Jerry: What were you trying to do? Make sense out of things? Bring
> order?
>
> (Edward Albee, *The Zoo Story*, 1962)

Peter and Jerry live in the same city and visit the same park, yet they inhabit different worlds. Transcending contrasts in social class and years of accumulated schooling, Peter and Jerry construct meaning in clearly distinct ways, each hanging in an evolutionary balance that gives rise to a different sense of personal identity and construction of the 'reality' of their chance afternoon meeting in Central Park. Peter makes meaning of his life and encounter with Peter through a conventional 'law and order' orientation. Life must be lived according to society's rules, and Jerry's disregard for the norms of social interchange and demand for Peter's park bench bring the latter to the very edge of his evolutionary stability: 'People can't have everything they want. You should know that; it's a rule; people can have some of the things they want, but they can't have everything' (Albee 1962: 136). Meanwhile Jerry has returned from the zoo, insistent upon telling this stranger his story: 'I've been to the zoo. *(Peter doesn't notice.)* I said, I've been to the zoo. MISTER I'VE BEEN TO THE ZOO!' he opens, and slowly manipulates Peter into a relationship meeting his own desired purposes (Albee 1962: 113). Alongside Albee's intended *Zoo Story* message regarding the violence lurking within the confines of both the literal and metaphorical zoos of the play, Kegan might argue that life is also a zoo in the colloquial sense of the term – in that experience of confusion which exists prior to the human activity of successful meaning-making.

Identity to Kegan is a matter of making (or, more accurately, creating) sense, the way in which Peter and Jerry and everyone interpret and make their worlds cohere. The 'same' view can be seen in many ways, the same sound heard in many forms. 'How we will understand what we hear – or better put, *what we actually do hear* – will be settled there where the event is made personal sense of, there where it actually *becomes* an event for us' (Kegan 1982: 3). That 'there' for Kegan is the machinery of identity construction and evolution which has been tapped until now primarily through social scientists' cognitive or affective probes. Aldous Huxley's (1972) axiom that experience is not what happens to you, but rather what you do with what happens to you, is the foundation upon which Kegan's identity (or meaning-making) theory is built. A self struggling to organize and make sense of its experience, with evolutionary constraints during each stage in this process, is what Kegan's constructive-developmental theory is about.

Kegan's work, to a greater or lesser degree, draws from all identity theorists discussed in this volume – from the more affectively oriented ego psychoanalytic psychology and object relations traditions to the cognitive developmental approaches of Piaget and Kohlberg. Yet Erikson, Blos, Mahler, Kohlberg or Loevinger, each considered in isolation, does not allow one to address that underlying 'zone of mediation where meaning is made', the essence of the self in Kegan's view. Each cognitively or affectively based approach we have examined to this point would seem to tap only one facet of identity, rather than portray the subtending structure which initially brings cognition and affect into existence. Having begun our enquiries into the nature of adolescent identity with Erikson, the first writer to attend carefully to its formation process, it is perhaps most appropriate now to conclude with the synthesizing work of Kegan, the most contemporary and integrative identity theorist to consider identity's evolutionary process.

Kegan the person

Robert Kegan describes himself as being born mid-century, in middle America (Minnesota), to middle-class parents, as a middle child, accumstomed to being in the middle of things (Otto 2000). As a Dartmoth College student in the late 1960s, Kegan described coming of age in this Vietnam era as one of his most formative experiences. It was a time when the United States was in the process of 'breaking open' and becoming much more reflective over governmental policies. Kegan had adopted strong pacifist views and was unwilling to serve in the Vietnam War. He took up a school teaching position that brought draft deferment each year. (He had to decline a graduate fellowship at Cambridge University in English, for such action would certainly have resulted in either his being forced to return to the United States to be drafted or to not being allowed to return to the US at all.) In the political sanctuary offered by the school classroom, Kegan became fascinated with students' hearts and minds and with the ways they did or did not develop. During this time, he began to reflect on his future and to construct the interdisciplinary kind of doctoral program he would wish to enter were he to pursue graduate study. Harvard approved the program he designed, and interdisciplinary interests have guided Kegan's work throughout his professional life.

Kegan wished to bring lifespan, phenomenological and existential dimensions into cognitive psychology. Initially, he hoped to create a richer developmental psychology for enhancing clinical practice and therapeutic contexts for development. In the years since his student days, Kegan's interests in what came to be known as constructive-developmental psychology have led him into many additional arenas, from clinical practice, to research, to organizational and administrative consulting. All of these commitments have sprung from his keen concern with the practical applications of the evolving self.

Robert Kegan is currently the William and Miriam Meehan Professor in Adult Learning and Professional Development at Harvard University's Graduate School of Education, Chair of the Institute for the Management and Leadership in Education, Harvard University, and co-director of a joint program with Harvard Medical School to bring constructive-developmental principles of learning to the reform of medical education. He is also co-director of a Gates Foundation funded project to develop a program at the Harvard Graduate School of Education for the training of change leadership coaches for school and district leaders. In addition, Kegan is a licensed, practicing clinical psychologist, a public speaker, lecturing widely to professional and lay audiences, and a consultant in the area of professional development.

Kegan's view of identity

Impressed with the contributions that Piaget had made to understanding the development of logical thinking in children as well as object relations theorists' delineation of the ego, Kegan's bold new construct of identity has emerged from the marriage of these two traditions. However, rather than addressing the marital relationship *between* cognition and affect (a time-honored developmental pursuit), Kegan has shifted psychological orientation completely by attending to the possible developmental process that *underlies* cognition and affect and initially brings both into being:

> We begin by asking not 'What is the relationship between affect and cognition?' but 'What is the relationship that "has" cognition and affect?' . . . If we begin by assuming that cognition and affect are not separable – that neither leads to or governs the other, that they are actually aspects of a common process – then we shift our attention from the relationship between them to the common process that subtends them.
>
> (Kegan *et al.* 1982: 105)

By analogy, Kegan considers a cylinder with two openings – if attention is focused on the openings, one could consider this geometric form as two holes connected by a glass tube. Yet such a construction of 'reality' does not really capture the essence of the cylinder – that entity which creates the two openings in the first place. 'Cognition and affect, similarly, might not have a relationship so much as they are created out of a bigger context that has them' (Kegan *et al.* 1982: 106). It is this larger context which Kegan addresses in defining identity.

Kegan's construct draws particularly upon cognitive-developmental notions of Piaget and Kohlberg as well as object relations theory in describing identity (or meaning-making) as the way 'the organism and the environment in which it is embedded keep reconstructing their relationship. . . . [Meaning-making is] a series of qualitative reconstructions of the relation between the subject and the object of experience' (Kegan *et al.* 1982: 107). Development, that process giving rise to both cognition and affect, is an activity that brings into being structures which define the boundaries between self and other. In other words, identity formation (or meaning-making) is an ongoing process in which the boundaries between self and other become structured, lost, and reformed. The activity of meaning-making, of organizing and making sense of the world, and then losing that coherence and sense of self to a newly emerging way of being and making sense are the foundations of the constructive-developmental approach; questions regarding the form and process of meaning-construction are this orientation's preoccupation.

More now about the meaning of 'self' and 'other' before addressing their changing relationship. 'Self' (or subject) to Kegan refers to that intrapsychic framework in which one is embedded and from which one is unable to create distance; it is not possible to have or to be aware of one's framework when embedded in it. For example, a young child *is* his or her impulses and perceptions; rather than *having* impulses and perceptions under the self's control, the 2-year-old's self *is* that which he or she perceives and desires. As for the meaning of 'other' (or object), Kegan's usage differs somewhat from that of object relations theorists reviewed in Chapter 3.

To the latter, *object* refers to an image or internalized representation of a person important to us that guides much of our present behavior. For Kegan, *object* refers not to our internalized representation of another person at all but rather to more general phenomena that we come to relinquish – 'to those feelings, thoughts, constructs, and relationships that we can step out of, observe, and thus manipulate' (Noam *et al.* 1983: 101). The term *object* means literally 'thrown away from'; for Kegan, identity or meaning-making is about the way in which we come to 'throw away' something that once was a part of the self and make it an object to a new restructured self so that what we once *were* we now *have*. Subject (self) and object (other) are in an ongoing process of change that may continue over the course of the lifespan.

For Kegan, understanding the balance (or lack thereof) between subject and object is crucial to untangling the process by which identity or the making of meaning evolves over the course of the lifespan. Development through the eyes of constructive-developmental theory is about the systematic way in which people change boundaries between that which is taken as self and that which is taken to be other, about that which gets thrown away. Furthermore, it is about how that which gets thrown away is later reintegrated into a new kind of relationship with the self. As development proceeds for the 2-year-old described earlier, perceptions and impulses move to the object side of the subject–object balance and come under the control of a more differentiated self. The 5- or 6-year-old is said to *have* rather than *be* his or her perceptions or impulses; that which was self has become object to a new self structure. While an old self (one which *was* its perceptions/impulses) has been 'thrown away', a new and more differentiated self, *having* its perceptions/ impulses, is gained. Thus, identity formation (meaning-making) is the process of balancing and rebalancing following a shift from the subject to object side of the subject–object relationship. Rather than occurring only during adolescence, it is a process having regularity in sequence, form, and movement that may continue its motion over the lifespan.

Kegan refers to a subject–object (self–other) relationship in balance as an *evolutionary truce*. More accurately, '[e]volutionary truces establish a balance between subject and object' (Kegan 1982: 28). Truces are a time when the world 'makes sense', though that sense it makes differs

markedly for individuals in different subject–object balances. Such is
the situation faced by Peter and Jerry in making sense of their afternoon chance encounter from different self–other balances. And such is
the situation responsible for an exasperated mother's ultimate realization in dealing with her young son in an example to follow. Kegan
anecdotally tells the tale of a mother with two sons squabbling over
their allocation of a dessert pastry. It seems the younger, a 4-year-old,
has received only one portion because he is smaller, while his 10-year-
old brother has received two. In total frustration following her failed
efforts to assure the younger child of his 'just dessert' when he is older,
the mother cuts her 4-year-old's pastry in half.

> 'You want two pieces? Okay, I'll give you two pieces. Here!' –
> whereupon she neatly cut the younger boy's pastry in half. Immedi-
> ately all the tension went out of him; he thanked his mother sin-
> cerely, and contentedly set upon his dessert. The mother and the
> older son were both astonished. They looked at the boy the way
> you would look at something stirring in a wastebasket. Then they
> looked at each other; and in that moment they shared a mutually
> discovered insight into the reality of their son and brother, a reality
> quite different from their own.
>
> (Kegan 1982: 27–28)

For this 4-year-old, no error or inconsistency is present in his judgment. 'The deep structure of the [evolutionary] truce, simply put, is that
the perceptions are on the side of the subject; that is, the child is *subject*
to his perceptions in his organization of the physical world' (Kegan
1982: 28–29). This youngster is unable to separate his self from his
impulses or perceptions; rather than *having* impulses and perceptions,
he *is* them. Embedded in his perceptions, this pre-operational child has
no self capable of organizing changed perceptions; thus it is the world
(and the two pieces of pastry it now appears to offer) rather than his
perceptions of it that change through mother's actions. 'Distinguishing
between how something appears and how something *is* is just what one
cannot do when one is subject to the perceptions' (Kegan 1982: 29).
This child's evolutionary truce, however, should soon change when that
which was self (impulses/perceptions) is 'thrown away' to become the
object in a new balance or evolutionary truce. Then and only then will
mother be foiled in her plot to provide 'more' dessert by cutting one
portion in half.

In contrast to many stage theorists, Kegan is also interested in the
transitions between stages of meaning-making. We spend much of our

lives being developmentally 'out of balance', moving from one state of subject–object balance to another, and it is to those who accompany another on such a journey of transition that Kegan's theory speaks particularly well. Implications for clinical as well as a more naturalistic modes of intervention emerge from this constructive-developmental view and will be described in a later section. Rather than 'breakdown' in one's meaning-making efforts, Kegan prefers the alternative concept of 'breakthrough' to capture the essence of change from an old to a new balance. Transition involves loss, a mourning of that loss, and experiencing a sense of vacuum prior to rebalance. 'All growth is costly. It involves leaving behind an old way of being in the world. Often it involves, at least for a time, leaving behind the others who have been identified with that old way of being' (Kegan 1982: 215). All transitions involve a period of time in which the self is not yet sufficiently differentiated from its old context of embeddedness to take that context as its new object. In a recent pilgrimage through files of old notes, I came across a poem, hand-scrawled, by a late adolescent student. It reflects very clearly that state of suspension between old and new equilibra, where it seems that 'nothing is, is now'. Like the commonly used analogy of an adolescent swinging in space between bars of two trapezes, this teenager has no framework between evolutionary balances from which to make the world cohere:

How to endure the space beyond time's next dot
Where nothing is
Is now
And all that was
Is no more
And that that is, isn't.

(Janine, aged 19)

The essence of transition between states of subject–object equilibrium is a 'recognition', an awareness that 'all [the me] that was, is no more'. When the balance as to what 'self' is 'me' shifts sufficiently to the object side of the subject–object balance, the new self takes as object its old framework of embeddedness, thereby granting 'me' the ability to reflect upon it. Thus, a poem by Janine in her new evolutionary truce might end, 'And all that was, *is* no more, but now I've grown to *have* it'.

Most recently, Kegan (1994) has turned to examine the fit between contemporary western culture's demands on its adolescents and adults and their developmental capacities actually to meet those demands. Kegan has argued that for at least some significant part of our lives there is a gross mismatch between the complexity of our culture's 'curriculum' and our mental capacity to 'grasp it' in the arenas of schooling, working, parenting, partnering and psychotherapy. He suggests that it is necessary to make explicit our culture's 'hidden curriculum', its expectations for adolescents and adults, in order both to increase sensitivity to subject–object balances that individuals may need to reach in order to satisfy cultural expectations, as well as to provide appropriate supports for the evolutionary process. These issues will be examined more fully in the section on the implications of constructive-developmental theory for social response.

The evolution of meaning-making

Kegan (1982: 81) proposes that the making of meaning evolves through a sequence of qualitatively different stages: 'I suggest that human development involves a succession of renegotiated balances, or "biologics", which come to organize the experience of the individual in qualitatively different ways.' The question that might well be asked now is: 'What are these qualitatively different ways that give rise to cognitive and affective structures, and what brings such ways into being?' Here, Kegan turns to Piaget and Kohlberg for their work on the development of meaning-making in the physical and social worlds; it is through these 'ways of knowing' that clues exist regarding a possible underlying organization that gives rise to developmental differences in children's logic in the first place. We too will turn briefly to these writers for a reinterpretation of meaning-making through Kegan's constructive-developmental lens. Following such excursions, we will journey in some detail through Kegan's subsuming stages of subject–object organization that he holds responsible for Piagetian and Kolbergian observations.

Believing Piaget to be a genius finding more than he sought, Kegan (1979, 1982) views the implications of Piaget's stages of cognitive change during childhood and adolescence as pointing the way towards a concept of personality (not merely cognition) as revolutionary as that of Freud. Each stage of cognitive understanding in Piaget's framework signifies that very underlying cylinder of self which makes the world cohere. In Piaget's sensori-motor infant, who uses a logic based on reflex action, Kegan finds a child living in its first developmental truce – that of *being* rather than *having* its reflexes and sensations. Here the child thinks by moving and sensing. As the subject–object balance tilts, the child comes to *have* rather than *be* its reflexes, and a new subjective is thereby created. Reflexes and sensations are now object for a self which is able to reflect upon its own sensations: 'When the child is able to have his reflexes rather than be them, he stops thinking he causes the world to go dark when he closes his eyes' (Kegan 1982: 31). This new self structure is that of Piaget's pre-operational child, now embedded in her perceptions and impulses but able to organize which sensations are me and which are not-me. The 4-year-old described earlier who received his 'just dessert' exemplifies a self embedded in (subject to) his perceptions. For the concrete operational child, Kegan asserts that perceptions/impulses (the old subject) have 'moved over' to become object to a self now embedded in a concrete construction of the physical world. Within the limits of this truce, physical properties of the self and world are explored; finding solutions to games of skill and knowledge become guiding quests. Through Kegan's framework, the final evolutionary truce Piaget describes is that of formal operational thought. When this new truce is negotiated, there appears the ability to reflect on that which *was* the concrete operational thinker – a self embedded in (or subject to) the 'actual'. Through the evolution of formal thought, the adolescent self is one which can now reflect upon the 'actual' as only one (rather boring) instance of a far greater range of 'possibles'. 'This new balance makes "what is" a mere instance of "what might be" ' (Kegan 1982: 38). And so hypothetico-deductive reasoning appears. The subject (self) has once again become the object of a new subjective, as the 'actual' becomes object to a subjective of the 'possible'.

The extension of Piaget's work by Lawrence Kohlberg (described in Chapter 4) also provides a lead into that underlying cylinder of the self, according to Kegan. As with Piaget's developmental account of meaning-making in the physical world, it is similarly possible to reinterpret Kohlberg's developmental scheme of moral meaning-making. Both accounts, Kegan argues, point to that process underlying and giving rise to both schemes in the first place. Young children's constructions of social meanings (morality) would appear governed by the same forces allowing them to make sense of the physical world. Kohlberg's first evolutionary truce (heteronomous morality) can be viewed as one in which the child's perceptions (both social and physical) are subject; the child's self here is embedded in its perceptions, thereby making impossible any understanding of another's intention. (This balance is Piaget's description of the pre-operational child.) As perception becomes object during the second evolutionary truce (individualism, instrumental purpose and exchange), we find a self able to appreciate that other people have perspectives of their own. Now, however, the self is embedded in its own needs and unable to orient one perspective to another. Those operating from the next balance, Kohlberg's stage 3 (interpersonal concordance) orientation, now have their needs as objects 'thrown from' the former self. Here, however, the self is not yet differentiated enough to *have* its relationships; rather, the self *is* its interpersonal affiliations. Early formal operations are required for reciprocal role taking. As subject 'moves over' in the transition to Kohlberg's 'law and order' orientation of stage 4, relationships now become object to the new 'me', a me *having* rather than *being* its interpersonal affiliations. Stage 4, however, also has its own self-embeddedness context. No longer bound to pleasing others in the immediate social group in order to construct one's notions of right and wrong, one is now embedded in a larger social order, or, more accurately, one creates a larger social order of embeddedness. Here, one *is* one's organizational affiliations. In transcending embeddedness in these social or ideological groups, the subject of post-conventional moral reasoners (stages 5 and 6) has once again 'moved over' – that organizational context defining the self of stage 4 individuals now becomes object to a new subjective *having* rather than *being* its corporate commitments. 'The result is that one comes to distinguish moral values apart from the authority of groups holding those values' (Kegan 1982: 67). Thus Kohlberg's stages of moral meaning-making may also be created by that underlying cylinder of personality giving rise to Piaget's stages of making sense of the physical world.

Kegan's constructive-developmental view holds that it is the individual's inability to satisfy itself which drives development. By attending to discrepant experiences found through exposure to different situations, the organism strives not to return to its old homeostatic state of subject–object balance but rather to create a new and more complex self (subject) able to make sense of and respond to the new reality. While no easy feat, each hard-won balance brings with it a new kind of recognition of how the world and the self have become more distinct while at the same time more related.

Self–other balancing is not something one pursues in isolation. The constructive-developmental framework suggests that a 'holding environment' or 'culture of embeddedness' with its own particular features and functions is crucial to one's successful emergence from embeddedness with what will become 'object' in the next balance: 'The infant, I have said, is embedded in its sensing and moving, but there is a real human environment in which it lives, with which it confuses its own sensing and moving' (Kegan 1982: 115). While, from the infant's view, mother is part of the self, she is also its holding environment, that 'real human environment' in which the child's self–other balancing takes place. Mother (or primary caretaker) provides the external medium for the infant's evolution, for its efforts at making the world cohere. Having learned something of the cylindrical openings observed by Piaget and Kohlberg leading to a vision of their underlying generator, let us now view that which may constitute the cylinder of identity itself, according to Kegan, and gives rise to the normative adolescent experience of 'I'.

The growth and loss of the incorporative self (stage 0)

Infants enter the world equipped with reflexes which have been adaptive in the prenatal environment; most of these responses are rather useful during the early months of terrestrial existence too. At this time, the infant *is* its reflexes and sensations, without awareness of a world separate from its self; the infant *is* its reflexes, all self and no object. Since there cannot yet be a subject–object balance, Kegan *et al.* (1982) have termed this incorporative phase, stage 0. This is the stage which gives birth to the object, and such is the structure underwriting Piaget's stage of sensori-motor intelligence. A self *having* rather than *being* its reflexes will gradually emerge from the incorporative balance. Such is the status of meaning-making for the stage 1 impulsive self. However, one is embedded in a new framework – that of one's perceptions and impulses.

The growth and loss of the impulsive balance (stage 1, or first order of consciousness)

Kegan (1982: 139) says of the child living in the stage 1 balance: 'An infant discovers that there is a world separate from him; but not until years later does the child discover that this separate world is not subject to him.' This summary is a beautifully simple yet eloquent description of life through the eyes of the 2- to 5-year-old child embedded in his or her perceptions and impulses. A world separate from the child has been created in its evolutionary process; yet at the same time, that world is at the mercy of the child's perceptions – with different views of something, it is the world (and not the child's perceptions of it) that changes.

Here it is just not possible to coordinate two or more differing views of the same thing, for there has not yet evolved a self differentiated from its perceptions to do the organizing of them. Thus, one is unable to take the role of another. Cognitively, there is no ability to reverse operations; affectively, there is no ability to experience ambivalence. The self or others can only be experienced as all good or all bad but not a mixture of both. A child now believes everyone sees things from his or her point of view. This ability to take the role of another, to see that others have perspectives of their own, involves a further reconstruction of the subject–object balance which lies a few years down the road for the preschooler in her present meaning-making balance.

Cognitive-developmental and psychoanalytic theories have noted important milestones occurring during the 2- to 5-year-old's lifespan. Kegan continues by reinterpreting cognitive-developmental observations of how the child learns to take the role of another as well as the psychoanalytic account of the Oedipus complex. Both phenomena can be read as a self subject to its own impulses and perceptions evolving within the holding environment of the family. We have earlier seen the results of a pre-operational child subject to his own perceptions – the world (and not his perceptions of it) changed when a dessert pastry was cut in half. The Freudian family romance may be no more than that – a child embedded in its own impulses playing them out within the context of its natural culture of embeddedness, the family. Kegan does not find it enlightening to consider the young child as wishing to have a parent as a lover; rather, it is the holding environment of the family that becomes the protector of the child's impulses and the recipient of its mode of loving. Indeed, the very fact that one parent often becomes the source of impulse gratification and the other an inhibitor really results from the child's inability to integrate 'hero and villain' in one person. Oedipal issues may so often arise in the free associations of adult patients, for the very practice of psychoanalysis itself encourages that fantasy-filled, representational, imaginative mode of thought characteristic of the pre-operational preschooler. Again, an underlying evolutionary cylinder giving rise to both cognitive and affective phenomena appears as a distinct possibility.

Transition from the balance of the impulsive self finds the child bringing impulses and perceptions under his own control; that which was subject becomes the object of a new subjective. In an anecdotal account of an expedition with several 6-year-olds to see the Disney film *Pete's Dragon*, Kegan (1985) captures the essence of the children's evolutionary transition. The film, partly fantasy and partly 'real' (like thought in the pre-operational to concrete operational transition), depicts the adventures of a young boy, Pete, and a dragon friend who eventually helps Pete obtain a pretty decent set of parents. Mission accomplished, the dragon takes leave of Pete and parents, who live happily ever after. Not so, however, for the children under Kegan's charge. In tears, one little girl cries, 'Why do these movies always have to end so sad? . . . Why can't he have both? Why can't he have the dragon *and* the nice parents? Why can't he have both?' (Kegan 1985: 180). For Kegan's young companions, pre-operational and Oedipal stages are in their final days; the world of concrete reality takes over as dragon life fades and the child comes to coordinate his or her impulses and perceptions to take on a more defined role within the family unit. One cannot, it seems, have both dragon and real world drama in the next evolutionary truce. Beyond the age 5 to 7 transition, a new balance with its own form of self-embeddedness once again appears; while *having* rather than *being* its impulses, the imperial self of stage 2 is now embedded in its own needs, interests and wishes.

The growth and loss of the imperial balance (stage 2, or second order of consciousness)

That imperial self of the concrete operational child comes to take over the function of impulse control previously exercised by the family. Both internal and external experience are now conserved. Stability of needs and habits becomes more evident in contrast to the whimsical lability of the preschooler's impulse life. Children hanging in the imperial balance become more self-sufficient, evidencing a 'self-containment' and sense of agency. In coordinating perceptions, the realization comes that others truly do have their own perspectives, and one's own is not automatically read and shared by all. Now one's own needs, interests and wishes *are* the self. That self cannot yet coordinate different wishes of others, for such capability comes only when subject (needs, interests, wishes) differentiates and becomes the object for a new interpersonal subjective in transition to stage 3's interpersonal balance.

In another anecdote, Kegan (1982) tells of his teaching experiences with a class of 12-year-olds, most of whom were embedded in this imperial balance. They were asked one day to describe the moral of Murray Heyert's short story, 'The New Kid'. In the story, it seems Marty is clumsy, always chosen last for the neighborhood's baseball team and always relegated to the outfield. During a game, Marty has his opportunity for glory – and, of course, blows it by failing to catch the ball and save his team from defeat, once again becoming the recipient of much scorn and abuse. Then one day a new kid arrives who, it seems, is even more of an oddity than Marty. He follows in Marty's footsteps, failing spectacularly at the crucial ball-catching moment. And low and behold, it is Marty who leads the humiliating attack on this newfound object of derision. Even more startling, however, were responses to what the story meant by the children in Kegan's classroom:

> The story is saying that people may be mean to you and push you down and make you feel crummy and stuff, but it's saying things

aren't really that bad because eventually you'll get your chance to push someone else down and then you'll be on top.

(Kegan 1982: 47)

In the imperial balance, these 12-year-olds could only make meaning from an embeddedness in their own needs and interests; the ability to coordinate their own interests with those of another is just what the imperial self cannot do, for the self has not yet differentiated to the point of being able to reflect upon its needs, taking them as object to be coordinated with those of others. Most children in Kegan's classroom evidenced simple reciprocity; yet, they could not consider how both Marty and the new kid felt, orienting one to the other. Such limits of meaning-making underlie Kohlberg's stage 2 hedonistic orientation towards morality.

The school and peer group become the culturing environment to those making meaning from the imperial balance; both can provide the supportive structure of expectations and response appealing to many young souls. Schools concerned about education without failure are providing a vital 'holding' function that helps set the tone for the child's evolutions to come. In the world beyond the family unit, it is the school and peer group which can now supply the respect and esteem due children in the process of making sense according to their own needs and interests. Such is the balance and culture of embeddedness for most primary school age children; such may also be the balance for the child behind the mask of the adult sociopath (Kegan 1986a).

The growth and loss of the interpersonal balance (stage 3, or third order of consciousness)

The adolescent is expected to be interpersonally trustworthy. This expectation arises from a long history of evolutionary activity and is possible only as the self–other balance tips so that needs and interests become the self's new object; now the self *has* (rather than *is*) its needs and is able to reflect upon them and coordinate them with those of others. Here, one is expected to be able to uphold a promise and generally become oriented towards mutuality in relationship. While reciprocal role taking seems to be the triumph of transition to this new balance, the interpersonal is its constraint. For the stage 3 interpersonal self, one does not *have* one's interpersonal relationships; the self *is* its relationships and very vulnerable to attitudes within the immediate social context:

A white teenager living in a liberal northern suburb may espouse values of racial egalitarianism if that is the prevailing peer ethic, only to become a holder of racist views among racist friends if her family relocates to a school and neighborhood in the South or closer to the action in the North. The prevailing wisdom here will be that the teenager has changed as a result of new friends and new influences; it would be as true to say, however, that the teenager's way of making meaning has remained the same.

(Kegan 1982: 57)

Kohlberg's interpersonal concordance orientation would seem to reflect this new balance, wherein the self is embedded in its need for another's approval and is unable to step out of this shared reality.

Kegan (1982) notes that it is often the person embedded in the interpersonal balance that the assertiveness trainer inappropriately targets. Assertiveness courses, with their emphasis on skills for declaring 'more independently' one's needs and wishes, miss the predicament of the interpersonal self. With no self yet differentiated from the interpersonal, there is no subject to do the asserting; it is thus to a vacuum that the assertiveness trainer speaks when addressing the stage 3 self. Similarly, it is often difficult for the interpersonal self to express anger, for such behavior threatens disruption of the very relationship which *is* the self. Often individuals in this balance may be victimized in relationships yet be unable to experience anger (or relinquish the relationship), for such action threatens that very self–other balance which one is. Qualitative differences in the way the self coheres must be appreciated and addressed for therapeutic intervention to be effective.

The interpersonal self is the normative subject–object truce of early and mid-adolescence; transition to a new form of independence from the interpersonal is the hallmark of late adolescent and young adult identity. During such transformation, however, the individual must once again undergo the loss of an old balance. This time, it is one's relationships which become object to the new self, now embedded in its institutional or ideological affiliations.

The growth and loss of the institutional balance (stage 4, or fourth order of consciousness)

In differentiating from the medium of the interpersonal, the institutional balance gives birth to a sense of self-authorship. *Having* rather than *being* its relationships, the self evolving to stage 4 again experiences the ability to internalize that which was previously external. Now the interpersonal is regulated by a self differentiated from others. Here, it is threats to personal autonomy rather than relationships which bring about defensive operations: 'The strength of stage 4 is its psychological self-employment, its capacity to own oneself, rather than having all the pieces of oneself owned by various shared contexts' (Kegan *et al.* 1982: 115).

A young man, Jonathon, whom I interviewed as part of a longitudinal study of identity formation during late adolescence, reflected on the changes he saw in himself during the two years covered by the study. He seemed unable to pinpoint very specifically just what had happened to him in his own development, but had the following to say:

> Well, they've changed [my beliefs and values], but in subtle ways. Whereas before I believed what I believed because I didn't know any different, now it's because I have some much more well thought-out ideas about why I believe what I believe, even though what I believe may not have changed tremendously.
>
> (Kroger, unpublished raw data 1995)

Kegan might argue that what has happened to Jonathon is the very emergence of a self coming to author itself. The old balance of 'believing what I believed because I didn't know any different' was limited by that form of knowing which *was* its interpersonal context. What was subject (the interpersonal) has shifted to the object side of the subject–object balance, enabling Jonathon now to reflect upon his former structure from the self-authorship balance of his present way of making sense.

Kegan quotes one of his clients, whom he feels very clearly lies in this stage 4 balance. There is a sense of self-ownership coming through Rebecca's words; yet it is the very rigidity of this self-ownership which limits this stage 4 evolutionary truce:

> I know I have very defined boundaries and I protect them very carefully. I won't give up the slightest control. In any relationship I decide who gets in, how far, and when.
>
> What am I afraid of? I used to think I was afraid people would find out who I really was and then not like me. But I don't think that's it anymore. What I feel now is – 'That's me. That's mine. It's what makes me. And I'm powerful. It's my negative side, maybe, but it's also my positive stuff – and there's a lot of that. What it is, is me, it's my self – and if I let people in maybe they'll take it, maybe they'll use it, and I'll be gone'.
>
> (Kegan 1979: 16)

Rebecca's self *is* the psychic organization she is trying to run smoothly. In the stage 4 balance, the self derives meaning from the organization rather than deriving the organization from one's own meaning or valuing system. Here, one *is* one's career, citizenship, religion. There is no broader or more encompassing framework within which to relativize one's organizational commitments, no self to organize its organizations. Piaget's stage of full formal operations and Kohlberg's 'law and order orientation' are the observables resulting from this evolutionary balance.

The culture of embeddedness for the institutional self is the larger social order – that public arena in which one is normatively received and recognized during late adolescence and adulthood. Without adequate recognition by such institutional holding environments, the evolutionary process is once again under threat. Transition to the interindividual balance sees the self with an increasing desire to question that which motivated its affiliations to those institutions with which it has been identified. There is thus a gradual and increasing differentiation from the value generator itself.

The growth of the interindividual balance (stage 5, or fifth order of consciousness)

The last evolutionary truce for which there is evidence is one in which the self is differentiated from its institutions – there is now a self which *has* rather than *is* its institutional affiliations. The new interindividual balance coordinates institutional selves and, in turn, is embedded in interindividuality. While one can feel manipulated by the stage 2 imperial self, devoured by the stage 3 interpersonal self, and 'mediated' by the stage 4 institutional self administrating its business, the stage 5 interindividual self is there, open to its own re-creation through ongoing contact and exchanges with other individuals and systems, open to change and redefinition.

From this last balance, one comes to *have* rather than *be* one's career, religion, nationality or other institutional affiliation. Institutions are no longer upheld as ends in themselves, for they no longer reign supreme (for example, career performance is no longer ultimate). Rather, a new structure of the self exists which looks to ways in which institutions might better serve the self's own purposes in growth. Kohlberg's post-conventional level is characterized by a self dislodged from its societal lodgings; at this stage, the legal system lies at the foot of a self capable of creating (rather than merely upholding) the law. This moral reasoning level Kegan finds governed by that deep structure of the interindividual balance. Similarly, there is evidence of a fifth Piagetian stage beyond formal operations, wherein there is the ability to stand outside a system and reflect on it, rather than using the system to be the means of one's reflecting. Kegan and his colleagues again find this stage of cognitive understanding governed by that deep structure of the interindividual balance (Souvaine *et al.* 1990).

Themes of differentiation and integration, of separation and inclusion, spiral throughout the balances and transitions of the evolving self. However, the relationship of these themes or *stylistic preferences* to one's actual *structure* of meaning-making has been clarified by Kegan (1994):

> Moreover, I confused *style* and *structure* throughout *The Evolving Self* by using an organizing metaphor or image I have since come to 'repent' (literally, 'to think again'). . . . I equated certain orders of consciousness (the first and the third [subject–object balance]) with the style of *connection* and other orders of consciousness (the second and the fourth [subject–object balance]) with the style of *separateness*. Unconfusing these sets of distinctions involves seeing that each order of consciousness can favour either of the two fundamental longings [for connection or separateness].
>
> (Kegan 1994: 221)

Thus, in any of Kegan's subject–object balances one might adopt a 'relational' or 'separate' style of approach to the developmental task of meaning construction.

While Mahler *et al.* (1975) and Blos (1967) have emphasized experiences of intrapsychic separation and connection, the birth and adolescent rebirth of the self, Kegan argues that the process not only of differentiation but also of integration occurs again and again over the course of the life cycle. Each renegotiation of the evolutionary balance between self and other means not only the death of an old self but the birth of a new. This process normatively occurs during early and late adolescence in transitions to stages 3 and 4, respectively. However, meaning-making to Kegan is a lifelong activity with rebalancing not restricted to the years of adolescence alone.

An optimal mode of meaning-making

Like others before him, Kegan too has shifted from a health/illness model of identity to one which views identity formation as a developmental phenomenon. For Kegan, definition of healthy identity holds dangers similar to that 'bag of virtues' approach to moral education described by Kohlberg; there can be no absolute model of good mental health. All definitions, from traditional psychiatry to humanistic psychology, are biased, reflecting attitudes of a particular reference group. An orientation towards development, on the other hand, provides a framework from which to generate more justifiable goals for intervention in that norms of growth can be addressed. During early and middle adolescence, one would expect to see youngsters generally making meaning from the imperial (stage 2) or interpersonal (stage 3) balances (or from the stage 2 to 3 transition). Late adolescents present a greater range of possibilities for meaning construction, and Kegan refrains from specifying normative age ranges for stages beyond the imperial-interpersonal transition. However, one might generally anticipate late adolescent meaning-making from the interpersonal or institutional balances (based on Kohlberg's longitudinal data) or from a place in the stage 3 to 4 transition. Certainly the educational system requires of all adolescents simple role-taking skills, and intervention will be needed if a young person is unable to make sense from at least the imperial balance by early adolescence.

Measuring meaning-making balance

Kegan and his colleagues (Lahey *et al.* 1987) have developed a semi-structured interview, lasting approximately one to one and a half hours, for the purpose of assessing one's current stage of meaning-making, or subject–object balance. An individual is shown a series of ten cards, each with a key word or phrase, and is asked to select several cards that evoke memories of recent events for further discussion. These ten cards have carefully selected words, all containing elements of self-reference and boundary (angry, success, anxious or nervous, strong stand or conviction, sad, torn, moved or touched, lost something, change, important to me).

After hearing about the situation that the key word evokes, the interviewer then carefully probes the interviewee's experiences to learn more about *how* the self must be constructed in order to feel the particular boundary violation the individual has expressed. Questions are asked, for example, about what the best/hardest part of the experience for the interviewee was, and what might have been lost/gained had the experience not taken place. The interviewer also frames questions in ways to offer the interviewee opportunity to construct meaning at the next higher step of meaning construction. If the respondent repeatedly does not do so, the assumption is made that the limits of his or her meaning construction complexity have been met. Interviews are taperecorded, transcribed, structural units identified, and one's predominant meaning-making stage is determined. In addition, the interview rating system also identifies four transition points along the continuum between all adjacent subject–object balances.

Lahey *et al.* (1987) report four studies of interrater reliability, one of test–retest reliability and one of inter-item consistency. When interrater agreement of subject–object balance is defined as falling within one discrimination unit (1/5 stage), agreement percentages between two raters were 82 per cent, 100 per cent, 100 per cent, and 100 per cent across the four studies. The one study of test–retest reliability reports a Pearson $r = 0.834$ ($p<.001$) when agreement is defined as falling within one discrimination unit (1/5 stage). The correlation of scores between two forms of the interview was 0.96 as reported in the one study which addresses the question of inter-item consistency. The subject–object interview has provided the means for assessing structures of meaning-making in the research which is described below.

Historical backdrop to Kegan's constructive-developmental model

Kegan's model has emerged from a long tradition of structural-developmental theories. Speicher and Noam (1999) have overviewed two strands of theories within the constructive-developmental tradition: 'minimalist' and 'maximalist' theories. While both strands have origins in Piaget's (1960) and Kohlberg's (1969) works, minimalist structural theories have retained their focus on cognitive dimensions of the self, while maximalist approaches have integrated dimensions of personality, emotions and individual biography to describe more global developments of the self. Minimalist models have retained original Piagetian and Kohlbergian assumptions for structural stages in development: there is an invariant and universal stage sequence, stages represent structural wholes, are hierarchically organized and involve increasing differentiation and complexity of structures of thought. Within this minimalist tradition, for example, Selman (1980) built on Kohlberg's and Piaget's work to describe and empirically validate a sequence of stages through which children and adolescents come to take the perspective of another (social role taking). Selman's work was the first attempt within this minimalist tradition to apply the features of cognitive development to children's and adolescents' understandings of the social world.

Maximalist approaches have taken constructive-developmental ideas in a somewhat different direction by not attempting to focus on the development of the self in purely cognitive terms. For example, Kegan (1982), Loevinger (1976) and Noam (1985) have all used structural principles to describe broader dimensions of self development in terms of personality, identity and/or ego development. While these works retain an understanding of stages in terms of developmental structures, there are many non-cognitive elements that stages incorporate, such as emotions and the ways in which one is close to other people. Loevinger (1976), in particular, describes stages partly in terms of structures, but also in terms of functions and motives related to coping and defending. Kegan (1994) has made efforts to detail the organizing principles by which general structural stages of thought and feeling are defined. He argues that a single, developmental process underlies developments within cognitive, social-cognitive and intrapersonal spheres (Kegan *et al.* 1998). Thus, Kegan's model has emerged from a strong background of structural-developmental theories to take a new path in the application of cognitive principles to the development of the self.

Criticism of Kegan's construct

Perhaps the most important contemporary criticism leveled at Kegan's constructive-developmental model has been against his claim for a central organizing tendency or meaning-making 'whole' in personality, which organizes its parts. Loevinger (1979b) and Noam (1988a), in particular, have questioned Kegan's claim to one underlying logic of development from which other domains of cognitive and ego functioning spring. In arguing for 'wholism' or 'consistency' among parts within general meaning-making structures, Kegan *et al.* (1998) begin by clarifying the meaning of consistency. Consistency, to Kegan, implies a consistency in the structure or order of complexity in one's ability to make sense (*how* one thinks). Consistency does *not* imply consistency in behavior or even in the contents of one's beliefs, values or preoccupying concerns (*what* one thinks).

Considerable empirical evidence now exists to show consistency in the use of meaning-making structure across a range of psychological domains. For example, Lahey (1986) has examined consistency of meaning-making structures within the domains of love and work. Despite differences in the ways in which people say they feel in these contexts, *how* they reason about conflicts in love and work have shown a very high degree of epistemological consistency. Lahey conducted 44 subject–object interviews with 22 adults (11 men and 11 women) to examine the degree of consistency among participants' constructions of the realms of work and intimacy. She found that subjects were no more than one discrimination unit (1/5 stage) apart in 18 of 22 cases – a remarkable show of consistency. Additional studies by Villegas-Reimers (1996), Walker (1995) and Dixon (1986) have all found support for the hypothesis that subject–object balances are the underlying basis for cognitive or social-cognitive stages of development.

Kegan *et al.* (1998) have responded to further commonly raised questions about the issue of consistency. Use of a 'mix' of various subject–object balances by some individuals, for example, does not violate the consistency hypothesis, Kegan argues, if people consistently use the same mix of meaning-making structures. Studies cited in the preceding paragraph suggest that they do. Any consistent 'mix' of subject–object balances is likely to reflect a transitional place in the evolutionary meaning-making process, where less complex and more complex meaning-making structures are simultaneously operating.

The phenomenon of temporary regression in times of stress has also been frequently raised as a possible violation of the consistency hypothesis. Yet, Kegan and his colleagues illustrate how even in times of stress when the self does not succeed in responding according to its most complex means of constructing sense, a principle of consistency is still in operation. For example, in situations where one 'loses it' and feels oneself to be returning to old patterns of thinking or feeling, one is also aware that one is 'losing it'. There is some higher order of meaning construction operating, Kegan argues, that enables one to evaluate that one is temporarily not using one's highest powers of making sense.

Clinically, Noam (1988b, 1990, 1992) has argued that split off, encapsulated or dissociated dimensions of our life experiences fail to be transformed into more complex meaning-making structures, thus violating Kegan's consistency hypothesis. Individual biography, Noam maintains, may necessitate the use of various defense mechanisms that cause distortions and give rise to various symptoms which may reflect earlier modes of meaning construction. Again, Kegan *et al.* (1998) argue that there is still a consistency of the whole system, rather than just a collection of dissociated parts, for there is still a larger system in existence and operating to keep out or hold back certain painful elements: '[I]ncreased complexity can also be put to the purpose of creating ever more elaborate ways to hold off unintegrated parts of the self's meaning-making' (Kegan *et al.* 1998: 58).

Kegan has also been criticized by feminist writers on the grounds that his hierarchical developmental model arbitrarily places women in a position of disadvantage; the stage 3 interpersonal balance may simply characterize a woman's way of organizing experience, while the stage 4 institutional balance may more aptly portray the experience of men. Kegan's (1994) clarification of stylistic and structural differences in meaning construction, however, greatly illuminates the ways in which the sexes may or may not adopt stylistic differences in the development of their actual structures of meaning-making.

Research findings on the evolving self

Constructive-developmental theory has been used to account for a variety of naturalistic, clinical and laboratory phenomena. However, the work of Kegan and colleagues is still in its infancy and requires the necessary complement of empirical study to verify more fully what a reinterpretation of existing research has begun to unravel. (See Kegan 1982, 1985, 1994 for empirical bases of the evolving self model.) While this section will overview existing research based specifically on Kegan's model, it will also discuss what is still needed to validate further this constructive-developmental approach.

The first empirical study making use of constructive-developmental concepts examined the relationship between depression and subject–object balance. Kegan (1979, 1982) has argued that depression is the companion of a subject–object balance in the process of transition. Different forms and experiences of depression might therefore be associated with transitions between different evolutionary truces. Based on a pilot study of 39 individuals during their stay on a hospital psychiatric ward, Kegan believed he and his colleagues had detected three qualitatively different forms of depression in descriptions patients provided of their predicaments.

These three types of depression all involved a self under threat. Type A ('self-sacrificing') depression was felt by those concerned over loss of their own needs or the increasing cost of keeping them at bay. Feelings of being constrained, controlled, deprived, interfered with or, alternatively, a mixture between feeling 'a slave to my own interests' and a 'loss of my own distinct personality' were often expressed by these individuals. 'With loss of the satisfaction of my wants, I may no longer be' seemed to be the root of this existential dilemma. Type B ('dependent') depression was felt by those experiencing a relationship under threat. Feelings of being abandoned, betrayed, forsaken and unbearably lonely were often experienced, as were alternations between feeling fused with another and then guilty for 'putting myself first'. The fundamental issue here seemed to be that with the loss of my relationships, I may cease to exist. Type C ('self-evaluative') depression was experienced as a blow to self-esteem, a failure to live up to the expectations people held for themselves. Subjectively, people here spoke of feeling humiliated, empty and out of control in an unfair world where life was meaningless; sometimes a mixture of emotions appeared, from identification with performance and feeling isolated to feeling weak, evil or unbounded. Here, the void looming large was that with the loss of my self-authorship, I may cease to be.

Each individual was rated according to one of these depression types by researchers blind as to the person's self–other differentiation rating. When depression types were compared with self–other differentiation ratings, a very strong association appeared. Those experiencing depression type A were rated as stage 2 or 2 to 3 transitional; those experiencing depression type B were rated as stage 3 or 3 to 4 transitional; those experiencing depression type C were rated as stage 4 or 4 to 5 transitional. Although small, this pilot study does point to a possible relationship between type of depression and way of making meaning (or, more accurately, failing to do so). These results fit in well with related studies of depression, countering criticism of Kegan's tautological thinking (Kegan 1983). Kegan (1982) also suggests that 'abandonment depression', characterized by separation anxiety, accompanies the stage 0 to 1 transition, and 'disillusioning depression', characterized by feelings of being shut out, sent away, distressed that others have gone into business for themselves, reflects the concerns of those in the stage 1 to 2 transition.

Research since this initial study has focused on a number of important issues in construct assessment and validation. A crucial move towards construct validation of Kegan's model has come by investigating the claim that progress through meaning-making stages occurs in a hierarchical and invariant sequence. Empirical support for this proposition has now emerged from a nine-year longitudinal study by Kegan and his colleagues (Kegan 1994). In this investigation, 22 adults were interviewed annually for four years and then re-interviewed again five years later. With few exceptions, intra-individual change from one data collection point to the next has involved movement in the direction of increasing complexity; without exception, changes were very gradual with no individual demonstrating a shift of more than two discrimination units (2/5 of a stage) over the course of one year. While further research is needed to verify the claim of an hierarchical and invariant sequence, results from these initial studies have been promising. Work by Baxter Magolda (1999b) over a 12-year timespan has produced similar results, though the Subject–Object Interview (Lahey *et al.* 1987) was not used to assess an individual's mode of meaning construction.

Over the past 15 years, the subject–object interview has been used in research to focus on a number of issues. In an interesting secondary analysis of comparable, randomly drawn research samples who had been given subject–object interviews, Kegan (1994) has made the point that at any given moment, around one-half to two-thirds of the adult population in the United States has not fully reached the fourth order of consciousness (the institutional balance). Given the cultural demands on late adolescents and adults for a fourth order of consciousness, Kegan observes this gap between demand and capacity and points to the enormous mental burden of modern life for the majority of late adolescents and adults in contemporary western culture.

Several studies have addressed the viability of the model in cultures outside the United States. Villegas-Reimers (1996) has examined the utility of the model for Venezuelan adolescents aged 12 to 18 years, and Kroger and Green (2004) have assessed subject–object balance among late adolescent New Zealanders aged 17 to 24 years. Both studies found the distribution of subject–object balances in their respective contexts comparable to distributions of subject–object balances within United States samples of adolescents in comparable age groups. Neither the Venezuelan nor New Zealand samples evidenced gender differences in the distribution of subject–object balances, supporting results from studies done in the United States (Kegan 1994). Beyond adolescence, the question of gender differences in subject–object scores has also been examined by Bar-Yam (1991), who failed to find any significant differences between the sexes in levels of self-evolvement for a sample of adults ranging in age from mid-twenties to mid-fifties. Her work was conducted with American men and women living in Europe and employed by the US military service.

Additional research has focused on issues as varied as constructions among college students of the drug and alcohol culture (Walker 1995), parenting (Kaufman 1985; Osgood 1991), work (Hsia 1992), present self and future time perspectives (Salyer 1995; Seymour 1991), friendships (Beykema 1990), autobiographical writing (Hodgson 1990), and social perspective taking (Dixon 1986). All of these studies have been grounded in constructive-developmental theory.

Current directions in constructive-developmental research

In order to continue the validation of Kegan's constructive-developmental model, how should assessment be undertaken? Kegan (1985) himself has suggested that individual studies might seek appraisals on a variety of relevant measures for subjects within varying age groups and contexts. Within the past decade, a number of studies have been undertaken for this purpose. Kroger and Green (2004) have examined the interrelationships among Kegan's measure of subject–object balance, Loevinger's measure of ego development and Marcia's measure of ego identity status for a group of 61 late adolescents. Findings indicated strong, positive correlations among all possible pairs of these three measures. A study by Pratt *et al.* (1991) has also examined the relationships among four systems of thinking about two personal life dilemmas. Adults aged 35 to 85 were each assessed via the coding schemes for Kohlberg's moral judgment interview, Kegan's subject–object interview, Gilligan's moral orientation interview, and a measure of integrative complexity. The Kohlberg, Kegan and integrative complexity codings of the dilemmas were positively related to each other. Thus, within at least several age ranges, there is empirical support for the validity of Kegan's model. Further such work towards validation might examine measures of cognitive performance on Piagetian tasks and Kohlberg and Selman assessments of social cognition in relation to subject–object balance. Additionally, longitudinal studies of such models need to be undertaken to examine the similarities and differences in developmental functioning across these varied structural approaches.

Attempts must also be made to validate Kegan's claim to a single, deep structure of meaning-making that gives rise to other developmental stage schemes. In 1987, Loevinger commented on the proliferation of stage theories in developmental research: 'If the stages [of moral reasoning and ego development] really reflect a common "deep structure", the stages of those variables should proceed in tandem' (Loevinger 1987: 242). She also raises the question, 'If they are not all evidence of the same structure, how many structures are there, and what should be the relations among them?' (Loevinger 1987: 242). For Kegan to claim a single, deep structure of meaning construction, the ability of subject–object balance to predict relationships with other constructive, affective and behavioral variables over time must be demonstrated.

Currently, Kegan and his associates are exploring the means by which individuals as well as organizations operate to manufacture non-change – almost a reverse engineering of the Buddhist idea that each moment brings opportunities for creating anew (Kegan and Lahey 2001). Rather, Kegan and his associates have found that in each moment one is frequently creating conditions to disallow change. They are currently working to develop practical means by which transformation of both individual and organizational meaning systems might be facilitated.

Implications for social response

We live in an age when counseling and psychotherapy are often regarded as the panaceas to life's ills. With all the complexities and divergences of current psychotherapeutic views and practices, Kegan offers some very simple advice – observe the wisdom of nature and the supports optimally provided through the family, peer group, work settings and love relationships. Then let these cultures of embeddedness serve as models not only for psychotherapeutic practice but also for more naturalistic models of intervention. Kegan looks to nature in attempting to specify requirements of optimal 'holding environments' or 'cultures of embeddedness' for assisting a self in its evolutionary business:

> Not only does an understanding of 'natural therapy' – those relations and human contexts which spontaneously support people through the sometimes difficult process of growth and change – offer 'preventative psychology' a sophisticated way to consider a person's supports, it offers a new guide to therapeutic practice by exposing some of the details of those interactions which it is quite possible successful therapy is replicating, whether it knows it or not.
>
> (Kegan 1982: 256)

With these thoughts, Kegan sees several characteristics and functions provided by natural holding environments. When it is functioning optimally, each culture of embeddedness: (1) holds securely (confirms and recognizes); (2) lets go at an appropriate time (contradicts and assists differentiation); (3) remains in place to see its guest through the transition to a new balance. A holding environment must begin by 'holding securely', acknowledging that self which is its guest and participating actively and intimately with the individual in his or her present meaning-making experience. But that environment must also provide contradiction to encourage differentiation. As we have seen, evolution of the self is driven by contradiction which cannot be integrated by the existing self–other balance. That contradiction must be at a level appropriate to its guest in her present meaning-making balance, however. In this way alone can the evolving self eventually take over the host's current functions in the next balance. Such contradiction often appears in the form of limit setting. Finally, the host culture must be there and remain available to support its guest's passage to a new self–other balance. It is primarily the job of the main caretaker, parents, family, school, peer group, work context or other public arena, and love relationship to act as holding environments for the incorporative, impulsive, imperial, interpersonal, institutional and the inter-individual selves, respectively, and thus assist the developmental passage of its guest by remaining intact and available throughout her evolutionary passage.

An example of one such culture of embeddedness, with the holding functions it successfully provides, might help us appreciate more fully the supports and contradictions which facilitate identity development. Kegan (1980) met 20-year-old Richard on a special program designed to prepare persons previously regarded as unemployable for jobs. Richard had given others the impression that he did not care about the program and was only in it for the money. Initially arriving late or irregularly, he would comment that he just could not make it and did not understand why he was being treated unfairly; a program that worked on a premise of cooperative decision making made little sense to Richard. Making meaning from the imperial balance, Richard found that people just got in his way and made life inconvenient. Earlier cultures of embeddedness had failed to meet this young man in the balance that he was. Fortunately this time, however, the special program gradually filled the three holding functions Richard needed for evolution from this balance.

It began by *meeting him in his balance and confirming him*. Tasks leading to financial reward and other personal gain were introduced to Richard by instructors teaching the necessary technical skills for completion of a marketable product. Richard's self-interested self was recognized and confirmed through the presentation of skills that would better his financial position. Once hooked into a task, however, Richard eventually met some *contradiction* in the instructor's expectation that Richard would soon regulate his work with others. The special program furthermore *remained in place* for the young man as he gained more than he bargained for. Through the course of the program, Richard actually underwent reconstruction of his self. Acknowledgment of his initial meaning-making state followed by contradiction had caused his old subject–object balance to become unhinged. Once successfully established in the interpersonal balance, Richard was able to reflect upon how he had changed. Kegan (1980: 378) gives the following account: '[A]t the beginning of the program he used to worry when he screwed up about what would happen to him, and now, when he screws up, he worries about other people being worried.' The holding environment had successfully fulfilled its three functions, though this match between Richard and the job program had occurred by accident. The implications from constructive-developmental theory, however, are that such provisions for growth can be planned and do not need to be a matter of chance occurrence at all.

What would be features of optimal holding environments for adolescents in the interpersonal and organizational balances? Kegan (1982) suggests that for the interpersonal self, the host culture of embeddedness (natural or psychotherapeutic) must initially recognize and confirm the adolescent's capacity for mutual, self-sacrificing, idealized relationships by sharing her feelings and internal experiences. Following such recognition, it must gradually insist on the recognition of its guest as a distinct and independent agent, responsible for her own self-authorship while still valuing closeness and remaining emotionally available through the transition process (for example, friend or therapist does not leave, the family does not shift locale and disrupt its teenager's relationships). For the organizational self, the environmental host (again natural or psychotherapeutic) must begin by recognizing and confirming its guest's own authorship in providing opportunities for expression, achievement and responsibility. Gradually, host must promote differentiation by insisting on relationship with the *person* running the show, refusing mediated, non-intimate forms of response. Finally, organizational supports must remain in place for a guest undergoing the process of intrapsychic separation from them (for example, one is not dismissed from work or a relationship at the very time of transition). Ultimately, the culture of intimacy meets the interpersonal self and enjoys that 'counterpointing of identities' which Erikson describes.

If we want to know another in any fundamental way, we as potential evolutionary hosts must recognize and confirm that balance in which our adolescent guest hangs. The act of joining another in his or her meaning-making system is the base from which subject–object differentiation can later spring. Kegan (1982) believes that Carl Rogers is a master of 'joiners'. The latter's client-centered approach of reflecting feelings at the 'cutting edge' of client awareness goes far beyond a simple parroting reply (an attack sometimes leveled at this technique). Rogers's empathic responding allows host intimately to join guest in the latter's unique as well as more universal way of making sense. Rather than making meaning from the host's agenda (for example, through interpretation of client attitudes), the constructive-developmental approach strongly advocates confirming and joining the guest's meaning-making system as the first order of business, followed by stimulating and accompanying the guest on its journey of self-evolution. Failure of a host environment to join and fully value its occupant's present meaning-making balance, to later let go and encourage differentiation while remaining in place to provide support can only serve to miscarry another's evolutionary life project.

In the early 1990s, Kegan (1994) turned to examine the demands placed upon adolescents and adults by contemporary western culture and has suggested some specific strategies that society and interested individuals may provide to assist teens into and through the process of structural transition. Demands for the interpersonal balance abound in the expectations that schools, families, employers and other social agents hold for adolescents. Adolescents are expected to take the needs and interests of others into account in their families and communities. In school, they are expected to think in connotative and denotative ways, to provide definitions rather than just examples; in employment they are expected to be reliable, loyal to the company and able to make commitments. In all of these arenas, there appears to be a common demand for a single, underlying (interpersonal) third order of consciousness. However, very few adolescents are likely to be constructing their realities in this way the moment they turn 13. Thus, teenagers are likely to be 'in over their heads' for at least a portion of their adolescent years. This situation is not necessarily bad, in Kegan's view, provided teens also experience effective support along the lines noted above. Such support can come through a variety of ways, but ideally it will foster developmental transition by anchoring the bridge from the second to third order of consciousness firmly at both ends. It is thus necessary within social contexts to build in features that will support this type of transition, without disdain for those at different points on the 'consciousness bridge'.

In the arena of education, for example, Henderson and Kegan (1989) and Kegan (1990) argue for a curriculum that will work to address the growth of the student's mind rather than providing merely a set of skills and information. A teacher might facilitate movement from the imperial to interpersonal balance (second to the third order of consciousness) in the following way. In an attempt to get across the concept of irony from an O'Henry story, a teacher might ask students for a definition. A student constructing from the second order of consciousness is likely to respond with an example. The teacher who responds that this is a good example of irony with a request for further examples and gradually asks what all these examples have in common does much to assist rather than discourage students in their struggle towards the interpersonal balance.

In late adolescence and young adulthood, cultural demands shift and the fourth order of consciousness (institutional balance) becomes a prerequisite for meeting societal expectations. Within the arena of employment, individuals are expected to be more self-initiating, self-correcting and self-evaluating, guided by their own visions or goals coordinated with those of their employer. In the family, people are expected to be psychologically independent of partners, transcending an idealized notion of love, and managing boundaries between the generations to support the development of others. As citizens, individuals are expected to be able to look at and evaluate the values and beliefs of cultural inheritance rather than be captive of them. Even within the arena of psychotherapy, Kegan observes that the approaches of Rogers, Perls and Ellis all demand greater self-support and self-direction. Such expectations require a fourth order of consciousness, and again the gap between cultural expectation and capacity looms large for many. From research noted earlier, Kegan (1994) estimates that approximately one-half to two-thirds of adults in the United States have not fully reached the fourth order of consciousness. Institutional demands for fourth-order construction may do much to encourage the developmental process, but again Kegan (1994) argues for the provision of necessary social supports to assist in the transition.

More recently, Kegan (1996) has focused on how societies can help to form better bridges between current and more complex orders of thought for individuals. He has addressed, for example, the issue of adolescent sexuality to illustrate how constructive-developmental psychology can promote a more effective bridging response to the enormous problem of teenage pregnancy than the current 'safe sex' or 'abstinence' cultural messages currently on offer. Kegan argues that, despite the grim picture presented by statistics on risks and consequences associated with unintended teen pregnancies, the new world of sexuality presents a tantalizing allure for most teenagers: 'Sex is what God gives to teenagers when the appeal of Disneyland starts to fade' (Kegan 1996: 127). The cultural message of 'abstinence' denies the allure of sexuality for teens, while the 'safe sex' cultural message assumes an order of consciousness capable of farsighted understandings of future cause–effect relationships, which most younger teens simply do not possess. For many younger teens, the future is simply what has not yet happened; what is commanding one's attention right now is what is ultimately most consuming for this individual.

Kegan argues for a bridging context that would provide a better fit between societal fears and concerns and teenage desires and mental capacities in the arena of sexuality. He suggests that within the limits of an individual's own comfort, the only line a culture should draw regarding an adolescent's sexual behavior is that intercourse be reserved for a serious relationship. A serious relationship is denoted by a different type of responsibility towards another, where the intention to remain together is in place, along with the desire to be perceived by the community as a couple and/or family unit. By conveying this new message of fully pleasurable sex without intercourse for adolescents, cultural concerns as well as teenage meaning-making constraints are both met: 'Nothing that calls adolescents to sexual expression requires genital penetration for its satisfaction' (Kegan 1996: 141). Lack of teenage sexual intercourse would reduce many of the negative consequences such as disease, pregnancy and failure to complete education currently associated with teenage sexuality. Kegan recognizes that the promotion of a new cultural norm is very hard work, but he believes the practice of sexuality within this provisional context for teens better addresses their own meaning-making realities than current cultural messages of 'abstinence' or 'safe sex'.

Writers through the past decade have begun examining the implications of Kegan's work in varied arenas impacting on adolescents. The arenas of education, career counseling, psychotherapy and the world of work have all been subjects for discussion in terms of the contributions that constructive-developmental psychology can make to furthering adolescent development. In education, for example, Baxter Magolda (1999b) and Ignelzi (2000) argue for an examination of fundamental assumptions about the role and abilities of students in traditional education curriculums. Baxter Magolda notes several basic challenges involved in creating effective learning environments in constructive-developmental terms: creating transitional environments for students holding absolute assumptions about knowledge, effectively facilitating conflicts that emerge when multiple perspectives are heard, and effectively assisting to connect multiple ways of meaning construction among students in the same course. Ignelzi examines ways by which one can more effectively support movement to fourth order consciousness in college environments.

In career counseling, the implications of constructive-developmental theory for career choice and implementation have been explored by McAuliffe (1993), and a consideration of how organizational cultures themselves can provide better holding environments to facilitate both individual and organizational growth have been elaborated by Van Buskirk and McGrath (1999) as well as Kegan and Lahey (2001). McAuliffe proposes strategies for supporting transformation of meaning-making through career counseling. He does not advocate that career counseling should always involve transformation of meaning systems. Rather, there may be situations wherein simple change from one occupation to another is most appropriate. Van Buskirk and

McGrath (1999) note that since organizational cultures must 'hold' individuals in a variety of 'developmental spaces', they should provide support in four ways: opportunity to be part of a greater whole; to enact me–not me boundaries; to have creative space; to provide a stable base. Kegan and Lahey's (2001) book is a constructive-developmental exploration of practical ways in which individuals can begin to challenge the fourth order level of consciousness assumptions in their employment settings. Its focus is primarily directed to adult growth and development, however, and is hence beyond the scope of the present volume.

Summary

Robert Kegan has proposed a constructive-developmental view of the identity formation process. This integrative theory suggests a process which drives cognitive and affective development and is responsible for generating logics tapped by Piaget and Kohlberg in the realms of physical and social cognition. The theory describes a sequence of balances and transitions in the relationship between that which is considered self and that taken to be other. Balances give rise to the meaning one makes of the world; transitions involve the loss of an old way of knowing. Adolescents gradually make meaning from the interpersonal balance, in which one *is* rather than *has* her relationships, and later from the organizational balance, in which one *is* rather than *has* one's institutional affiliations, or from transitions to or from each of these balances. A self optimally evolves to a new balance in a holding environment which has three characteristics: holding securely, letting go, and remaining in place. Any intervention through natural or psychotherapeutic means must come to know an individual in his or her initial meaning-making balance, contradict at an appropriate time with an appropriate response, and remain in place during its guest's evolutionary passage for optimal development to proceed.

Further reading

Kegan, R., Lahey, L. and Souvaine, E. (1998) 'From taxonomy to ontogeny: thoughts on Loevinger's theory in relation to subject–object psychology', in P. M. Westenberg, A. Blasi and L. D. Cohn (eds) *Personality Development: Theoretical, Empirical, and Clinical Investigations of Loevinger's Conception of Ego Development*, Mahwah, NJ: Lawrence Erlbaum Associates, (pp. 39–58).

Kegan, R. (1996) 'Neither "safe sex" nor "abstinence" may work – Now what?: Toward a third norm for youthful sexuality', in D. Cicchetti and S. L. Toth (eds) *Adolescence, Opportunities and Challenges. Rochester Symposium on Developmental Psychopathology*, vol. 7, Rochester, NY: University of Rochester Press, (pp. 125–148).

Kegan, R. (1994) *In Over Our Heads: The Mental Demands of Modern Life*, Cambridge, MA: Harvard University Press.

Kegan, R. (1982) *The Evolving Self: Problems and Process in Human Development*, Cambridge, MA: Harvard University Press.

Rogers, L. and Kegan, R. (1990) 'Mental growth and mental health as distinct concepts in the study of developmental psychopathology: theory, research and clinical implications', in H. Rosen and D. Keating (eds) *Constructive Approaches to Psychopathology*, Hillsdale, NJ: Lawrence Erlbaum Associates.

7   Towards integration and conclusions

> I was losing myself. The ground, once so firm beneath my feet, now quivered; the path below disappeared. And then I met the abyss, where my own name and possessions became strangers, unfamiliar baggage in this formless place. But this very abyss, where all was lost, somehow, somewhere gave rise to what I now dare to call 'me'.
>
> (A 16-year-old voyager)

I once overheard a well-liked teacher in a quiet moment of reflection comment to a distraught soul in a 16-year-old's form that there is no map when it comes to matters of maturing; even Frost's road less traveled, described in his well-known poem by that name, is more defined in form than the course this teenager must plot. While there are undoubtedly no detailed relief maps laying out the finer contours of our individual identity pathways, there do appear to be some major general thoroughfares in the identity formation process that, when recognized, might have given both the adolescent wayfarer and sympathetic bystander above some assurance of a teenage future that would once again cohere, albeit in a new way. Plottings of general normative routes provided by Erikson, Blos, Kohlberg, Loevinger and Kegan not only allow us to glimpse the next developmental roadside resting point (identity stage) but also provide guides as to the most useful means of unblocking developmental arrest as well as assisting the already engaged traveler on his or her own life journey.

Having studied the maps of five identity theorists to chart the evolution of the self, ego and identity, one might now wish to collate such plottings in search of common ground. While theorists have converged on the phenomenon of identity from somewhat different approaches, the stage features of Erikson, Blos, Kohlberg, Loevinger and Kegan do lend themselves to ready comparison. Though each theorist uses somewhat different mechanisms to account for the developmental process of identity formation during adolescence, it is instructive to trace commonalities in stage features across the five chartings.

Commonalities across theoretical models

Erikson's more generic probe of the identity versus role confusion task of adolescence has been elaborated by both Kegan (1982) and Marcia (1966) in such a way as to allow more detailed comparisons with other frameworks. Kegan has noted that Erikson's identity versus role confusion stage, with its orientation to a self in search of vocational, ideological and sex role commitments, captures the energy of late adolescents but does not adequately describe the adolescent of earlier times. Following Erikson's childhood stage of industry versus inferiority, Kegan suggests a stage of affiliation versus abandonment to encompass the pursuits of 'connection, inclusion, and highly invested mutuality' more characteristic of younger adolescents. Marcia's foreclosure and diffusion identity statuses, most prominent in early adolescence, describe individuals concerned with maintaining or attaining identificatory relationships. Interesting parallels exist between these statuses and the psychosocial dilemma of the affiliation versus abandonment stage suggested by Kegan. With Kegan's addition to the Erikson scheme, identity models viewed in this volume suggest stages which fall into rather intriguing alignments when plotted across theories. Such patterns, in turn, point to what may be different underlying intrapsychic organizations or 'deep structures' of adolescent identity development. Table 7.1 overviews the course of identity development from the five orientations presented in this volume.

From Table 7.1, one can see how the Eriksonian industry versus inferiority conflict of the later primary school years, with its focus on mastery, is described psychodynamically by Blos in terms of latency, with its time of Oedipal consolidation, and preadolescence, with increases in sexual and aggressive drives. These two theoretical maps both depict a self in the process of seeking and serving its own interests. For Kohlberg, Loevinger and Kegan respectively, strong parallels exist between the instrumental orientation of moral logic and the self-protective stage and imperial balance of ego functioning. All of these stages again blueprint a self whose own needs are primary, whose interests are self-protective. All five models sketch a preadolescent self with a sense of agency, striving to meet its own needs, taking over the function of impulse control previously exercised by the family but not yet capable of coordinating its own needs with those of other people.

Table 7.1 The normative developmental course of identity during adolescence from five theoretical perspectives

Identity theorist	Stages of development				
Erikson	Industry/inferiority	(Affiliation/Abandonment)*	Identity/Role confusion		Intimacy/Isolation
Marcia		Foreclosure/Diffusion	Moratorium	Achievement	
Blos	Latency, Pre-adolescence	Early adolescence	Adolescence proper	Late adolescence	Post-adolescence
Object relations adaptation		Adolescent symbiosis	Differentiation Practicing Rapprochement	Object constancy	
Kohlberg	Instrumental orientation	Interpersonal concordance orientation		Social system orientation	Principled orientation
Loevinger	Self-protective stage	Conformist stage		Conscientious stage	Autonomous stage
Kegan	Imperial balance	Interpersonal balance		Institutional balance	Interindividual balance

*Note: It is the opinion of Kegan (1982) that Erikson overlooks a stage between 'Industry' and 'Identity' in the identity formation process. Kegan terms this stage 'Affiliation vs. Abandonment' to capture the period of 'highly invested mutuality' which occurs in early adolescence, prior to the late adolescent quest for individual identity.

With the addition of Kegan's affiliation versus abandonment conflict to Erikson's stage scheme, the five theoretical thoroughfares again coincide to point towards a new state of intrapsychic organization. Where isolated self-interest marked the structure of preceding times, early adolescence marks a time of affiliation. With an underlying structural organization which now enables young people to orient to others, Marcia's foreclosure status denotes the formation of an identity through identification, a distinct style of other orientation. (The diffusion status reflects a non-normative failure in this process.) Blos's early adolescence, with its object relations counterpart of adolescent symbiosis, captures a self embedded in its internalized object representations and only later coming to differentiate from them. Kohlberg, Loevinger and Kegan also describe a self embedded in some way in an interpersonal matrix. The moral logic of Kohlberg's interpersonal concordance orientation finds right action to be that which pleases others and brings their approval. Loevinger's conformist stage depicts a self bound to the dictates of the immediate social group, while Kegan's interpersonal balance describes a self unable to distance from or step out of a shared reality. Across the five identity maps, early adolescence seems to reflect a focus on affiliation, in both the intrapsychic and external object relations realms.

Mid to late adolescence has been the main focus of Erikson's writings on identity. Across all five identity thoroughfares, one can now see a self distancing from an embeddedness in the affiliations of early adolescence and focused on generating its own aims while at the same time coordinating such aims with those of others. Marcia's moratorium and achievement identity statuses reflect states of searching for and finding satisfying vocational, ideological and sexual commitments within a social order. Adolescent differentiation, practicing and rapprochement subphases of disengagement from internalized object ties would seem to underlie the moratorium identity status, with the achievement status reflecting an intrapsychic organization of adolescent self–other constancy. Kohlberg, Loevinger and Kegan all describe a corresponding state of late adolescent self-organization as one bound by a sense of duty to uphold the larger social order while at the same time able to experience a sense of self-ownership and authorship. A heightened sensitivity to questions of 'Who am I?' are concomitant features of late adolescence. Again, all five models in some way depict a self loosened from its earlier interpersonal moorings, more self-aware than ever while remaining oriented toward a larger social order.

It is not until postadolescence that the self may attain yet another stage of structural organization. Erikson's stage of intimacy versus isolation, Blos's postadolescence, Kohlberg's principled orientation, Loevinger's autonomous stage and Kegan's interindividual balance all detail a self orienting to others from an even more differentiated intrapsychic position. As Erikson describes intimacy to be a counterpointing of identities (possible only when identities have become reasonably well established), so too does Blos suggest postadolescence to be a time of character consolidation as boundaries between self and others firm. Then and only then does Blos suggest that mature and intimate extrafamilial love relationships can form. Kohlberg, Loevinger and Kegan all describe a young adult self more autonomous in its organization and, at the same time, more capable of instigating community reform on issues of social justice as well as experiencing mutuality in relationship. Adulthood, for all reviewed theorists, can be a time in which a more differentiated than ever sense of 'I' makes possible a more intimate than ever sense of 'we'.

Contrasts across theoretical models

While some striking similarities in the themes and content of stages appear across the five models of development reviewed in this volume, there are also some noteworthy differences in the orientations and general assumptions about identity that each model makes. Erikson's psychosocial orientation and Blos's more traditional psychoanalytic perspective view identity (or character) in terms of a reciprocal relationship between an individual's needs, wishes, fears and biological capacities and the surrounding context. In large measure, *emotions* (and defenses against them) are active ingredients in the strivings for autonomy, relationship and roles in the world. Kohlberg and Kegan's models, by contrast, are based primarily on *cognitive* orientations to the self. Though Kohlberg does not relate his model to identity formation directly, he does describe cognitive changes in the development in moral reasoning, an important element of the ego (in his view). Kegan considers the development of the self to be subsumed both by cognition and emotion, inseparable components that give rise to various organizations of understanding through which individuals come to make sense of themselves and their external worlds. However, Kegan's model describes a series of cognitive differences in perspective taking, and his work is based on how one comes to *make sense* of the world and one's place in it. While Loevinger includes a *cognitive* organizational component in her model of ego development, she also includes elements of *affective* and *emotional states*, personal orientations to and investments in others. Loevinger's structures of ego development might be located somewhere in between psychoanalytic (Erikson and Blos) and cogni-tive-developmental (Kohlberg and Kegan) positions, though Loevinger aligns her model more with cognitive-developmental views (Loevinger 1987).

Because of these varied orientations across the stage models, there is a somewhat different understanding of what an intrapsychic structure or mental organization that gives rise to each stage actually *is*. The more cognitively based theories of Kohlberg and Kegan view mental struc-tures in terms of rational, logically based understandings of meaning. Each stage is definable according to developmental variations in per-spective taking and a striving toward equilibrium. The more psycho-analytic orientations of Erikson, Blos and later object relations writers, on the other hand, view mental structures more in terms of relational orientations toward internalized others as well as those in the external world. (Separation and individuation for Blos and introjection, internalization, identity formation for Erikson.) Loevinger's structures of ego development appear to be based on a combination of these elements.

Though all models have a state of equilbrium (balance) as their goal in individual development, they also have somewhat different under-standings of what drives the developmental process toward that end. Kohlberg, Loevinger, Kegan and some identity status researchers would suggest the developmental process to be driven by Piagetian processes of assimilation and accommodation – the striving to interpret one's understandings of the world in terms of existing structures and grad-ually drawing upon more complex cognitive processes in order to reach a new state of understanding. Erikson would suggest that changing social demands coupled with changes in individual biological capacities and psychological needs drive the developmental process forward. Object relations writers would argue that the second separation–individuation process of adolescence is driven by one's press for emo-tional and interpersonal autonomy coupled with social circumstances supportive of that individuation process.

A further difference across the five models lies in the issue of regres-sion. The more psychodynamically oriented models of Erikson, Blos and later object relations writers view regression as an important part of the developmental process. Blos (1967: 173), for example, indicates that regression in adolescent development is normative, universal and necessary: 'Regression in adolescence is not, in and of itself, a defense, but it constitutes an essential psychic process that, despite the anxiety it engenders, must take its course.' He further implies that when regression does not occur during adolescence, there is some fault in development. Erikson similarly describes 'retrogressions' at each stage in his psychosocial developmental scheme. By contrast, Kohlberg and Kegan do not recognize the process of regression in their developmental models. Kegan (1994), for example, observes that the ability of individuals to take a perspective on their regressed states of thinking or feeling in their own accounts of this experience indicates that true regression (the *actual* return to an earlier mode of thinking or feeling) has not occurred. Kohlberg, similarly, does not consider regression (again in the sense of the return to an earlier mode of thinking) possible in his developmental model of sequentially organized, hierarchical stages. In her early writings, Loevinger and others found evidence for the sequentiality of her stages of ego development and hence did not discuss the issue of regression (e.g. Redmore and Loevinger 1979). However, subsequent research has indicated that regression to an earlier stage of ego development does occur at a rate greater than might be explained by measurement error alone (e.g. Hauser *et al.* 1991; Westenberg and Gjerde 1999). Thus, in more recent years, Manners and Durkin (2001) acknowledge and have called for further investigation into the phenomenon of regression in both adolescent and adult ego development.

I have suggested that researchers consider three different forms of regression that may be operating in longitudinal studies, in order to clarify its functions in such developmental schemes (Kroger 1996). These types of regression are:

- *regression of disequilibrium* (transitory in nature and involved in transition to a more complex and differentiated structural organization
- *regression of rigidification* (more stable in nature, involving return to more immediately familiar, less complex and more secure mode of reasoning in which adaptation is not greatly impaired
- *regression of disorganization*, more stable in nature, destructuring to a far less complex stage in which adaptation is greatly impaired.

Different types of life events and/or contextual issues may be associated with these different regression forms.

Table 7.2 summarizes some key similarities and differences in focus, structural assumptions, drivers of development and views of regression for the five developmental models reviewed in this volume.

Table 7.2 Key concepts for five theoretical perspectives on self, ego and identity

Identity theorist	Focus	Assumptions about Mental Structures	Drivers of Development	Role of Regression
Erikson Marcia	Emotions as central in strivings for autonomy, relationship and social roles	Based on relational orientations toward internalized and external others	Individual needs, biological givens, social demands	Vital to development
Blos Object relations adaptation	Emotions as central in strivings for autonomy, relationship and social roles	Based on relational orientations toward internalized others	Individual needs, biological drives	Vital to development
Kohlberg	Cognition as central in strivings for making sense of moral issues	Based on rational, logical understandings of morality	Assimilation, accommodation	Not possible in development
Loevinger	Cognition plus emotion as central in strivings for meaning	Based on both logical and relational orientations toward external others	Assimilation, accommodation	Possible, more research necessary
Kegan	Cognition as central in autonomy, relationship, and social role	Based on rational, logical understandings of meaning	Assimilation, accommodation	Not possible in development

Commonalities and contrasts in implications for social response

With many commonalities in contours of the five theoretical approaches, are there any similarities among theorists' varied calls for social response to the identity formation process during adolescence? Perhaps the most crucial common denominator across models is the importance that all approaches attach to the need for accurate identification of the young person's present stage of identity development in planning effective support or intervention to facilitate change. Marcia, Blos and object relations theorists, Kohlberg, Loevinger and Kegan all begin by stressing the importance of differential social response to adolescents in various stages of the identity formation process. As intrapsychic organizations differ through the normative stages of development, so too must social response vary to meet the very unique demands presented by each phase of mental organization.

Beyond this common denominator, theorists vary in the emphasis placed on the desirability of facilitating movement to more mature stages of organization. While the advantages of facilitating development for those with identity structures arrested in childhood seem clear, Loevinger in particular questions the ultimate value of interventions designed to advance functional ego stages to more mature forms in late adolescent and adult life. For Loevinger, designing educational and psychotherapeutic responses tailored to meet a client in his or her current ego stage of functioning without necessarily facilitating further structural development are appropriate end goals.

Among those theorists who do place high premium on interventions to promote more mature forms of identity organization, all acknowledge the importance of adolescent readiness before attempting to stimulate change. Even Piaget, on whose work Kohlberg and Kegan models are based, suggests an optimal time of readiness for change:

> I have a hypothesis which I am so far incapable of proving: probably the organization of operations has an optimal time. ... It is probably possible to accelerate intellectual development, but maximal acceleration is not desirable. There seems to be an optimal time. What this optimal time is will surely depend on each individual and on the subject matter. We still need a great deal of research to know what the optimal time would be.
>
> (Piaget 1967: 1)

It is the research of Kohlberg and colleagues which has offered some guidelines on recognition of readiness. As indicated in Chapter 4, development (at least to a higher stage of moral reasoning) appears most easily stimulated in children 'who have been at a particular moral judgment stage some intermediate length of time than in those who have just entered a new stage or those who have remained at the same stage beyond some optimal period' (Colby *et al.* 1977: 102). In his theoretical writings, Kegan too emphasizes the importance of timing in efforts to stimulate further development; promoting differentiation too soon can sabotage another's life project. In reporting the experiences of a first-year university student still hanging in the interpersonal balance, Kegan illustrates the critical role of timing in social response:

> The subtle and overt messages a college freshman gets that he is on his own in the conduct of his academic and private life can serve to honor that newly emerging voice in the development of personality. But for a person who has not yet begun this emergence, the same messages – which professors and advisers may think of as confirmations of the student's adulthood – can be experienced as an abandonment, a refusal to care and a disorienting vacuum of expectation. This new embeddedness culture is not yet called for, and the old one has been lost.
>
> (Kegan 1982: 186)

Mahler and other object relations theorists have also stressed the ill effects on infant and later adolescent and adult personality organization when the primary caretaker expedites differentiation before that optimal time of readiness on the part of the individual in his care.

With these cautions in mind, how might progress to a more mature stage of identity organization be best promoted? A common thread weaving its way through approaches concerned with this issue seems to be the bystander's introduction of dialogue aimed at creating a state of intrapsychic disequilibrium in the youthful traveler while at the same time remaining in place to provide a supportive relationship. Kohlberg and his associates have advocated exposure to reasoning at the next stage of moral logic, while Kegan and object relations theorists similarly suggest the provision of experiences which both refuse to confirm the old intrapsychic balance and at the same time recognize and meet the new. Marcia likewise aims gradually to facilitate progress to a more mature identity status for foreclosure and moratorium adolescents by promoting a degree of unstructuredness within a supportive framework that permits freedom for the adolescents' experimentation and exploration. If stimulating a more mature identity organization is a desired aim, it would seem that initially meeting a structure growing ready for change and then deliberately contradicting this organization while remaining supportively in place as the new comes into being are the most facilitative means of promoting further identity development.

Empirical comparisons across models

Loevinger (1987) asked a critical question, reviewed in Chapter 5. Commenting on the proliferation of stage models in various arenas of human development, she noted that 'if the stages really reflect a common "deep structure", the stages of those variables should all proceed in tandem' (Loevinger 1987: 242). She continued: 'If they are not all evidence of the same structure, how many structures are there, and what should be the relations among them?' (Loevinger 1987: 242). Given strong similarities in the contents of stages across the five models described in this volume, a following question one might ask would be 'What, if any, empirical links have been found across these models?' Furthermore, 'Do these results suggest any common "deep structures" of identity?'

At this point in time, evidence has been accumulating that indicates strong empirical relationships across the five stage models of development. While no study to date has examined interrelationships among all five models – identity status (Marcia), adolescent separation–individuation (Blos), moral reasoning (Kohlberg), ego development (Loevinger), or meaning-making balance (Kegan), a number of studies have explored empirical links between two or three of these stage schemes.

Strong associations between identity status and the following variables have all been found: separation–individuation, moral reasoning, ego development and meaning-making balance. Individuals on the verge of young adulthood and scoring as foreclosed in identity status have evidenced difficulties in the second separation-individuation process of adolescence. Such difficulties have included either strong separation anxiety or detached attachment patterns, in contrast to the secure attachment patterns of the identity achieved (e.g. Perosa *et al.* 1996; Kroger 1985, 1995; Papini *et al.* 1989). Identity diffuse or foreclosed individuals have generally scored at preconventional or conventional levels of moral reasoning, while moratorium and achieved adolescents have scored at conventional or post-conventional levels (e.g. Foster and LaForce 1999; Hult 1979; Rowe and Marcia 1980). Less mature (foreclosed and diffuse) adolescents have most frequently scored at the pre-conventional or conventional stages of ego development and at or below the interpersonal meaning-making balance. Moratorium and achieved adolescents have most frequently scored at self-aware, conscientious and individualistic stages of ego development and at or in transition to the institutional meaning-making balance (e.g. Berzonsky and Adams 1999; Kroger and Green 2004).

Associations have also appeared between moral reasoning (in terms of both ethics of justice and ethics of care assessments) and ego development (e.g. Kitchener *et al.* 1984; Skoe and von der Lippe 2002). Links have also been found between measures of separation–individuation and ego development (e.g. Bell and Bell 1983) and between moral reasoning and meaning-making balance (Pratt *et al.* 1991); in both of these latter areas, however, only one published study of each relationship has been undertaken.

In addition, meta-analyses in the areas of both ego development and moral reasoning point to some interesting patterns of interrelationships between these two constructs during and beyond adolescence. Snarey (1998) obtained individual case records from nine prior investigations of ego development and moral reasoning involving 567 persons. Participants ranged from 11 to 82 years of age and represented a variety of educational levels. Snarey found that ego development and moral reasoning constructs are significantly related to one another across the lifespan. However, complex patterns of relationships appeared between these two constructs over time. In general, greater strides were made in ego development compared with moral reasoning during adolescence, while greater strides were made in moral reasoning compared with ego development during early adulthood. There was stability in the ego–moral reasoning development relationship during and beyond mid-adulthood.

While it is not possible to answer Loevinger's opening question at the present time, theoretical similarities of stage structures appear supported by empirical links across the five models. Snarey's (1998) meta-analysis of ego development and moral reasoning literatures, however, indicates the importance of long-term longitudinal studies and attention to factors that may be mediating such relationships during adulthood.

Development in context

In the years since the second edition of this volume was published, each developmental model reviewed herein has experienced a burgeoning of research interest in how the model's developmental patterns and stage distributions are related to varied contextual conditions. While some studies addressing such issues have been presented in each of the five theoretical chapters of this volume, I attempt below to draw some general conclusions regarding contextual factors that appear associated with stability, progression and regression within the identity status arena. Space limitations, unfortunately, will not allow a full discussion of such factors for all models.

One consistent finding across most of the five models under review here is that some variation in identity, separation–individuation, moral reasoning, ego and self–other balance distributions and/or patterns of development are apparent when adolescents in different contextual conditions are observed. Within the *identity status* model, a growing number of studies have been examining identity status distributions and patterns of development in varied lifestyle, social and cultural circumstances. Early contextual studies by Adams and Fitch (1983) and Costa and Campos (1989) found students differentially attracted to academic departments by identity status. Munro and Adams (1977) and later Danielsen *et al.* (2000) found different identity distributions for university students compared with working youths of the same age. More recent studies have examined identity status distributions and patterns of development in more varied cultural and social circumstances. In Scandinavia, for example, three studies have found lower levels of both identity exploration as well as identity commitment among late adolescent male and female university students, compared with North American counterparts (Adamson *et al.* 2000; Stegarud *et al.* 1999; Jensen *et al.* 1998). All authors note that this pattern may arise due to greater social pressures toward social conformity in Scandinavia than in the United States. (This cultural attitude is so deeply rooted that it has been given the name *Jante Law* in Norway.) Particular events may also be associated with identity status changes. Dunkel (2002), for example, found greater anxiety among those US adolescents exploring identity options following the terrorist attacks of 9/11 than those not in the process of exploring identity options. Anthis (2002) found stressful life events more generally predicted increases in identity exploration over time. Identity status development appears strongly linked to contextual circumstances. In particular, progressive identity status movement is associated with environmental conditions that produce both experiences of conflict and social support (Bosma and Kunnen 2001).

Given the strong links between identity and context, Marcia (1993) has noted that the next logical step in research should be to try to specify environmental conditions linked with specific types of identity resolutions. He has called for a taxonomy of environments that would transcend local situations (e.g. college, workplace, military) to focus instead upon important trans-situational circumstances. Such circumstances might include facilitation or discouragement of self-expression, social role prescriptions and introduction to diversity or homogeneity of ideas. Knowledge of optimum contextual circumstances for identity development would provide an important framework for the establishment of intervention and social programs aimed at serving youth. Yoder's (2000) efforts to consider various forms of contextual 'barriers' that may limit identity potential are an important step in this direction.

Balance between self and other: new directions for identity theory and research

In this volume, five developmental models have been presented which describe the phenomenon of identity formation during adolescence. Though each approaches the nature of the 'I' from a somewhat different direction, all models have in some way addressed the phenomenon of intrapsychic differentiation and a rebalancing of the relationship between that considered as self and that taken to be other, alongside the new forms of external relationships that such changes bring. Erikson and Marcia have described the structural shift of an adolescent self derived through its identificatory relationships to one incorporating yet transcending such form to a new configuration greater than the sum of its parts. Rebalancing, in Erikson's scheme, involves the loss of a self structured primarily through its identifications to be replaced by one more integrated in form, delineated in its own boundaries. Blos characterizes the second individuation process of adolescence as an intrapsychic feat in which the parental introjects, internalized and regarded as self, are gradually relinquished; an old self structure gives way to the new, with a heightened sense of distinctiveness from others emerging in the exchange, within selected developmental contexts. The development of moral reasoning, one subdomain of ego functioning, has been described by Kohlberg as a series of qualitatively more complex structural organizations, whereby authority becomes increasingly internalized. With each successive stage, a self more distinct from yet at the same time concerned about a widening circle of others comes into being. To Loevinger, ego development is again an ongoing process of rebalancing that taken as self and that considered to be other. Earlier stages of ego organization in Loevinger's scheme reflect a self-interested self, exclusive in its attention to personal needs and impulses; a self derived from group standards and later operating according to its own authority are the hallmarks of adolescents' and adults' increasing differentiation from and new ways of relating to others. Finally, Kegan's stage sequence reflects a self embedded in a series of contexts, increasingly differentiated from the individual's own functioning; the self of the neonate, embedded in its own reflexes, gives way through successive reorganizations to the young adolescent, embedded in his or her interpersonal matrix. Progression through organizational and interpenetrating systems marks the full course of development during late adolescent and adult life. Given the evolutionary nature of the identity formation process, it is surprising that greater attention has not been directed to mechanisms involved in stage transitions. Kegan (1994) is one of few researchers who has attempted to detail regularities in this process.

Phenomenological accounts of self–other rebalancing, the essence of the identity formation process, have been eloquently presented by many writers attempting to capture and convey the experience. Certainly Janine's poem (Chapter 6), an account of being in an intrapsychic space 'where nothing is, is now—And all that was, is no more, and that that is, isn't', conveys the sense of inner vacuum associated with such rebalancing. It is perhaps in Sartre's *Nausea* that we have one of the most brilliant first-person accounts of the breakdown in one's customary way of experiencing self and object. In this novel, Roquentin is overcome by a feeling of localized nausea in his hand as he becomes aware of a changed relationship to objects in touching a pebble on the ground:

> I think it's I who has changed: that's the simplest solution, also the most unpleasant. . . . If I am not mistaken, and if all the signs which are piling up are indications of a fresh upheaval in my life, well then, I am frightened.
>
> (Sartre 1965: 14, 15)

Less dramatic, though no less an indication of structural transformation, is a statement by Hamish, a late adolescent (moratorium) university student whom I interviewed as part of a two-year longitudinal study of identity formation:

> [What's brought about that change in your political opinions?] I would guess the reduction in the influence of my father who has a very, very strong political orientation and the realization that one doesn't have to be firmly attached to any point of view and that a 'don't know' is as good an opinion as a firm belief.

That 'reduction in the influence of my father' can be interpreted as relinquishment of the internalized father, no longer needed to provide the architecture for Hamish's self; that newly emerging self, however, has yet to clearly define its own values. Through such literary and worldly accounts, a number of questions arise regarding the nature of self–other rebalancing.

Many issues beg research attention in future efforts to chart identity development over time. Particularly important to illuminating transformation processes are the following issues:

- delineating possible steps in structural reorganization
- detailing functions of regression for development
- understanding reasons for the elusiveness of developmental complexity
- adopting appropriate research methodologies.

These issues, all of relevance to passages during the second decade of life, are also of relevance to other times of rebalancing during the lifespan.

The process of structural change in context

As noted in Chapter 3, Margaret Mahler and her associates (Mahler *et al.* 1975) have attempted to delineate specific separation–individuation subphases in the infant's differentiation of its self from its caretaker, the basis for a new form of relatedness. Blos (1967) has suggested that a second individuation process may be occurring during adolescence in the differentiation of self from an internalized other, though he has not similarly detailed movement subphases. I have suggested that the Marcia identity status framework along with measures of separation anxiety provide us with opportunities for indexing possible subphases of any adolescent separation–individuation process. Kegan and his associates (Lahey *et al.* 1987) have also proposed a sequence of steps involved in leaving an old self–other balance and creating a new. Might one catalogue the developmental transformations of adolescence in each of the stage models examined by this volume in terms of sequentially predictable processes? What individual and contextual factors are associated with engagement in and resolution of this intrapsychic and interpersonal feat?

Examination of a single case study by Kroger (1993) has suggested some steps and possible factors that may be associated with successful navigation, at least, of Erikson's identity formation process. Awareness of conflict or discrepancy between personal desire and perceived role expectation begin to cause discomfort. Outward action, however, begins only at a time of readiness, when there is sufficient ego strength to withstand the withdrawal of earlier external and internal 'props' which have served to define the self. This action is assisted by a significant other who can bridge both sides of the internal dialogue but ultimately support the newly emerging self. Initial steps in this intrapsychic process are focused on desires for escape and separation, coupled with fears of dissolution. Later, desire for exploring one's own potentials, coupled with feelings of guilt, replace earlier themes. The ability to withstand both the fear of death (dissolution) and guilt appear central to successful negotiation of the identity formation process. From a major review of determinants and mechanisms of ego identity development, structural change appears to be an iterative process of person–context transactions (Bosma and Kunnen 2001). Important determinants of change are factors that enhance one's openness to new experiences and other personality variables, environmental support and one's own history of coping and resilience. Greater attention to the actual process of structural transformation implicit within each of the structural-developmental models examined here alongside contextual features associated with change would seem a fruitful direction for future research.

The role of regression

Mahler (1983: 6) has noted: 'To go forward and to reach a higher degree of integration, a temporary phase of regression, of disorganization, of outright minor crisis – a chaotic state – has to occur.' Similarly, Blos (1967: 173) has pointed to the adaptive function of regression during adolescence, though this phenomenon has generally been considered a sign of pathology during other life stages. Through times of developmental transformation, regression may operate normatively in the restructuring process. While most stage theorists would argue against the concept of structural regression, transitory retrograde movement during times of self–other rebalancing has been frequently observed and inadequately explored.

Turiel (1974) initially helped to clarify the different meanings that regression may have. He notes that regression may refer to a temporary state of disorganization, not implying the return to an earlier developmental stage of functioning but rather reflecting a developmentally less advanced structure in the process of transition; or regression may also refer to the use of prior developmental structures that suggest earlier stages remain unchanged, with each succeeding organization layered on top of earlier ones. A third meaning of regression more frequently found in psychoanalytic literature connotes the re-experiencing of abandoned ego states which once constituted special ways of coping with stress; this type of regression is usually defensive in nature. Temporary disorganization may be a normative and necessary part of structural reorganization. Regression in the psychodynamic sense, however, may occur when contextual issues reactivate earlier developmental trauma and impair structural advance (Noam 1988a). I have also proposed at least three different forms of regression that may be occurring in longitudinal investigations of identity and ego development, indicated in a previous section of this chapter (Kroger 1996). The possible adaptive and non-adaptive forms and roles of regression are in need of clarification, particularly in the study of self, ego and identity development over time.

The elusiveness of developmental complexity

Longitudinal studies over adolescence and young adulthood have now been conducted in the arenas of identity status studies (Marcia's model), the second separation–individuation process (derived from Blos's proposal), moral reasoning (Kohlberg's paradigm), ego development (Loevinger's model) and subject–object balance (Kegan's theory). In all of these researches, large percentages of late adolescents or young adults have failed to attain the more complex levels of structural organizations that the respective theories describe. Large percentages (approximately 50 per cent) of individuals leave late adolescence in foreclosed or diffuse identity statuses (e.g. Cramer 1998; Fitch and Adams 1983; Kroger 1995). Similar percentages of youth have evidenced failure in completing the adolescent separation–individuation transition, showing patterns of high separation anxiety or dependency denial alongside low levels of healthy separation (e.g. Kroger 1995). Only a small number of young adults attain principled moral reasoning, while the self-aware level is the modal level of ego development within the United States (e.g. Colby *et al.* 1983; Holt 1980).

Though longitudinal studies of subject–object balance have been more limited in number, they too suggest that few attain institutional or interpersonal balances by young adulthood (Kegan 1994). Where longitudinal studies involving the five models discussed in this volume have been extended into middle adulthood, further development has been the exception rather than the rule. Why is it that the most complex stages of development are so rarely reached? Research into this issue is an important arena for future investigations.

Research strategies

Attempts to tap any existing underlying 'deep structure' of identity are at present limited not only by our conceptions of developmental stages and our almost exclusive focus on times of equilibrium, but also by our research methodologies. Developmental processes, particularly those operating during times of structural transformation, are not particularly amenable to measurement. Longitudinal efforts to chart changing self–other balances through extensive in-depth interviews and clinical observations would seem an excellent means of approaching this research challenge. Lahey *et al.*'s (1987) guide to subject–object interviews, Noam's (1985) stage-phase-and-style interview, which in part examines how a subject's self and interpersonal boundaries become set, and efforts to probe in more detail the exploration, revision, commitment and maintenance processes in identity status interviews are important starting points in this venture. Furthermore, assessments at reasonably frequent time intervals are crucial to an understanding of the developmental processes involved in transitions of identity. Qualitative as well as quantitative modes of evaluation should provide the most powerful combination of tools suited to charting such structural reorganizations.

Conclusions

Through this volume, there has been an overview of the work of five theorists who have contributed to our understanding of identity during adolescence. Each in his or her own way has approached the 'I' from a developmental perspective, setting forth stages through which the self differentiates and becomes 're-related' to others over the course of the lifespan. Adolescence has been identified by all approaches as a time of heightened activity for most in the loss and creation of new balances. Many questions remain in attempts to tap any 'deep structure' of identity through various measurement frameworks. If such an underlying identity organization does exist, mechanisms of transition as well as stability must be more clearly delineated to enable those working with adolescents to provide assistance at optimal times in optimal ways. Further exploration of circumstances associated with developmental arrest is also essential to undertake, such that contexts may be structural to facilitate development in optimal ways. Ultimately, however, it is only

one's own ease with the process of change that will allow one to aid and
not hinder another on his or her own life journey:

> For this is the journey that men [and women] make: to find them-
> selves. If they fail in this, it doesn't matter much what else they find.
>
> (Michener, *The Fires of Spring*, 1972)

Bibliography

Adams, G. R. (1994) 'Revised classification criteria for the extended objective measure of ego identity status: a rejoinder', *Journal of Adolescence* 17: 551–556.

——(1999) 'The objective measure of ego identity status: a manual on theory and test construction', unpublished manuscript, University of Guelph, Ontario, Canada.

Adams, G. R. and Fitch, S. A. (1981) 'Ego stage and identity status development: a cross-lag analysis', *Journal of Adolescence* 4: 163–171.

——(1982) 'Ego stage and identity status development: a cross-sequential analysis', *Journal of Personality and Social Psychology* 43: 574–583.

——(1983) 'Psychosocial environments of university departments: effects on college students' identity status and ego stage development', *Journal of Personality and Social Psychology* 44: 1266–1275.

Adams, G. R. and Jones, R. M. (1983) 'Female adolescents identity development: age comparisons and perceived child rearing experience', *Developmental Psychology* 19: 249–256.

Adams, G. R. and Marshall, S. (1996) 'A developmental social psychology of adolescence: understanding the person-in context', *Journal of Adolescence* 19: 429–442.

Adams, G. R. and Shea, J. A. (1979) 'The relationship between identity status, locus of control, and ego development', *Journal of Youth and Adolescence* 8: 81–89.

Adams, G. R., Bennion, L. and Huh, K. (1989) 'Objective measure of ego identity status: a reference manual', unpublished manuscript, University of Guelph, Ontario, Canada.

Adams, G. R., Montemayor, R. and Brown, B. B. (1992) 'Adolescent ego-identity development: an analysis of patterns of development and the contributions of the family to identity formation during middle and late adolescence', unpublished manuscript, University of Guelph.

Adamson, L., Björk, M. and Karimi, K. (2001) 'Ego identity status in a Swedish sample of late adolescents', in L. Adamson and J. Kroger (co-convenors). New approaches to self and identity. Symposium presented at the biennial meetings of the European Association of Developmental Psychology, Uppsala, Sweden, 24 August.

Adelson, J. and Doehrman, M. J. (1980) 'The psychodynamic approach to adolescence', in J. Adelson (ed.) *Handbook of Adolescent Psychology*, New York: Wiley.

Akers, J. F., Jones, R. M. and Coyl, D. D. (1998) 'Adolescent friendship pairs: similarities in identity status development, behaviors, attitudes, and intentions', *Journal of Adolescent Research* 13: 178–201.

Albee, E. (1962) *The Zoo Story and Other Plays*, London: Jonathan Cape (originally published 1958).

Alisho, K. C. and Schilling, K. M. (1984) 'Sex differences in intellectual and ego development in late adolescence', *Journal of Youth and Adolescence* 13: 213–224.

Allen, J. P., Hauser, S. T., Bell, K. L. and O'Connor, T. G. (1994) 'Longitudinal assessment of autonomy and relatedness in adolescent–family interactions as predictors of adolescent ego development and self-esteem', *Child Development* 65: 179–194.

Anderson, S. A. and Fleming, W. M. (1986) 'Late adolescents' home-leaving strategies: predicting ego identity and college adjustment', *Adolescence* 21: 453–459.

Anthis, K. S. (2002) 'On the calamity theory of growth: the relationship between stressful life events and changes in identity over time', *Identity* 2: 229–240.

Archer, S. L. (1994) *Interventions for Adolescent Identity Development*. Newbury Park, CA: Sage.

Armon, C. and Dawson, T. L. (1997) 'Developmental trajectories in moral reasoning across the life span', *Journal of Moral Education* 26: 433–453.

Armstrong, J. G. and Roth, D. M. (1989) 'Attachment and separation difficulties in eating disorders: a preliminary investigation', *International Journal of Eating Disorders* 8: 141–155.

Bagnold, E. (1972) 'The door of life', in E. D. Landau, S. L. Epstein and A. P. Stone (eds) *Child Development through Literature*, New Jersey: Prentice-Hall (originally published 1938).

Barrett, T. C. and Harren, V. A. (1979) 'Perspectives on self-theory: a comment on Loevinger and Kegan', *The Counseling Psychologist* 8: 34–39.

Bartle-Haring, S. and Strimple, R. E. (1996) 'Association of identity and intimacy: an exploration of gender and sex-role orientation', *Psychological Reports* 79: 1255–1264.

Bartle-Haring, S., Brucker, P. and Hock, E. (2002) 'The impact of parental separation anxiety on identity development in late adolescence and early adulthood', *Journal of Adolescent Research* 17: 439–450.

Bartolomucci, E. and Taylor, J. (1991) 'Preliminary reliability and validity of an instrument measuring separation–individuation outcomes', *Psychological Reports* 69: 391–398.

Bar-Yam, M. (1991) 'Do women and men speak in different voices? A comparative study of self-evolvement', *International Journal of Aging and Human Development* 32: 247–259.

Baumeister, R. F. (1986) *Identity: Cultural Change and the Struggle for Self*, New York: Oxford University Press.

——(1987) 'How the self became a problem: a psychological review', *Journal of Personality and Social Psychology* 52: 163–176.

Baumeister, R. F. and Muraven, M. (1996) 'Identity as adaptation to social, cultural, and historical context', *Journal of Adolescence* 19: 405–416.

Baxter Magolda, M. B. (1999a) 'Constructing adult identities', *Journal of College Student Development* 40 (6): 629–644.

——(1999b) *Creating Contexts for Learning and Self Authorship: Constructive-Developmental Pedagogy*, Nashville, TN: Vanderbilt University Press.

Bell, D. C. and Bell, L. G. (1983) 'Parental validation and support in the development of adolescent daughters', *New Directions for Child Development* 22: 27–42.

Bellew-Smith, M. and Korn, J. H. (1986) 'Merger intimacy status in adult women', *Journal of Personality and Social Psychology* 50: 1186–1191.

Benson, M. J., Harris, P. B. and Rogers, C. S. (1992) 'Identity consequences of attachment to mothers and fathers among late adolescents', *Journal of Research on Adolescence* 2: 187–204.

Bergman, R. (2002). 'Why be moral? A conceptual model from developmental psychology', *Human Development* 45: 104–124.

Berzonsky, M. D. and Adams, G. R. (1999) 'Reevaluating the identity status paradigm: still useful after 35 years', *Developmental Review* 19: 557–590.

Berzonsky, M. D. and Kuk, L. S. (2000) 'Identity status, identity processing style, and the transition to university', *Journal of Adolescent Research* 15: 81–98.

Bettelheim, B. (1969) *The Children of the Dream*, London: Macmillan.

Beykema, S. (1990) 'Women's best friendships: their meaning and meaningfulness', unpublished doctoral dissertation, Harvard Graduate School of Education.

Bjornsen, C. A. (2000) 'The blessing as a rite of passage in adolescence', *Adolescence* 35: 357–363.

Blasi, A. (1980) 'Bridging moral cognition and moral action: a critical review of the literature', *Psychological Bulletin* 88: 1–45.

——(1988) 'Identity and the development of the self', in D. K. Lapsley and F. C. Power (eds) *Self, Ego, and Identity: Integrative Approaches*, New York: Springer-Verlag.

Blasi, A. (1990) 'Kohlberg's theory and moral motivation', in D. Schrader (ed.) *The Legacy of Lawrence Kohlberg, New Directions for Child Development* 47: 51–57.

——(1998) 'Loevinger's theory of ego development and its relationship to the cognitive-developmental approach', in P. M. Westenberg, A. Blasi and L. D. Cohn (eds) *Personality Development: Theoretical, Empirical, and Clinical Investigations of Loevinger's Conception of Ego Development*, Mahwah, NJ: Lawrence Erlbaum Associates.

Blasi, A. and Glodis, K. (1995) 'The development of identity. A critical analysis from the perspective of the self as subject', *Developmental Review* 15: 404–433.

Blass, R. B. and Blatt, S. J. (1996) 'Attachment and separateness in the experience of symbiotic relatedness', *Psychoanalytic Quarterly* 65: 711–746.

Blatt, M. (1969) 'The effects of classroom discussion programs upon children's level of moral judgment', unpublished doctoral dissertation, University of Chicago.

Blatt, R. B. and Blatt, S. J. (1996) 'Attachment and separateness in the experience of symbiotic relatedness', *Psychoanalytic Quarterly* 65: 711–746.

Blatt, M. and Kohlberg, L. (1975) 'The effects of classroom moral discussion upon children's moral judgment', *Journal of Moral Education* 4: 129–161.

Blos, P. (1962) *On Adolescence: A Psychoanalytic Interpretation*, New York: Free Press.

——(1967) 'The second individuation process of adolescence', *Psychoanalytic Study of the Child* 22: 162–186.

——(1968) 'Character formation in adolescence', *Psychoanalytic Study of the Child* 23: 245–263.

——(1970) *The Young Adolescent: Clinical Studies*, New York: Free Press.

——(1971) 'The child analyst looks at the young adolescent', *Daedalus* 100: 961–978.

——(1976) 'When and how does adolescence end?', *Adolescent Psychiatry* 5: 5–17.

——(1979) *The Adolescent Passage: Developmental Issues*, New York: International Universities Press.

——(1980) 'Modifications in the traditional psychoanalytic theory of female adolescent development', *Adolescent Psychiatry* 8: 8–24.

——(1983) 'The contribution of psychoanalysis to the psychotherapy of adolescents', *Psychoanalytic Study of the Child* 38: 577–600.

——(1985) *Son and Father: Before and Beyond the Oedipus Complex*, New York: Free Press.

——(1989) 'The place of the adolescent process in the analysis of the adult', *Psychoanalytic Study of the Child* 44: 3–18.

Blum, L. (1999) 'Race, community and moral education: Kohlberg and Spielberg as civic educators', *Journal of Moral Education* 28: 125–143.

Blustein, D. L. and Phillips, S. D. (1990) 'Relation between ego identity statuses and decision-making styles', *Journal of Counseling Psychology* 37: 160–168.

Blustein, D. L., Ellis, M. V. and Devenis, L. E. (1989) 'The development and validation of a two-dimensional model of the commitment to career choices process', *Journal of Vocational Behavior* 35: 342–378.

Blustein, D. L., Wallbridge, M. M., Friedlander, M. L. and Palladino, D. E. (1991) 'Contributions of psychological separation and parental attachment to the career development process', *Journal of Counseling Psychology* 38: 39–50.

Boles, S. A. (1999) 'A model of parent representations, second individuation, and psychological adjustment in late adolescence', *Journal of Clinical Psychology* 55: 497–512.

Borders, L. D. (1989) 'Developmental cognitions of first practicum supervisees', *Journal of Counseling Psychology* 36: 163–169.

——(1998) 'Ego development and counselor development', in P. M. Westenberg, A. Blasi and L. D. Cohn (eds) *Personality Development: Theoretical,*

Empirical, and Clinical Investigations of Loevinger's Conception of Ego Development, Mahwah, NJ: Lawrence Erlbaum Associates.

Bosma, H. A. and Gerrits R. S. (1985) 'Family functioning and identity status in adolescence', *Journal of Early Adolescence* 5: 69–80.

Bosma, H. A. and Kunnen, E. S. (2001) 'Determinants and mechanisms in ego identity development: a review and synthesis', *Developmental Review* 21: 39–66.

Bosma, H. A., Graafsma, T. L. G., Grotevant, H. D. and de Levita, D. J. (eds) (1994) *Identity and Development: An Interdisciplinary Approach*, Newbury Park, CA: Sage.

Bowlby, J. (1969) *Attachment*, New York: Basic Books.

Boyes, M. C. and Chandler, M. (1992) 'Cognitive development, epistemic doubt, and identity formation in adolescence', *Journal of Youth and Adolescence* 21: 277–304.

Boyes, M. C. and Walker, L. J. (1988) 'Implications of cultural diversity for the universality claims of Kohlberg's theory of moral reasoning', *Human Development* 31: 44–59.

Brandt, D. E. (1977) 'Separation and identity in adolescence', *Contemporary Psychoanalysis* 13: 507–518.

Breger, L. (1974) *From Instinct to Identity: The Development of Personality*, Englewood Cliffs, NJ: Prentice-Hall.

Brenman-Gibson, M. (1986) *Clinical Implications of Erik Erikson's Work* (cassette recording no. 100-297-86), Washington, DC: American Psychological Association.

Brickfield, L. (1989) 'Identity development from late adolescence to adulthood: a study of ego identity status, object representation and self-esteem in women', unpublished doctoral dissertation, Adelphi University.

Broughton, J. and Zahaykevich, M. K. (1988) 'Ego and ideology: a critical review of Loevinger's theory', in D. K. Lapsley and F. C. Power (eds) *Self, Ego, and Identity*. New York: Springer-Verlag.

Brown, L. and Gilligan, C. (1992) *Meeting at the Crossroads: Women's Psychology and Girls' Development*, Cambridge, MA: Harvard University Press.

Brown, L., Debold, E., Tappan, M. and Gilligan, C. (1991) 'Reading narratives of conflict and choice for self and moral voices: a relational method', in W. M. Kurtines and J. L. Gewirtz (eds) *Handbook of Moral Behavior and Development, vol. 2: Research*, Hillsdale, NJ: Lawrence Erlbaum Associates.

Browning, D. L. (1987) 'Ego development, authoritarianism, and social status: an investigation of the incremental validity of Loevinger's Sentence Completion Test (Short Form)', *Journal of Personality and Social Psychology* 53: 113–118.

Campbell, E., Adams, G. R. and Dobson, W. R. (1984) 'Familial correlates of identity formation in late adolescence: a study of the predictive utility of connectedness and individuality in family relations', *Journal of Youth and Adolescence* 13: 509–525.

Candee, D. and Kohlberg, L. (1987) 'Moral judgment and moral action: a reanalysis of Haan, Smith, and Block's (1968) free speech movement data', *Journal of Personality and Social Psychology* 52: 554–564.

Caplan, P. J. (1979) 'Erikson's concept of inner space: a data-based reevaluation', *American Journal of Orthopsychiatry* 49: 100–108.

Carlozzi, A. F., Campbell, N. J. and Ward, G. R. (1982) 'Dogmatism and externality in locus of control as related to counselor trainee skill in facilitative responding', *Counselor Education and Supervision* 21: 227–236.

Carlozzi, A. F., Gaa, J. P. and Liberman, D. B. (1983) 'Empathy and ego development', *Journal of Counseling Psychology* 30: 113–116.

Carlsson, V. and Westenberg, P. M. (1998) 'Cross-cultural applications of the WUSCT', in J. Loevinger (ed.) *Technical Foundations for Measuring Ego Development: the Washington University Sentence Completion Test*, Mahwah, NJ: Lawrence Erlbaum Associates.

Carpendale, J. I. (2000) 'Kohlberg and Puiget on stages and moral reasoning', *Developmental Review* 20: 181–205.

Carpendale, J. I. and Krebs, D. L. (1992) 'Situational variation in moral judgment: in a stage or on a stage?', *Journal of Youth and Adolescence* 21: 203–224.

——(1995) 'Variations in level of moral judgment as a function of type of dilemma and moral choice', *Journal of Personality* 63: 289–213.

Carroll, J. L. and Rest, J. R. (1982) 'Moral development', in B. B. Wolman (ed.) *Handbook of Developmental Psychology*, Englewood Cliffs, NJ: Prentice-Hall.

Cebik, R. J. (1985) 'Ego development theory and its implications for supervision', *Counselor Education and Supervision* 24: 226–233.

Chandler, M. (1997) 'Stumping for progress in a post-modern world', in E. Amsel and K. A. Renninger (1997) *Change and Development: Issues of Theory, Method, and Application*, Mahwah, NJ: Lawrence Erlbaum Associates.

Chapman, J. W. and Nicholls, J. G. (1976) 'Occupational identity status, occupational preference, and field dependence in Maori and Pakeha boys', *Journal of Cross-Cultural Psychology* 7: 61–72.

Choi, K. H. (2002) 'Psychological separation–individuation and adjustment to college among Korean American students: the roles of collectivism and individualism', *Journal of Counseling Psychology* 49: 468–475.

Christenson, R. M. and Wilson, W. P. (1985) 'Assessing pathology in the separation–individuation process by an inventory: a preliminary report', *Journal of Nervous and Mental Disease* 173: 561–565.

Ciaccio, N. V. (1971) 'A test of Erikson's theory of ego epigenesis', *Developmental Psychology* 4: 306–311.

Cohn, L. D. (1991) 'Sex differences in the course of personality development: a meta-analysis', *Psychological Bulletin* 109: 252–266.

Cohn, L. D. (1998) 'Age trends in personality development: a quantitative review', in P. M. Westenberg, A. Blasi and L. D. Cohn (eds) *Personality Development: Theoretical Empirical, and Clinical Investigations of Loevinger's Conception of Ego Development*, Mahwah, NJ: Lawrence Erlbaum Associates.

Colby, A. (2002) 'Moral understanding, motivation, and identity', *Human Development* 45: 130–135.

Colby, A. and Damon, W. (1992) *Some Do Care: Contemporary Lives of Moral Commitment*, New York: Free Press.

Colby, A. and Kohlberg, L. (1987) *The Measurement of Moral Judgment*, vol. 1, Cambridge, MA: Cambridge University Press.

Colby, A., Kohlberg, L., Fenton, E., Speicher-Dubin, B. and Lieberman, M. (1977) 'Secondary school moral discussion programs led by social studies teachers', *Journal of Moral Education* 6: 90–111.

Colby, A., Kohlberg, L., Gibbs, J. and Lieberman, M. (1983) 'A longitudinal study of moral judgment', *Monographs of the Society for Research in Child Development* 48: 1–124.

Colby, A., Kohlberg, L., Speicher, B., Hewer, A., Candee, D., Gibbs, J. and Power, C. (1987) *The Measurement of Moral Judgement*, vol. 2, Cambridge: Cambridge University Press.

Coleman, J. C. (1974) *Relationships in Adolescence*, London: Routledge and Kegan Paul.

Coles, R. (1970) *Erik H. Erikson: The Growth of His Work*, Boston: Little Brown.

Constantinople, A. (1967) 'Perceived instrumentality of the college as a measure of attitudes toward college', *Journal of Personality and Social Psychology* 5: 196–210.

——(1969) 'An Eriksonian measure of personality development in college students', *Developmental Psychology* 1: 357–372.

Coonerty, S. (1989) 'An exploration of change in separation–individuation themes in the borderline disorder', paper presented at Annual Meeting of the Division of Psychoanalysis, American Psychological Association, Boston, April.

Coppolillo, H. P. (1984) 'Integration, organization, and regulation in late adolescence', in D. D. Brockman (ed.) *Late Adolescence: Psychoanalytic Studies*, New York: International Universities Press.

Costa, M. E. and Campos, B. P. (1989) 'University area of study and identity development: a longitudinal study', paper presented at Biennial Meeting of the Society for the Study of Behavioral Development, Jyvaskyla, Finland, July.

Costa, P. T. and McCrae, R. R. (1993) 'Ego development and trait models of personality', *Psychological Inquiry* 4: 20–23.

Costos, D. (1986) 'Sex role identity in young adults: its parental antecedents and relation to ego development', *Journal of Personality and Social Psychology* 50: 602–611.

Costos, D. (1990) 'Gender role identity from an ego developmental perspective', *Sex Roles* 22: 723–741.

Côté, J. E. (1993) 'Foundations of a psychoanalytic social psychology: neo-Eriksonian propositions regarding the relationship between psychic structure and cultural institutions', *Developmental Review* 13: 31–53.

——(1996) 'Identity: a multidimensional analysis', in G. R. Adams,

R. Montemayor and T. Gullotta (eds) *Psychological Development in Adolescence*, Newbury Park, CA: Sage.

Côté, J. E. and Levine, C. (1983) 'Marcia and Erikson: the relationship among ego identity status, neuroticism, dogmatism, and purpose in life', *Journal of Youth and Adolescence* 12: 43–53.

——(1988) 'A critical examination of the ego identity status paradigm', *Developmental Review* 8: 147–184.

——(1989) 'An empirical test of Erikson's theory of ego identity formation', *Youth and Society* 20: 388–415.

——(2002) *Identity Formation, Agency, and Culture: A Social Psychological Synthesis*, Mahwah, NJ: Lawrence Erlbaum Associates.

Côté, J. E. and Schwartz, S. J. (2002) 'Comparing psychological and sociological approaches to identity: identity status, identity capital, and the individualization process', *Journal of Adolescence*, 25: 571–586.

Cramer, P. (1995) 'Identity, narcissism, and defense mechanisms in late adolescence', *Journal of Research in Personality* 29: 341–361.

——(1998) 'Freshman to senior year: a follow-up study of identity, narcissism, and defense mechanisms', *Journal of Research in Personality* 34: 42–72.

——(1999) 'Ego functions and ego development: defense mechanisms and intelligence as predictors of ego level', *Journal of Personality* 67: 735–760.

Cushman, P. (1990) 'Why the self is empty', *American Psychologist* 45: 599–611.

Czyzowska, D. and Niemczynski, A. (1996) 'Universality of socio-moral development: a cross-sectional study in Poland', *Journal of Moral Education* 25: 441–454.

da Ponte, L. (1929) *Memoirs*. Philadelphia: J. S. Lippincott.

Danielsen, L. M., Lorem, A. E. and Kroger, J. (2000) 'The impact of social context on the identity-formation process of Norwegian late adolescents', *Youth and Society* 31: 332–362.

Darley, J. (1993) 'Research on morality: possible approaches, actual approaches', *Psychological Science* 4: 353–365.

Day, J. M. and Tappen, M. B. (1996) 'The narrative approach to moral development: from the epistemic subject to dialogical selves', *Human Development* 39: 67–82.

Denton, K. and Krebs, D. (1990) 'From the scene to the crime: the effect of alcohol and social context on moral judgment', *Journal of Personality and Social Psychology* 59: 242–248.

Dill, D. L. and Noam, G. G. (1990) 'Ego development and treatment requests', *Psychiatry* 53: 85–91.

Dixon, J. W. (1986) 'The relation of social perspective stages to Kegan's stages of ego development', unpublished doctoral dissertation, University of Toledo.

Dolan, B. M., Evans, C. and Norton, K. (1992) 'The separation–individuation inventory: association with borderline phenomena', *Journal of Nervous and Mental Disease* 180: 529–533.

Douvan, E. and Adelson, J. (1996) *The Adolescent Experience*, New York: Wiley.

Dreyer, P. H. (1994) 'Designing curricular identity interventions for secondary schools', in S. L. Archer (ed.) *Interventions for Adolescent Identity Development*, Newbury Park, CA: Sage.

Dubow, E. F., Huesmann, L. R. and Eron, L. D. (1987) 'Childhood correlates of adult ego development', *Child Development* 58: 859–869.

Dunkel, C. S. (2002) 'Terror management theory and identity: the effect of the 9/11 terrorist attacks on anxiety and identity change', *Identity: An International Journal of Theory and Research* 2: 287–301.

Dunkel, C. S. and Anthis, K. S. (2001) 'The role of possible selves in identity formation: a short-term longitudinal study', *Journal of Adolescence* 24: 765–776.

Dyk, P. H. and Adams, G. R. (1990) 'Identity and intimacy: an initial investigation of three theoretical models using cross-lag panel correlations', *Journal of Youth and Adolescence* 19: 91–109.

Edward, J., Ruskin, N. and Turrini, P. (1992) *Separation–Individuation: Theory and Application*, 2nd edn, New York: Brunner/Mazel.

Edwards, C. P. (1986) 'Cross-cultural research on Kohlberg's stages: the basis for consensus', in S. Modgil and C. Modgil (eds) *Lawrence Kohlberg: Consensus and Controversy*, London: Falmer Press.

Eisenberg, N. and Strayer, J. (eds) (1987) *Empathy and its Development*, Cambridge: Cambridge University Press.

Eisenberg, N. and Mussen, P. (1989) *The Roots of Prosocial Behavior in Children*, Cambridge: Cambridge University Press.

Ellis, A. (1962) *Reason and Emotion in Psychotherapy*, New York: Lyle Stuart.

Enright, R. D., Lapsley, D. K., Drivas, A. E. and Fehr, L. A. (1980) 'Parental influences on the development of adolescent autonomy and identity', *Journal of Youth and Adolescence* 9: 529–546.

Erickson, V. L. (1990) 'Deliberate psychological education for women: a curriculum follow-up study', in V. L. Erickson and J. M. Whitely (eds) *Developmental Counseling and Teaching*, Monterey, CA: Brooks/Cole.

Erikson, E. H. (1956) 'The problem of ego identity', *Journal of the American Psychoanalytic Association* 4: 56–121.

——(1959) 'Identity and the life cycle,' *Psychological Issues* 1 [Monograph 1]. New York: International Universities Press.

——(1963) *Childhood and Society*, 2nd edn, New York: Norton.

——(1968) *Identity, Youth, and Crisis*, New York: Norton.

——(1970) 'Autobiographic notes on the identity crisis', *Daedalus* 99: 730–759.

——(1975) *Life History and the Historical Moment*, New York: Norton.

——(1976) 'Reflections on Dr. Borg's life cycle', *Daedalus* 105: 1–28.

——(1977) *Toys and Reasons: Stages in the Ritualization of Experience*, New York: Norton.

——(1983) 'Concluding remarks: infancy and the rest of life', in J. D. Call, E. Galenson and R. L. Tyson (eds) *Frontiers of Infant Psychiatry*, New York: Basic Books.

——(1984) 'Reflections on the last stage – and the first', *Psychoanalytic Study of the Child* 39: 155–165.

Esman, A. H. (1980) 'Adolescent psychopathology and the rapprochement phenomenon,' *Adolescent Psychiatry* 8: 320–331.

——(1997) 'Obituary: Peter Blos (1903–1997)', *International Journal of Psychoanalysis* 78: 813–814.

Evans, R. I. (1967) *Dialogue with Erik Erikson*, New York: Harper and Row.

Feldberg, A. (1983) 'Adolescent separation, individuation, and identity (re)-formation: theoretical extensions and modifications', unpublished doctoral dissertation, California School of Professional Psychology, Fresno.

Fitch, S. A. and Adams, G. R. (1983) 'Ego identity and intimacy status: replication and extension', *Developmental Psychology* 19: 839–845.

Flum, H. and Blustein, D. L. (2000) 'Reinvigorating the study of vocational exploration: a framework for research', *Journal of Vocational Behavior* 56: 380–404.

Foster, J. D. and LaForce, B. (1999) 'A longitudinal study of moral, religious, and identity development in a Christian liberal arts environment', *Journal of Psychology and Theology* 27: 52–68.

Frank, S. J., Pirsh, L.A. and Wright, V. C. (1990) 'Late adolescents' perceptions of their relationships with their parents: relationships among de-idealization, autonomy, relatedness, and insecurity and implications for adolescent adjustment and ego identity status', *Journal of Youth and Adolescence* 19: 571–588.

Franz, C. E. and White, K. M. (1985) 'Individuation and attachment in personality development: extending Erikson's theory', *Journal of Personality* 53: 224–256.

Friedlander, M. L. and Siegel, S. M. (1990) 'Separation–individuation difficulties and cognitive-behavioral indicators of eating disorders among college women', *Journal of Counseling Psychology* 37: 74–78.

Friedman, L. J. (1999) *Identity's Architect: A Biography of Erik H. Erikson*, New York: Scribner.

Fromm, E. (1955) *The Sane Society*, New York: Fawcett Premier.

Furman, E. (1982) 'Mothers have to be there to be left', *Psychoanalytic Study of the Child* 37: 15–28.

Garmon, L. C., Basinger, K. S., Gregg, V. R. and Gibbs, J. C. (1996) 'Gender differences in stage and expression of moral judgment', *Merrill-Palmer Quarterly* 42: 418–437.

Gergen, K. J. (1991). *The Saturated Self: Dilemmas of Identity in Contemporary Life*, New York: Basic Books.

Gfellner, B. M. (1986a) 'Changes in ego and moral development in adolescents: a longitudinal study', *Journal of Adolescence* 9: 281–302.

——(1986b) 'Ego development and moral development in relation to age and grade level during adolescence', *Journal of Youth and Adolescence* 15: 147–163.

Gilligan, C. (1982a) *In a Different Voice: Psychological Theory and Women's Development*, Cambridge, MA: Harvard University Press.

——(1982b) 'Why should a woman be more like a man', *Psychology Today* 16: 1982.

——(1985) 'Response to critics', paper presented to the Biennial Meeting of the Society for Research in Child Development, Toronto, April.

——(1989) *Making Connections: The Relational Worlds of Adolescent Girls at Emma Willard School*, Cambridge, MA: Harvard University Press.

——(1998) 'Remembering Larry', *Journal of Moral Education* 27: 125–140.

Gilligan, C. and Attanucci, J. (1988) 'Two moral orientations: gender differences and similarities', *Merrill-Palmer Quarterly* 34: 223–237.

Gilligan, C., Brown, C. and Rogers, A. (1990a) 'Psyche embedded: a place for body, relationships, and culture in personality theory', in A. I. Rabin, R. Zucker, R. Emmons and S. Franks (eds) *Studying Persons and Lives*, New York: Springer-Verlag.

Gilligan, C., Murphy, J. M. and Tappan, M. B. (1990b) 'Moral development beyond adolescence', in C. N. Alexander and E. J. Langer (eds) *Higher Stages of Human Development: Perspectives on Adult Growth*, New York: Oxford University Press.

Gilligan, C., Rogers, A. and Tolman, D. (1991) *Women, Girls, and Psychotherapy: Reframing Resistance*, New York: Haworth Press.

Ginsburg, S. D. and Orlofsky, J. L. (1981) 'Ego identity status, ego development, and locus of control in college women', *Journal of Youth and Adolescence* 10: 297–307.

Gnaulati, E. and Heine, B. J. (2001) 'Separation–individuation in late adolescence: an investigation of gender and ethnic differences', *Journal of Psychology* 135: 59–70.

Goossens, L. (2001) 'Global verses domain-specific statuses in identity research: a comparison of two self-report measures', *Journal of Adolescence* 24: 681–699.

Goossens, L., Beyers, W., Emmen, M. and van Aken, M. A. G. (2002) 'The imaginary audience and personal fable: factor analyses and concurrent validity of the "New Look" measures', *Journal of Research on Adolescence* 12: 193–215.

Greenberg, J. R. and Mitchell, S. A. (1983) *Object Relations in Psychoanalytic Theory*, Cambridge, MA: Harvard University Press.

Gregg, V., Gibbs, J. C. and Basinger, K. S. (1994) 'Patterns of developmental delay in moral judgment by male and female delinquents', *Merrill-Palmer Quarterly* 40: 538–553.

Grotevant, H. D. and Cooper, C. R. (1985) 'Patterns of interaction in family relationships and the development of identity exploration in adolescence', *Child Development* 56: 415–428.

——(1986) 'Individuation in family relationships', *Human Development* 29: 82–100.

Group for the Advancement of Psychiatry (1968) *Normal Adolescence*, vol. 6, report no. 68, New York: Group for the Advancement of Psychiatry.

Haan, N. (1974) 'The adolescent antecedents of an ego model of coping and defense and comparisons with Q-sorted ideal personalities', *Genetic Psychology Monographs* 89: 273–306.

Habermas, J. (1975) 'Moral development and ego identity', in J. Habermas (ed.) *Communication and the Evolution of Society*, Boston: Beacon.

Hamachek, D. E. (1988) 'Evaluating self concept and ego development within Erikson's psychosocial framework: a formulation', *Journal of Counseling and Development* 66: 354–360.

——(1989) 'Evaluating self-concept and ego status in Erikson's last three psychosocial stages', paper presented at the Annual Conference of the American Association for Counseling and Development, Boston, March.

Hansburg, H. G. (1980a) *Adolescent Separation Anxiety: A Method for the Study of Adolescent Separation Problems*, vol. 1, New York: Robert E. Krieger.

——(1980b). *Adolescent Separation Anxiety: Separation Disorders*, vol. 2, New York: Robert E. Krieger.

Harré, R. (1987) 'Grammar, psychology and moral rights', in M. Chapman (ed.) *Meaning and Growth of Understanding*, Berlin: Springer-Verlag.

Hartmann, H. (1958) *Ego Psychology and the Problem of Adaptation*, New York: International Universities Press.

Hauser, S. T. (1976) 'Loevinger's model and measure of ego development: a critical review', *Psychological Bulletin* 83: 928–955.

Hauser, S. T., Powers, S. I., Noam, G. G., Jacobson, A. M., Weiss, B. and Follansbee, D. J. (1984) 'Familial contexts of adolescent ego development', *Child Development* 55: 195–213.

Hauser, S. T., Powers, S. I., and Noam, G. G. (1991) *Adolescents and their Families: Paths of Ego Development*, New York: The Free Press.

Henderson, A. F. and Kegan, R. (1989) 'Learning, knowing, and the self: a constructive developmental view', in K. Field, B. J. Cohler and G. Wool (eds) *Emotions and Behavior Monographs*, monograph no. 6, Madison, CO: International Universities Press.

Henton, J., Lamke, L., Murphy, C. and Haynes, L. (1980) 'Crisis reactions of college freshman as a function of family support systems', *Personnel and Guidance Journal* 58: 508–511.

Hesse, H. (1980) 'Siddhartha', in *Hermann Hesse. Six Novels with Other Stories and Essays*, London: Collins (first published 1950).

Hickey, L. and Scharf, P. (1980) *Toward a Just Correctional System*, San Francisco: Jossey Bass.

Higgins, A. (1991) 'The just community approach to moral education: evolution of the idea and recent findings', in W. M. Kurtines and J. L. Gewirtz (eds) *Handbook of Moral Behavior and Development, Vol 2: Research*, Hillsdale, NJ: Lawrence Erlbaum Associates.

Hock, E., Eberly, M., Bartle-Haring, S., Ellwanger, P. and Widaman, K. (2001) 'Separation anxiety in parents of adolescents: theoretical significance and scale development', *Child Development* 72: 284–298.

Hodgson, T. O. (1990) 'Constructive developmental analysis of autobiographical writing', unpublished doctoral dissertation, University of Massachusetts.

Hoffer, E. (1951) *The True Believer*, New York: Harper and Row.

Hoffman, J. A. (1984) 'Psychological separation of late adolescents from their parents', *Journal of Counseling Psychology* 31: 170–178.

Holmbeck, G. N. and Leake, C. (1999) 'Separation–individuation and psychological adjustment in late adolescence', *Journal of Youth and Adolescence* 28: 563–581.

Holmbeck, G. N. and McClanahan, G. (1994) 'Construct and content validity of the separation–individuation test of adolescence: a reply to Levine', *Journal of Personality Assessment* 62: 169–172.

Holmbeck, G. N. and Wandrei, M. L. (1993) 'Individual and relational predictors of adjustment in first-year college students', *Journal of Counseling Psychology* 40: 73–78.

Holt, R. R. (1980) 'Loevinger's measure of ego development: reliability and national norms for male and female short forms', *Journal of Personality and Social Psychology* 39: 909–920.

Hopkins, J. R. (1995) 'Erik Homburger Erikson (1902–1994)', *American Psychologist* 50: 796–797.

Horner, T. M. (1985) 'The psychic life of the young infant', *American Journal of Orthopsychiatry* 55: 324–344.

Hsia, L. C. (1992) 'Learning in conflicts', unpublished doctoral dissertation, Harvard Graduate School of Education.

Hult, R. E. (1979) 'The relationship between ego identity status and moral reasoning in university women', *Journal of Psychology* 103: 203–207.

Humphreys, C. N. and Davidson, W. B. (1997) 'Individuation of self and stereotyping of others', *Psychological Reports* 81: 1252–1254.

Hunsberger, B., Pratt, M. and Pancer, S. M. (2001) 'Adolescent identity formation: religious exploration and commitment', *Identity: An International Journal of Theory and Research* 1: 365–386.

Hurtig, A. L., Petersen, A. C., Richards, M. H. and Gitelson, I. B. (1985) 'Cognitive mediators of ego functioning in adolescence', *Journal of Youth and Adolescence* 14: 435–450.

Huxley, A. (1972) 'Visionary experience', in J. White (ed.) *The Highest State of Consciousness*, New York: Archer.

Hy, L. X. and Loevinger, J. (1996) *Measuring Ego Development*, 2nd edn, Mahwah, NJ: Lawrence Erlbaum Associates.

Ignelzi, M. (2000) 'Meaning-making in the learning and teaching process', *New Directions for Teaching and Learning* 82: 5–14.

Isay, R. A. (1980) 'Late adolescence: the second separation stage of adolescence', in S. I. Greenspan and G. H. Pollock (eds) *The Course of Life: Psychoanalytic Contributions Toward Understanding Personality Development, Vol. II: Latency, Adolescence, and Youth*, Washington, DC: NIMH.

Ivey, A. E. (1976) 'Counseling psychology, the psychoeducator model, and the future', *The Counseling Psychologist* 6: 72–75.

Jacobsen, E. (1964) *The Self and the Object World*, New York: International Universities Press.

Jennings, A. G. and Armsworth, M. W. (1992) 'Ego development in women with histories of sexual abuse', *Child Abuse and Neglect* 16: 553–565.

Jennings, W. S. and Kohlberg, L. (1983) 'Effects of a just community program on the moral development of youthful offenders', *Journal of Moral Education* 12: 33–50.

Jensen, M., Kristiansen, I., Sandbekk, M. and Kroger, J. (1998) 'Ego identity status in cross-cultural context: a comparison of Norwegian and United States university students', *Psychological Reports* 83: 455–460.

Johnson, P., Buboltz, W. C. and Seemann, E. (2003) 'Ego identity status: a step in the differentiation process', *Journal of Counseling and Development* 81: 191–195.

Jones, R. M. (1994) 'Curricula focused on behavioral deviance', in S. L. Archer (ed.) *Interventions for Adolescent Identity Development*, Newbury Park, CA: Sage.

Jordan, D. (1970) 'Parental antecedents of ego identity formation', unpublished master's thesis, State University of New York at Buffalo.

Josselson, R. (1980) 'Ego development in adolescence', in J. Adelson (ed.) *Handbook of Adolescent Psychology*, New York: Wiley.

——(1982) 'Personality structure and identity status in women viewed through early memories', *Journal of Youth and Adolescence* 11: 293–299.

——(1987) *Finding Herself: Pathways to Identity Development in Women*, San Francisco: Jossey-Bass.

——(1988) 'The embedded self: I and thou revisited', in D. K. Lapsley and F. C. Power (eds) *Self, Ego, and Identity: Integrative Approaches*, New York: Springer-Verlag.

Kacerguis, M. A. and Adams, G. R. (1980) 'Erikson stage resolution: the relationship between identity and intimacy', *Journal of Youth and Adolescence* 9: 117–126.

Kalsner, L. and Pistole, M. C. (2003) 'College adjustment in a multiethnic samåle: attachment, separation–individuation, and ethnic identity', *Journal of College Student Development* 44: 92–109.

Kaly, P. W. (2000) 'Examining the effects of a ship-based adventure program on adolescent self-esteem and ego-identity development', *Dissertation Abstracts International: Section B, The Sciences and Engineering* 60(9-B): 4891.

Kaplan, A. and Klein, R. (1985) *The Relational Self in Late Adolescent Women*, Wellesley, MA: Wellesley College, Stone Center for Developmental Services and Studies.

Kaufman, K. S. (1985) 'Parental discipline and constructive-developmental psychology', unpublished doctoral dissertation, Harvard Graduate School of Education.

Kegan, R. (1979) 'The evolving self: a process conception for ego psychology', *The Counseling Psychologist* 8: 5–38.

——(1980) 'Making meaning: the constructive-developmental approach to persons and practice', *The Personnel and Guidance Journal* 58: 373–380.

——(1982) *The Evolving Self: Problem and Process in Human Development*, Cambridge, MA: Harvard University Press.

——(1983) 'A neo-Piagetian approach to object relations', in B. Lee and G. G. Noam (eds) *Developmental Approaches to the Self*, New York: Plenum.

——(1985) 'The loss of Pete's dragon: developments of the self in the years five to seven', in R. L. Leahy (ed.) *The Development of the Self*, New York: Academic Press.

——(1986a) 'The child behind the mask: sociopathy as developmental delay', in W. H. Reid, D. Dorr, J. I. Walker and J. W. Bonner III (eds) *Unmasking the Psychopath: Antisocial Personality and Related Syndromes*, New York: Norton.

——(1986b) 'Kohlberg and the psychology of ego development: a predominantly positive evaluation', in S. Modgil and C. Modgil (eds) *Lawrence Kohlberg: Consensus and Controversy*, London: Falmer Press.

——(1986c) 'Interchange: Kegan replies to Loevinger', in S. Modgil and C. Modgil (eds) *Lawrence Kohlberg: Consensus and Controversy*, London: Falmer Press.

——(1990) 'Minding the curriculum: of student epistemology and faculty conspiracy', unpublished manuscript, Harvard Graduate School of Education.

——(1991) 'Developmental approaches to professional development', paper presented at the Conference of the Clinical-Developmental Institute, Cambridge, MA, June.

——(1994) *In Over Our Heads: The Mental Demands of Modern Life*, Cambridge, MA: Harvard University Press.

——(1996) 'Neither "safe sex" nor abstinence may work – Now what?: toward a third norm for youthful sexuality', in D. Cicchetti, and S. L. Toth (eds) *Adolescence, Opportunities and Challenges. Rochester Symposium on Developmental Psychopathology*, vol. 7. Rochester, NY: University of Rochester Press, pp. 125–148.

Kegan, R. and Lahey, L. L. (2001) *How the Way We Talk Can Change the Way We Work*, San Francisco: Jossey Bass.

Kegan, R., Noam, G. G. and Rogers, L. (1982) 'The psychologic of emotion: a neo-Piagetian view', in D. Cicchetti and P. Hesse (eds) *New Directions for Child Development: Emotional Development*, San Francisco: Jossey Bass.

Kitchener, K. S., King, P. M., Davison, M. L., Parker, C. A. and Wood, P. K. (1984) 'A longitudinal study of moral and ego development in young adults', *Journal of Youth and Adolescence* 13: 197–211.

Kohlberg, L. (1958) 'The development of modes of thinking and choices in years 10 to 16', unpublished doctoral dissertation, University of Chicago.

——(1969) 'Stage and sequence: the cognitive-developmental approach to socialization', in D. A. Goslin (ed.) *Handbook of Socialization Theory and Research*, Chicago: Rand McNally.

——(1973) 'Continuities in childhood and adult moral development revisited', in P. B. Baltes and K. W. Schaie (eds) *Life-Span Developmental Psychology: Personality and Socialization*, New York: Academic Press.

——(1975) 'Counseling and counselor education: a developmental approach', *Counselor Education and Supervision* 14: 1975.

——(1980a) 'Stages of moral development as a basis for education', in B. Munsey (ed.) *Moral Development, Moral Education, and Kohlberg*, Birmingham, AL: Religious Education Press.

——(1980b) 'Educating for a just society: an updated and revised statement', in B. Munsey (ed.) *Moral Development, Moral Education, and Kohlberg*, Birmingham, AL: Religious Education Press.

——(1981) *Essays in Moral Development, Vol. 1: The Philosophy of Moral Development*, San Francisco: Harper and Row.

——(1984) *Essays in Moral Development, Vol. 2: The Psychology of Moral Development*, San Francisco: Harper and Row.

Kohlberg, L. and Gilligan, C. (1971) 'The adolescent as a philosopher: the discovery of the self in a postconventional world', *Daedelus* 100: 1051–1086.

Kohlberg, L. and Kramer, R. (1969) 'Continuities and discontinuities in childhood and adult moral development', *Human Development* 12: 93–120.

Kohlberg, L. and Turiel, E. (1971) 'Moral development and moral education', in G. S. Lesser (ed.) *Psychology and Educational Practice*, London: Scott, Foresman.

Kohlberg, L. and Wasserman, E. R. (1980) 'The cognitive-developmental approach and the practicing counselor: an opportunity for counselors to rethink their roles', *The Personnel and Guidance Journal* 58: 559–567.

Kraemer, D. L. (1958) 'Problems of identity', *Journal of the American Psychoanalytic Association* 6: 131–142.

Kraemer, S. (1982) 'Leaving home and the adolescent family therapist', *Journal of Adolescence* 5: 51–62.

Krebs, D. L. and Vermeulen, S. C. (1994) 'Gender and perspective differences in moral judgment and moral orientation', *Journal of Moral Education* 23: 17–26.

Krebs, D. L., Vermeulen, S. C. A., Carpendale, J. I. and Denton, K. (1991) 'Structural and situational influences on moral judgment: the interaction between stage and dilemma', in W. M. Kurtines and J. L. Gewirtz (eds) *Handbook of Moral Behavior and Development, Vol. 1: Theory*, Hillsdale, NJ: Lawrence Erlbaum Associates.

Krebs, D. L., Wark, G. and Krebs, D. (1995) 'Lessons from life: toward a functional model of morality', *Moral Education Forum* 20: 22–29.

Krebs, D. L., Denton, K. and Wark, G. (1997) 'The forms and functions of real-life moral decision-making', *Journal of Moral Education* 26: 131–145.

Krettenauer, T., Ullrich, M., Hofmann, V. and Edelstein, W. (2003) 'Behavioral problems in childhood and adolescence as predictors of ego level attainment in early adulthood', *Merrill-Palmer Quarterly* 49: 125–153.

Kroger, J. (1983) 'I knew who I was when I got up this morning', *SET Research Information for Teachers* 1: 1–6.

——(1985) 'Eriksonian ego identity: implications for counselling in the secondary schools', paper presented at the Joint Conference of the Australian/New Zealand Psychological Societies, Christchurch, New Zealand, August.

——(1990) 'Ego structuralization in late adolescence as seen through early memories and ego identity status', *Journal of Adolescence* 13: 65–77.

——(1992) 'Intrapsychic dimensions of identity during late adolescence', in G. R. Adams, T. P. Gullotta and R. Montemayor (eds) *Adolescent Identity Formation: Advances in Adolescent Development*, vol. 4 Newbury Park, CA: Sage.

Kroger, J. (1993) 'On the nature of structural transition in the identity formation process', in J. Kroger (ed.) *Discussions on Ego Identity*, Hillsdale, NJ: Lawrence Erlbaum Associates.

—— (1995) 'The differentiation of "firm" and "developmental" foreclosure identity statuses: a longitudinal study', *Journal of Adolescent Research* 10: 317–337.

—— (1996) 'Identity, regression and development', *Journal of Adolescence* 19: 203–222.

—— (1997) 'Gender and identity: the intersection of structure, content, and context', *Sex Roles* 36: 747–770.

—— (1998) 'Adolescence as a second-separation-individuation process: critical review of an object relations approach', in E. Skoe and A. von der Lippe (eds) *Personality Development in Adolescence: A Cross National and Life Span Perspective*, London: Routledge.

—— (2003) 'Identity in adolescence', in G. R. Adams and M. D. Berzonsky (eds) *Blackwell Handbook of Adolescence*, Oxford: Oxford University Press.

Kroger, J. and Green, K. (1994) 'Factor analytic structure and stability of the separation–individuation test of adolescence', *Journal of Clinical Psychology* 50: 772–779.

—— (1996) 'Events associated with identity status change', *Journal of Adolescence* 19: 477–490.

—— (2004) 'The convergence among self, ego and identity during late adolescence', a Rasch analysis. Manuscript submitted for publication.

Kroger, J. and Haslett, S. J. (1987) 'A retrospective study of ego identity status change from adolescence through middle adulthood', *Social and Behavioral Sciences Documents* 17 (ms no. 2797).

—— (1988) 'Separation–individuation and ego identity status in late adolescence: a two-year longitudinal study', *Journal of Youth and Adolescence* 17: 59–81.

Kurtines, W. M. and Gewirtz, J. L. (eds) (1991a) *Handbook of Moral Behavior and Development: Theory*, vol. 1, Hillsdale, NJ: Lawrence Erlbaum Associates.

—— (eds) (1991b) *Handbook of Moral Behavior and Development: Research*, vol. 2, Hillsdale, NJ: Lawrence Erlbaum Associates.

—— (eds) (1991c) *Handbook of Moral Behavior and Development: Application*, vol. 3, Hillsdale, NJ: Lawrence Erlbaum Associates.

Kurtines, W. and Greif, E. B. (1974) 'The development of moral thought: review and evaluation of Kohlberg's approach', *Psychological Bulletin* 81: 453–470.

Kutnick, P. (1986) 'The relationship of moral judgment and moral action: Kohlberg's theory, criticism, and revision', in S. Modgil and C. Modgil (eds) *Lawrence Kohlberg: Consensus and Controversy*, London: Falmer Press.

Jordan, D. (1971) 'Identity status: a developmental model as related to parental behavior', unpublished doctoral dissertation, State University of New York at Buffalo.

Lahey, L. L. (1986) 'Males' and females' construction of conflict in work and love', unpublished doctoral dissertation, Harvard Graduate School of Education.

Lahey, L., Souvaine, E., Kegan, R., Goodman, R. and Felix, S. (1987) 'A guide to the subject–object interview: its administration and interpretation', unpublished manuscript, Harvard Graduate School of Education.

Langford, P. E. (1994) 'Do senior secondary students possess the moral maturity to negotiate class rules?', *Journal of Moral Education* 23: 387–407.

——(1997) 'Separating judicial from legislative reasoning in moral dilemma interviews', *Child Development* 68: 1105–1116.

Lapsley, D. K. (1992) 'Toward an integrated theory of adolescent ego development: the "new look" at adolescent egocentrism', *American Journal of Orthopsychiatry* 63: 562–571.

Lapsley, D. K. and Edgerton, J. (2002) 'Separation–individuation, adult attachment style, and college adjustment', *Journal of Counseling and Development* 80: 484–492.

Lapsley, D. K. and Lasky B. (2001) 'Prototypic moral character', *Identity: An International Journal of Theory and Research* 1: 345–363.

Lapsley, D. K. and Rice, K. (1988) 'The "new look" at the imaginary audience and personal fable: towards an integrative model of adolescent ego development', in D. K. Lapsley and F. C. Power (eds) *Self, Ego, Identity: Integrative Approaches*, New York: Springer-Verlag.

Lapsley, D. K., Aalsma, M. C. and Varshney, N. M. (2001) 'A factor analytic and psychometric examination of pathology of separation-individuation', *Journal of Clinical Psychology* 57: 915–932.

Larson, R. W. (1997) 'The emergence of solitude as a constructive domain of experience in early adolescence', *Child Development* 68: 80–93.

LaVoie, J. (1994) 'Identity in adolescence: issues of theory, structure and transition', *Journal of Adolescence* 17: 17–28.

Leaper, C., Hauser, S. T., Kreman, A. *et al.* (1989) 'Adolescent–parent interactions in relation to adolescents' gender and ego development pathway: a longitudinal study', *Journal of Early Adolescence* 9: 335–61.

Lee, H. Y. and Hughey, K. F. (2001) 'The relationship of psychological separation and parental attachment to the career maturity of college freshmen from intact families', *Journal of Career Development* 27: 279–293.

Leming, J. S. (1986) 'Kohlbergian programs in moral education: a practical review and assessment', in S. Modgil and C. Modgil (eds) *Lawrence Kohlberg: Consensus and Controversy*, London: Falmer Press.

Lerner, R. (1993) 'A developmental contextual view of human development', in S. C. Hayes, L. J. Hayes, H. W. Reese and T. R. Sarbin (eds) *Varieties of Scientific Contextualism*, Reno, NV: Context Press.

——(2003) 'Applying developmental science for youth and families: historical and theoretical foundations' in R. M. Lerner, F. Jacobs and D. Wertleib (eds) *Handbook of Applied Development Science: Promoting Positive Child, Adolescent, and Family Development through Research, Policies, and Programs*, vol. 1, Newbury Park, CA: Sage.

Levine, J. B. (1994) 'On McClanahan and Holmbeck's construct validity study of the separation–individuation test of adolescence', *Journal of Personality Assessment* 62: 166–168.

Levine, J. B. and Saintonge, S. (1993) 'Psychometric properties of the separation–individuation test of adolescence within a clinical population', *Journal of Clinical Psychology* 49: 492–507.

Levine, J. B., Green, C. J. and Millon, T. (1986) 'Separation–individuation test of adolescence', *Journal of Personality Assessment* 50: 123–137.

Levitz-Jones, E. M. and Orlofsky, J. L. (1985) 'Separation–individuation and intimacy capacity in college women', *Journal of Personality and Social Psychology* 49: 156–169.

Loevinger, J. (1976) *Ego Development: Conceptions and Theories*, San Francisco: Jossey-Bass.

——(1979a) 'The idea of the ego', *The Counseling Psychologist* 8: 3–5.

——(1979b) 'Reply to Kegan', *The Counseling Psychologist* 8: 39–40.

——(1979c) 'Construct validity of the sentence completion test of ego development', *Applied Psychological Measurement* 3: 281–311.

——(1980) 'Some thoughts on ego development and counseling', *Personnel and Guidance Journal* 58: 389–390.

——(1982) 'Confessions of an iconoclast', invited address to symposium sponsored by Psi Chi and American Psychological Association Committee on Women, Washington, DC, August.

——(1983) 'On ego development and the structure of personality', *Developmental Review* 3: 339–350.

——(1984) 'On the self and predicting behavior', in R. A. Zucker, J. Aronoff and A. I. Rabin (eds) *Personality and the Prediction of Behavior*, Orlando, FL: Academic Press.

——(1985) 'Revision of the Sentence Completion Test for ego development', *Journal of Personality and Social Psychology* 48: 420–427.

——(1987) *Paradigms of Personality*, New York: W. H. Freeman.

——(1991) 'Personality structure and the trait–situation controversy: on the use of low correlations', in W. M. Grove and D. Cicchetti (eds) *Thinking about Psychology*, vol. 2, Minneapolis: University of Minnesota Press.

——(1992) 'A century of character development', in S. Koch and D. E. Leary (eds) *Development*, Baltimore, MD: American Psychological Association.

——(1993a) 'Conformity and conscientiousness: one factor or two stages?' in D. C. Funder, R. D. Parke and C. Tomlinson-Keasy (eds) *Studying Lives Through Time: Personality and Development*, Washington, DC: American Psychological Association.

——(1993b) 'Measurement of personality: true or false?' *Psychological Inquiry* 4: 1–16.

——(1994) 'Has psychology lost its conscience?', *Journal of Personality Assessment* 62: 2–8.

——(1997) 'Stages of personality development', in R. Hogan, J. Johnson and S. Briggs (eds) *Handbook of Personality Psychology*, San Diego, CA: Academic Press.

——(1998a) 'History of the Sentence Completion Test (SCT) for ego development', in J. Loevinger (ed.) *Technical Foundations for Measuring Ego Devel-*

opment: The Washington University Sentence Completion Test, Mahwah, NJ: Lawrence Erlbaum Associates.

——(ed.) (1998b) *Technical Foundations for Measuring Ego Development: The Washington University Sentence Completion Test*, Mahwah, NJ: Lawrence Erlbaum Associates.

——(2002) 'Confessions of an iconoclast: at home on the fringe', *Journal of Personality Assessment* 78: 195–208.

Loevinger, J. and Blasi, A. (1991) 'Development of the self as subject,' in J. Strauss and G. R. Goethals (eds) *The Self: Interdisciplinary Approaches*, New York: Springer-Verlag.

Loevinger, J. and Wessler, R. (1970) *Measuring Ego Development*, vol. 1, San Francisco: Jossey-Bass.

Loevinger, J., Wessler, R. and Redmore, C. (1970) *Measuring Ego Development*, vol. 2, San Francisco: Jossey-Bass.

Loevinger, J., Cohn, L. D., Redmore, C. D., Bonneville, L. P., Streich, D. D. and Sargent, M. (1985) 'Ego development in college', *Journal of Personality and Social Psychology* 48: 947–962.

Logan, R. D. (1986) 'A reconceptualization of Erikson's theory: the repetition of existential and instrumental themes', *Human Development* 29: 125–136.

Lourenço, O. (1996) 'Reflections on narrative approaches to moral development', *Human Development* 39: 83–99.

McAuliffe, G. J. (1993) 'Constructive development and career transition: implications for counseling', *Journal of Counseling and Development* 72: 23–28.

McCarthy, J. B. (1995) 'Adolescent character formation and psychoanalytic theory', *American Journal of Psychoanalysis* 55: 245–267.

McClanahan, G. and Holmbeck, G. N. (1992) 'Separation–individuation, family functioning, and psychological adjustment in college students: a construct validity study of the separation–individuation test of adolescence', *Journal of Personality Assessment* 59: 468–485.

McCullers, C. (1946) *Member of the Wedding*, Boston: Houghton Mifflin.

McKinney, J. P. and McKinney, K. G. (1999) 'Prayer in the lives of late adolescents', *Journal of Adolescence* 22: 279–290.

Mahler, M. S. (1983) 'The meaning of developmental research of earliest infancy as related to the study of separation–individuation', in J. D. Call, E. Galenson and R. L. Tyson (eds) *Frontiers of Infant Psychiatry*, New York: Basic Books.

Mahler, M. S., Pine, F. and Bergman, A. (1975) *The Psychological Birth of the Human Infant*, New York: Basic Books.

Makros, J. and McCabe, M. P. (2001) 'Relationships between identity and self-representations during adolescence', *Journal of Youth and Adolescence* 30: 623–639.

Manners, J. and Durkin, K. (2000) 'Processes involved in adult ego development: a conceptual framework', *Developmental Review* 20: 475–513.

Manners, J. and Durkin, K. (2001) 'A critical review of the validity of ego development theory and its measurement', *Journal of Personality Assessment* 77: 541–567.

Mansfield, K. (1972) 'Prelude', in E. Bowen (ed.) *34 Short Stories*, London: Collins (originally published 1918).

Marcia, J. E. (1966) 'Development and validation of ego identity status', *Journal of Personality and Social Psychology* 3: 551–558.

——(1967) 'Ego identity status: relationship to change in self-esteem, "general maladjustment," and authoritarianism', *Journal of Personality* 35: 118–133.

——(1976a) 'Identity six years after: a follow-up study', *Journal of Youth and Adolescence* 5: 145–160.

——(1976b) 'Studies in ego identity', unpublished research monograph, Simon Fraser University, Burnaby, Canada.

——(1979) 'Identity status in late adolescence: description and some clinical implications', Identity Development Symposium, Gröningen, The Netherlands, June.

——(1980) 'Identity in adolescence', in J. Adelson (ed.) *Handbook of Adolescent Psychology*, New York: Wiley.

——(1983) 'Some directions for the investigation of identity formation in early adolescence', *Journal of Early Adolescence* 3: 215–223.

——(1986) 'Clinical implications of the identity status approach within psychosocial developmental theory', *Cadernos de Consulta Psicologica* 2: 23–34.

——(1993) 'Relational roots of identity', in J. Kroger (ed.) *Discussions on Ego Identity*, Hillsdale, NJ: Lawrence Erlbaum Associates.

——(1994) 'Ego identity and object relations', in J. Masling and R. F. Bornstein (eds) *Empirical Perspectives on Object Relations Theory*, Washington, DC: American Psychological Association.

——(2002) 'Identity and psychosocial development in adulthood', *Identity: An International Journal of Theory and Research* 2: 7–27.

——(2004). 'Why Erikson?', in K. R. Hoover (ed.) *The Future of Identity: Centennial Reflections on the Legacy of Erik Erikson*, Lanham, MD: Lexington Books.

Marcia, J. E. and Friedman, M. (1970) 'Ego identity status in college women', *Journal of Personality* 38: 249–263.

Marcia, J. E., Waterman, A. S., Matteson, D. R., Archer, S. L. and Orlofsky, J. L. (1993) *Ego Identity: A Handbook for Psychosocial Research*, New York: Springer-Verlag.

Markstrom-Adams, C. and Smith, M. (1996) 'Identity formation and religious orientation among high school students from the United States and Canada', *Journal of Adolescence* 19: 247–261.

Markstrom-Adams, C., Ascione, F. R., Braegger, D. and Adams, G. R. (1993) 'Promotion of ego identity development: can short-term intervention facilitate growth?', *Journal of Adolescence* 16: 217–224.

Markstrom-Adams, C., Sabino, V., Turner, B. and Berman, R. (1994) 'Adolescent ego resiliency: the Eriksonian measure of ego strengths', paper presented at the Biennial Meeting of the International Society for the Study of Behavioral Development, Amsterdam.

Marsden P., Meyer, C., Fuller, M. and Waller G. (2002) 'The relationship between eating psychopathology and separation–individuation in young nonclinical women', *Journal of Nervous and Mental Diseases* 190: 710–713.

Maslach, C., Stapp, J. and Santee, R. T. (1985) 'Individuation: conceptual analysis and assessment', *Journal of Personality and Social Psychology* 49: 729–738.

Masterson, J. F. (1986) 'Creativity as a vehicle to establish a real self: Jean Paul Sartre, Edvard Munch, Thomas Wolfe', in J. F. Masterson (ed.) *The Real Self: A Developmental and Object Relations Approach* (cassette recording 4), New York: Masterson Group.

Masterson, J. F. and Costello, J. L. (1980) *From Borderline Adolescent to Functioning Adult: The Test of Time*, New York: Brunner/Mazel.

Mazor, A., Alfa, A. and Gampel, Y. (1993) 'On the thin line between connection and separation: the individuation process, from cognitive and object-relations perspectives, in kibbutz adolescents', *Journal of Youth and Adolescence* 22: 641–669.

Meeus, W. and Dekovic, M. (1994) 'Identity development, parental and peer support in adolescence: results of a national Dutch survey', unpublished manuscript, Utrecht University, The Netherlands.

Michener, J. (1972) *The Fires of Spring*, New York: Random House.

Miller-Tiedeman, A. and Tiedeman, D. V. (1972) 'Decision-making for the 70s', *Focus on Guidance* 1: 1–15.

Millis, S. R. (1984) 'Separation–individuation and intimacy status in young adulthood', unpublished doctoral dissertation, University of Cincinnati.

Milne, L. C. and Lancaster, S. (2001) 'Predoctors of depression in female adolescents', *Adolescence* 36: 207–223.

Mitchell, V. (1993) 'The synthetic function in the study of personality', *Psychological Inquiry* 4: 37–40.

Modgil, S. and Modgil, C. (1986) *Lawrence Kohlberg: Consensus and Controversy*, London: Falmer Press.

Moore, D. and Hotch, D. F. (1981) 'Late adolescents' conceptualizations of home leaving', *Journal of Youth and Adolescence* 10: 1–10.

——(1982) 'Adolescent–parent separation: the role of parental divorce', *Journal of Youth and Adolescence* 11: 115–119.

——(1983) 'The importance of different home-leaving strategies to late adolescents', *Adolescence* 18: 413–416.

Moustakas, C. E. (1974) *Portraits of Loneliness and Love*, Englewood Cliffs, NJ: Prentice-Hall.

Munro, G. and Adams, G. R. (1977) 'Ego identity formation in college students and working youth', *Developmental Psychology* 13: 523–524.

Narvaez, D. (1998) 'The influence of moral schemas on the reconstruction of moral narratives in eighth graders and college students', *Journal of Educational Psychology* 90: 13–24.

Neill, A. S. (1972) *Summerhill: A Radical Approach to Child Rearing*, Harmondsworth: Penguin.

Nelson, J. R., Smith, D. J. and Dodd, J. (1990) 'The moral reasoning of juvenile delinquents: a meta-analysis', *Journal of Abnormal Child Psychology* 18: 231–239.

Nettles, E. J. and Loevinger, J. (1983) 'Sex role expectations and ego level in relation to problem marriages', *Journal of Personality and Social Psychology* 45: 676–687.

Nin, A. (1978) *Linotte: The Early Diary of Anaïs Nin*, New York: Harcourt Brace Jovanovich.

Noam, G. (1985) 'Stage, phase, and style: the developmental dynamics of the self', in M. Berkowitz and F. Oser (eds) *Moral Education*, Mahwah, NJ: Lawrence: Erlbaum Associates.

——(1988a) 'The self, adult development, and the theory of biography and transformation', in D. K. Lapsley and F. C. Power (eds) *Self, Ego, and Identity: Integrative Approaches*, New York: Springer-Verlag.

——(1988b) 'A constructivist approach to developmental psychology', in E. Nannis and P. Cowan (eds) *Developmental Psychopathology and its Treatment*, San Francisco: Jossey Bass, pp. 91–122.

——(1990) 'Beyond Freud and Piaget: biographical worlds – interpersonal self' in T. E. Wren (ed.) *The Moral Domain*, Cambridge, MA: MIT Press.

——(1992) 'Development as the aim of clinical intervention', *Development and Psychopathology* 4: 679–696.

——(1998) 'Solving the ego development–mental health riddle', in P. M. Westenberg, A. Blasi and L. D. Cohn (eds) *Personality Development: Theoretical, Empirical, and Clinical Investigations of Loevinger's Conception of Ego Development*, Mahwah, NJ: Lawrence Erlbaum Associates.

——(1999) 'Clinical and developmental perspectives on adolescent coping', *Child Psychiatry and Human Development* 30: 87–101.

Noam, G. G., Kohlberg, L. and Snarey, J. (1983) 'Steps toward a model of the self', in B. Lee and G. G. Noam (eds) *Developmental Approaches to the Self*, New York: Plenum.

Noam, G. G., Powers, S. I., Kilkenny, R. and Beedy, J. (1991a) 'The interpersonal self in lifespan developmental perspective: theory, measurement and longitudinal case analyses', in P. B. Baltes, D. L. Featherman and R. M. Lerner (eds) *Lifespan Development and Behavior* 10: 59–104.

Noam, G. G., Recklitis, C. J. and Paget, K. F. (1991b) 'Pathways of ego development: contributions to maladaptation and adjustment', *Development and Psychopathology* 3: 311–328.

Novy, D. M. (1993) 'An investigation of the progressive sequence of ego development levels', *Journal of Clinical Psychology* 49: 332–338.

Novy, D. M., Gaa, J. P., Frankiewicz, R. G., Liberman, D. and Amerikaner, M. (1992) 'The association between patterns of family functioning and ego development of the juvenile offender', *Adolescence* 105: 25–35.

Novey, D. M., Frankiewicz, R. G., Francis, D. J., Liberman, D., Overall, J. E. and Vincent, K. R. (1994) 'An investigation of the structural validity of Loevinger's model and measure of ego development', *Journal of Personality* 62: 87–118.

O'Brien, K. M. (1996) 'The influence of psychological separation and parental attachment on the career development of adolescent women', *Journal of Vocational Behavior* 48: 257–274.

Offer, D. (1991) 'Adolescent development: a normative perspective', in S. I. Greenspan and G. H. Pollock (eds) *The Course of Life, Vol. IV: Adolescence*, New York: International Universities Press.

Offer, D. and Offer, J. (1974) 'Normal adolescent males: the high school and college years', *Journal of the American College Health Association* 22: 209–215.

Orlofsky, J. L. (1976) 'Intimacy status: relationship to interpersonal perception', *Journal of Youth and Adolescence* 5: 73–88.

Orlofsky, J. and Frank, M. (1986) 'Personality structure as viewed through early memories and identity status in college men and women', *Journal of Personality and Social Psychology* 50: 580–586.

Orlofsky, J. L., Marcia, J. E. and Lesser, I. M. (1973) 'Ego identity status and the intimacy versus isolation crisis of young adulthood', *Journal of Personality and Social Psychology* 27: 211–219.

Oser, F. K. (1996) 'Kohlberg's dormant ghosts: the case of education', *Journal of Moral Education* 25: 253–275.

Osgood, C. (1991) 'Readiness for parenting teenagers: a structural-developmental approach', unpublished doctoral dissertation, University of Massachusetts.

Otto, C. (2000) 'Grabbing the tiger by the tail, a conversation with Robert Kegan'. Available http://www.dialogonleadership.org/interviewKegan.html (accessed 6 July 2004).

Palmer, T. B. (1974) 'The youth authority's community treatment project', *Federal Probation* 38: 3–14.

Papini, D. R., Micka, J. C. and Barnett, J. K. (1989) 'Perceptions of intra-psychic and extrapsychic functioning as bases of adolescent ego identity status', *Journal of Adolescent Research* 4: 462–482.

Perosa, L. M., Perosa, S. L. and Tam, H. P. (1996) 'The contribution of family structure and differentiation to identity development in females', *Journal of Youth and Adolescence* 25: 817–837.

——(2002) 'Intergenerational systems theory and identity development in young adult women', *Journal of Adolescent Research* 17: 235–259.

Perron, J., Vondracek, F. W., Skorikov, V. B., Tremblay, C. and Corbiere, M. (1998) 'A longitudinal study of vocational maturity and ethnic identity development', *Journal of Vocational Behavior* 52: 409–424.

Phinney, J. S. (1989) 'Stages of ethnic identity development in minority group adolescents', *Journal of Early Adolescence* 9: 34–49.

——'Understanding ethnic diversity: the role of ethnic identity', *American Behavioral Scientist* 40: 143–152.

Phinney, J. S. and Chavira, V. (1992) 'Ethnic identity and self esteem: an exploratory longitudinal study', *Journal of Adolescence* 15: 271–281.

Phinney, J. S. and Rosenthal, D. A. (1992) 'Ethnic identity in adolescence: process, content, and outcome', in G. R. Adams, T. P. Gullotta and R. Montemayor (eds) *Adolescent Identity Formation: Advances in Adolescent Development*, vol. 4, Newbury Park, CA: Sage.

Piaget, J. (1932) *The Moral Judgment of the Child*, London: Kegan Paul.

——(1952) *The Child's Conception of Number*, New York: Norton.

——(1967) 'On the nature and nurture of intelligence', invited address delivered at New York University, March.

——(1969) *The Psychology of the Child*, New York: Harper Torchbooks.

Pine, F. (1985) *Developmental Theory and Clinical Process*, New Haven: Yale University Press.

——(1990) *Drive, Ego, Object, and Self*, New York: Basic Books.

——(1992) 'Some refinements of the separation–individuation concept in light of research on infants', *Psychoanalytic Study of the Child* 45: 179–194.

Pinquart, M. and Silbereisen, R. K. (2002) 'Changes in adolescents' and mothers' autonomy and connectedness in conflict discussions: an observation study', *Journal of Adolescence* 25: 509–522.

Podd, M. H. (1972) 'Ego identity status and morality: the relationship between two developmental constructs', *Developmental Psychology* 6: 497–507.

Podd, M. H., Marcia, J. E. and Rubin, B. M. (1970) 'The effects of ego identity and partner perception on a prisoner's dilemma game', *Journal of Social Psychology* 82: 117–126.

Power, C. (1991) 'Lawrence Kohlberg: the vocation of a moral psychologist and educator. Part 1', in W. M. Kurtines and J. L. Gewirtz (eds) *Handbook of Moral Behavior and Development Vol. 1: Theory*, Hillsdale, NJ: Lawrence Erlbaum Associates.

Prager, K. J. and Bailey, J. M. (1985) 'Androgyny, ego development, and psychosocial crisis resolution', *Sex Roles* 13: 525–536.

Pratt, M. W., Diessner, R., Hunsberger, B., Pancer, S. M. and Savoy, K. (1991) 'Four pathways in the analysis of adult development and aging: comparing analyses of reasoning about personal-life dilemmas', *Psychology and Aging* 6: 666–675.

Quintana, S. M. and Kerr, J. (1993) 'Relational needs in late adolescent separation–individuation', *Journal of Counseling and Development* 71: 349–354.

Quintana, S. M. and Lapsley, D. K. (1990) 'Rapprochement in late adolescent separation–individuation: a structural equations approach', *Journal of Adolescence* 13: 371–385.

Rapaport, D. (1960) The structure of psychoanalytic theory: a systematizing attempt, *Psychological Issues* [Monograph 6], New York: International Universities Press.

Raskin, P. M. (1994) 'Identity and the career counselling of adolescents: the development of vocational identity', in S. L. Archer (ed.) *Interventions for Adolescent Identity Development*, Newbury Park, CA: Sage.

Rattansi, A. and Phoenix, A. (1997) 'Rethinking youth identities: modernist and postmodernist frameworks' in J. Bynner, L. Chisholm and A. Furlong (eds) *Youth, Citizenship and Social Change in a European Context*, Aldershot: Ashgate.

Recklitis, C. J. and Noam, G. G. (1999) 'Clinical and developmental perspectives on adolescent coping', *Child Psychiatry and Human Development* 30: 87–101.

Redmore, C. D. (1983) 'Ego development in the college years: two longitudinal studies', *Journal of Youth and Adolescence* 12: 301–306.

Redmore, C. D. and Loevinger, J. (1979) 'Ego development in adolescence: longitudinal studies', *Journal of Youth and Adolescence* 8: 1–20.

Redmore, C. D., Loevinger, J. and Tamashiro, R. (1978) 'Measuring ego development: scoring manual for men and boys', unpublished manuscript, St. Louis, MO: Washington University.

Rest, J. (1979a) *Development in Judging Moral Issues*, Minneapolis: University of Michigan Press.

——(1979b) *Revised Manual for the Defining Issues Test*, Minneapolis: Minnesota Moral Research Projects.

Rest, J., Turiel, E. and Kohlberg, L. (1969) 'Relations between level of real judgment and preference and comprehension of the moral judgments of others', *Journal of Personality* 37: 225–252.

Rest, J., Power, C. and Brabeck, M. (1988) 'Lawrence Kohlberg (1927–1987)', *American Psychologist* 43: 399–400.

Rest, J., Narvaez, D., Bebeau, M. J. and Thoma, S. J. (1999) *Postconventional Moral Thinking: A Neo-Kohlbergian Approach*, Mahwah, NJ: Lawrence Erlbaum Associates.

Rhodes, B. and Kroger, J. (1992) 'Parental bonding and separation–individuation difficulties among late adolescent eating disordered women', *Child Psychiatry and Human Development* 22: 249–263.

Rice, K. (1990) 'Attachment in adolescence: a narrative and meta-analytic review', *Journal of Youth and Adolescence* 19: 511–538.

Rice, K. G. (1991) 'Attachment and separation–individuation: a time-sequential study of late adolescents', paper presented at the Biennial Meeting of the Society for Research in Child Development, Seattle, April.

Rice, K. G., Cole, D. A. and Lapsley, D. K. (1990) 'Separation–individuation, family cohesion, and adjustment to college: measurement validation and test of a theoretical model', *Journal of Counseling Psychology* 37: 195–202.

Richmond, M. B. and Sklansky, M. A. (1984) 'Structural change in adolescence', in D. D. Brockman (ed.) *Late Adolescence: Psychoanalytic Studies*, New York: International Universities Press.

Rierdan, J. (1998) 'Ego development, pubertal development, and depressive symptoms in adolescent girls', in P. M. Westenberg, A. Blasi and L. D. Cohn (eds) *Personality Development: Theoretical, Empirical and Clinical Investigations of Loevinger's Conception of Ego Development*, Mahwah, NJ: Lawrence Erlbaum Associates.

Rogers, A. G. (1998) 'Understanding changes in girls' relationships and in ego development: three studies of adolescent girls', in P. M. Westenburg, A. Blasi and L. D. Cohn (eds) *Personality Development: Theoretical, Empirical, and Clinical Investigations of Loevinger's Conception of Ego Development*, Mahwah, NJ: Lawrence Erlbaum Associates.

Rogers, C. R. (1983) *Freedom to Learn for the 80's*, Columbus: Charles E. Merrill.

Rosenthal, D. A., Gurney, R. M. and Moore, S. M. (1981) 'From trust to intimacy: a new inventory for examining Erikson's stages of psychosocial development', *Journal of Youth and Adolescence* 10: 526–537.

Rossi, J. A. (1996) 'Creating strategies and conditions for civil discourse about controversial issues', *Social Education* 60: 15–21.

Rowe, I. and Marcia, J. E. (1980) 'Ego identity status, formal operations, and moral development', *Journal of Youth and Adolescence* 9: 87–99.

Rubin, K. H. and Trotter, K. T. (1977) 'Kohlberg's moral judgment scale: some methodological considerations', *Developmental Psychology* 13: 535–536.

Sabatelli, N. R. and Williams, D. E. (1993) 'A factor analytic examination of the adolescent individuation measure', paper presented at the Biennial Meeting of the Society for Research in Child Development, New Orleans, April.

Saintone, S., Achille, P. A. and Lachance, L. (1998) 'The influence of big brothers on the separation–individuation of adolescents from single parent families', *Adolescence* 33: 343–353.

Salyer, B. K. (1995) 'Adolescent self perceptions and developmental theory', unpublished doctoral dissertation, Harvard Graduate School of Education.

Sanders, J. L. (1998) 'Religious ego identity and its relationship to faith maturity', *Journal of Psychology* 132: 653–658.

Santos, P. J. and Coimbra, J. L. (2000) 'Psychological separation and dimensions of career indecision in secondary school students', *Journal of Vocational Behavior* 56: 346–362.

Sartre, J. P. (1964) *Words*, London: Hamish Hamilton.

——(1965) *Nausea*, Harmondsworth: Penguin (originally published 1938).

Schafer, R. (1973) 'Concepts of self and identity and the experience of separation–individuation in adolescence', *Psychoanalytic Quarterly* 42: 42–59.

Scharf, M. (2001) 'A "natural experiment" in child rearing ecologies and adolescents' attachment and separation representations', *Child Development* 72: 236–251.

Schenkel, S. and Marcia, J. E. (1972) 'Attitudes toward premarital intercourse in determining ego identity status in college woman', *Journal of Personality* 3: 472–482.

Schwarz, K. and Robins, C. J. (1987) 'Psychological androgyny and ego development', *Sex Roles* 16: 71–81.

Selles, T., Markstrom-Adams, C. and Adams, G. R. (1994) 'Identity formation and risk for suicide among older adolescents', paper presented at the Biennial Meeting of the Society for Research on Adolescence, San Diego, February.

Selman, R. L. (1980) *The Growth of the Interpersonal Understanding: Developmental and Clinical Analyses*, New York: Academic Press.

Seymour, R. D. (1991) 'Constructing a personal future time perspective', unpublished doctoral dissertation, Harvard Graduate School of Education.

Shaw, G. B. (1966) 'Major Barbara', in R. Cohn and B. Dukore (eds) *Twentieth Century Drama: England, Ireland, and the United States*, New York: Random House (first published in 1907).

Shulkin, A. (1990) 'Separation–individuation and identity status among late adolescent college students', unpublished doctoral dissertation, University of Minnesota.

Shulman, S. and Klein, M. M. (1993) 'Distinctive role of the father in adolescent separation–individuation', *New Directions for Child Development* 62: 41–57.

Silverberg, S. B. and Steinberg, L. (1987) 'Adolescent autonomy, parent–adolescent conflict, and parental well-being', *Journal of Youth and Adolescence* 16: 293–312.

Simmons, D. D. (1983) 'Identity achievement and axiological maturity', *Social Behavior and Personality* 11: 101–104.

Simpson, E. L. (1974) 'Moral development research: a case study of scientific cultural bias', *Human Development* 17: 81–106.

Skoe, E. E. (1993) Sex role orientation and its relationship to the development of identity and moral thought', *Scandinavian Journal of Psychology* 36: 235–245.

——(1993) 'The ethic of care interview manual', unpublished manuscript, University of Tromsø, Norway.

Skoe, E. E. and Diessner, R. (1994) 'Ethic of care, justice, identity, and gender: an extension and replication', *Merrill-Palmer Quarterly* 40: 272–289.

Skoe, E. E. and Gooden, A. (1993) 'Ethic of care and real-life moral dilemma content in male and female early adolescents', *Journal of Early Adolescence* 13: 154–167.

Skoe, E. E. and Marcia, J. E. (1991) 'A measure of care-based morality and its relation to ego identity', *Merrill-Palmer Quarterly* 37: 289–304.

Skoe, E. E. and von der Lippe, A. L. (2002). 'Ego development and the ethics of care and justice: the relations among them revisited', *Journal of Personality* 70: 485–508.

Skorikov, V. and Vondracek, F. W. (1998) 'Vocational identity development: its relationship to other identity domains and to overall identity development', *Journal of Career Assessment* 6: 13–35.

Slugoski, B. R. and Ginsburg, G. P (1989) 'Ego identity and explanatory speech', in J. Shotter and K. J. Gergen (eds) *Texts of Identity*, London: Sage.

Slugoski, B. R., Marcia, J. E. and Koopman, R. F. (1984) 'Cognitive and social interactional characteristics of ego identity statuses in college males', *Journal of Personality and Social Psychology* 47: 646–661.

Smolak, L. and Levine, M. P. (1993) 'Separation–individuation difficulties and the distinction between bulimia nervosa and anorexia nervosa in college women', *International Journal of Eating Disorders* 14: 33–41.

Snarey, J. (1985) 'Cross-cultural universality of social-moral development: a critical review of Kohlbergian research', *Psychological Bulletin* 97: 202–232.

Snarey, J. (1998) 'Ego development and the ethical voices of justice and care; an Eriksenian interpretation' in P. M. Westenberg, A. Blasi and L. D. Cohn (eds) *Personality Development: Theoretical, Empirical, and Clinical Investigations of Loevinger's Conception of Ego Development*, Mahwah, NJ: Lawrence Erlbaum Associates.

Snarey, J. and Keljo, K. (1991) 'In a *Gemeinschaft* voice: the cross-cultural expansion of moral development theory', in W. M. Kurtines and J. L. Gewirtz (eds) *Handbook of Moral Behavior and Development, Volume 3: Theory*, Hillsdale, NJ: Lawrence Erlbaum Associates.

Snarey, J., Kohlberg, L. and Noam, G. (1983) 'Ego development in perspective: structural stage, functional phase, and cultural age-period models', *Developmental Review* 3: 303–338.

Snarey, J., Friedman, K. and Blasi, J. (1986) 'Sex role strain among kibbutz adolescents and adults: a developmental perspective', *Journal of Youth and Adolescence* 15: 223–242.

Sochting, I., Skoe, E. E. and Marcia, J. E. (1994) 'Care-based moral reasoning and prosocial behavior: a question of gender or sex role orientation?', *Sex Roles* 31: 131–147.

Soldz, S. (1988) 'The construction of meaning: Kegan, Piaget, and psychoanalysis', *Journal of Contemporary Psychotherapy* 18: 46–59.

Souvaine, E., Lahey, L. L. and Kegan, R. (1990) 'Life after formal operations: implications for a psychology of the self', in C. N. Alexander and E. J. Langer (eds) *Higher Stages of Human Development: Perspectives on Adult Growth*, New York: Oxford University Press.

Speicher, B. and Noam, G. G. (1999) 'Clinical-developmental psychology', in R. L. Mosher, D. J. Youngman and J. M. Day (eds) *Human Development across the Life Span: Educational and Psychological Applications* Westport, CN: Praeger, pp. 105–129.

Sprinthall, N. A. (1994) 'Counseling and social role taking: promoting moral and ego development', in J. R. Rest and D. Narvaez (eds) *Moral Development in the Professions: Psychology and Applied Ethics*, Hillsdale, NJ: Lawrence Erlbaum Associates.

Stegarud, L., Solheim, B., Karlsen, M. and Kroger, J. (1999). 'Ego identity status in cross-cultural context: a replication study', *Psychological Reports* 85: 457–461.

Stephen, J., Fraser, E. and Marcia, J. E. (1992) 'Moratorium-achievement (Mama) cycles in lifespan identity development: value orientations and reasoning system correlates', *Journal of Adolescence* 15: 283–300.

Sterling, C. M. and Van Horn, K. R. (1989) 'Identity and death anxiety', *Adolescence* 23: 321–326.

Stern, D. N. (1985) *The Interpersonal World of the Infant*, New York: Basic Books.

Stevens, R. (1983) *Erik Erikson: An Introduction*, Oxford: Open University Press.

Streitmatter, J. (1993) 'Gender differences in identity development: an examination of longitudinal data', *Adolescence* 28: 55–66.

Sullivan, E. V. (1977) 'A study of Kohlberg's structural theory for moral development: a critique of liberal social science ideology', *Human Development* 20: 352–376.

Sullivan, H. S. (1953) *The Interpersonal Theory of Psychiatry*, New York: Norton.

Sullivan, K. and Sullivan, A. (1980) 'Adolescent–parent separation', *Developmental Psychology* 16: 93–99.

Swensen, C. H. (1980) 'Ego development and a general model for counseling and psychotherapy', *Personnel and Guidance Journal* 58: 382–388.

Tan, A. L., Kendis, R. J., Fine, J. T. and Porac, J. (1977) 'A short measure of Eriksonian ego identity', *Journal of Personality Assessment* 41: 279–284.

Teo, T., Becker, G. and Edelstein, W. (1995) 'Variability in strucctured wholeness: context factors in L. Kohlberg's data on the development of moral judgment', *Merrill-Palmer Quarterly* 41: 381–392.

Tesch, S. A. and Cameron, K. A. (1987) 'Openness to experience and development of adult identity', *Journal of Personality* 55: 615–630.

Thoma, S. J. (1994) 'Trends and issues in moral judgment research using the defining issues test', *Moral Education Forum* 19: 1–7.

Tokar, D. M., Withrow, J. R., Hall, R. J. and Moradi, B. (2003) 'Psychological separation, attachment security, vocational self-concept crystallization, and career indecision: a structural equation analysis', *Journal of Counseling Psychology* 50: 3–19.

Triandis, H. C. (1989) 'The self and social behavior in differing cultural contexts', *Psychological Review* 96: 506–520.

Tupuola, A. M. (1993) 'Critical analysis of adolescent development – a Samoan women's perspective', unpublished masters thesis, Victoria University of Wellington, New Zealand.

Turiel, E. (1966) 'An experimental test of the sequentiality of developmental stages in the child's moral judgments', *Journal of Personality and Social Psychology* 3: 611–618.

——(1969) 'Developmental processes in the child's moral thinking', in P. H. Mussen, J. Langer and M. Covington (eds) *Trends and Issues in Developmental Psychology*, New York: Holt, Rinehart and Winston.

——(1974) 'Conflict and transition in adolescent moral development', *Child Development* 45: 14–29.

——(1990) 'Moral judgment, action, and development', in D. Schrader (ed.) *The Legacy of Lawrence Kohlberg. New Directions for Child Development* 47: 31–49.

Vaillant, G. E. and Milofsky, E. (1980) 'Natural history of male psychological health: IX. Empirical evidence for Erikson's model of the life cycle', *American Journal of Orthopsychiatry* 137: 1348–1359.

Van Buskirk, W. and McGrath, D. (1999) 'Organizational cultures as holding environments: a psychodynamic look at organizational symbolism', *Human Relations* 52: 805–832.

Van Hoof, A. (1999). 'The identity status field re-reviewed: an update of unresolved and neglected issues with a view on some alternative approaches', *Developmental Review* 19: 497–556.

Vartanian, L. R. (1997) 'Separation–individuation, social support, and adolescent egocentrism: an exploratory study', *Journal of Early Adolescence* 17: 245–270.

Verhoef, H. and Michel, C. (1997) 'Studying morality within the African context: a model of moral analysis and construction', *Journal of Moral Education* 26: 389–407.

Villegas-Reimers, E. (1996) 'Self development of Venezuelan adolescents: a test of Kegan's theory and subject-object interview with another culture', *Journal of Cross-Cultural Psychology* 27: 25–36.

von der Lippe, A. L. (2000) 'Family factors in the ego development of adolescent girls', *Journal of Youth and Adolescence* 29: 373–393.

von der Lippe, A. L. and Møller, I. U. (2000). 'Negotiation of conflict, communication patterns, and ego development in the family of adolescent daughters', *International Journal of Behavioral Development* 24: 59–67.

Vondracek, F. W., Schulenberg, J., Skorikov, V. Gillespie, L. K. and Walheim, C. (1995) 'The relationship of identity status to career indecision during adolescence', *Journal of Adolescence* 18: 17–29.

Walker, L. (1980) 'Cognitive and perspective taking prerequisites for moral development', *Child Development* 51: 131–139.

——(1984) 'Sex differences in the development of moral reasoning: a critical review', *Child Development* 55: 677–691.

——(1989) 'A longitudinal study of moral reasoning', *Child Development* 60: 157–166.

——(1991) 'Sex differences in moral reasoning', in W. M. Kurtines and J. L. Gewirtz (eds) *Handbook of Moral Behavior and Development: Research*, vol. 2, Hillsdale, NJ: Lawrence Erlbaum Associates.

——(1995a) 'Sexism in Kohlberg's moral psychology?' in W. M. Kurtines and J. L Gewirtz (eds) *Moral Development: An Introduction*, Boston: Allyn and Bacon.

——(1995b) 'Whither moral psychology?', *Moral Educational Forum* 20: 1–8.

Walker, S. J. (1995) 'College students, alcohol, and drugs, and culture: an application of the theories and practices of Robert Kegan and Paulo Freire', unpublished doctoral dissertation, Harvard Graduate School of Education.

Wallerstein, R. S. (1998) 'Erikson's concept of ego identity reconsidered', *Journal of the American Psychoanalytic Association* 46: 229–247.

Walsh, C. (1999) 'Reconstructing Larry: assessing the legacy of Lawrence Kohlberg', *Harvard Education Bulletin* 43: 6–13.

Waterman, A. S. and Goldman, J. A. (1976) 'A longitudinal study of ego identity development at a liberal arts college', *Journal of Youth and Adolescence* 5: 361–369.

Waterman, A. S. and Whitbourne, S. K. (1981) 'The inventory of psychosocial development: a review and evaluation', *JSAS Catalog of Selected Documents in Psychology* 11 (ms. no. 2179).

Waterman, A. S., Geary, P. S. and Waterman, C. K. (1974) 'Longitudinal study of changes in ego identity status from the freshman to the senior year at college', *Developmental Psychology* 10: 387–392.

Welker, J. N. (1971) 'Observations and comments concerning young children in a preschool', unpublished manuscript, University of California, Davis.

Westenberg, P. M. and Gjerde, P. F. (1999) 'Ego development during the transition from adolescence to young adulthood: a 9-year longitudinal study', *Journal of Research in Personality* 33: 233–252.

Westenberg, P. M., Blasi, A. and Cohn, L. D. (1998a) *Personality Development: Theoretical, Empirical, and Clinical Investigations of Loevinger's Conception of Ego Development*, Mahwah, NJ: Lawrence Erlbaum Associates.

Westenberg, P. M., Jonckheer, J., Treffers, P. D. A. and Drewes, M. J. (1998b) 'Ego development in children and adolescents: another side of the impulsive, self-protective, and conformist ego levels', in P. M. Westenberg, A. Blasi and L. D. Cohn (eds) *Personality Development: Theoretical, Empirical, and Clinical Investigations of Loevinger's Conception of Ego Development*, Mahwah, NJ: Lawrence Erlbaum Associates.

Westenberg, P. M., Treffers, P. D. A. and Drewes, M. J. (1998c) 'A new version of the WUSCT: the sentence completion test for children and youths (SCT-Y)', in J. Loevinger (ed.) *Technical Foundations for Measuring Ego Development*, Mahwah, NJ: Lawrence Erlbaum Associates.

Westenberg, P. M., van Strien, S. D. and Drewes, M. J. (2001) 'Revised description and measurement of ego development in early adolescence: an artifact of the written procedure?', *Journal of Early Adolescence* 21: 470–493.

White, M. S. (1985) 'Ego development in adult women', *Journal of Personality* 85: 561–574.

White, R. (1959) 'Motivation reconsidered: the concept of competence', *Psychological Review* 66: 297–333.

Willemsen, E. W. and Waterman, K. K. (1991) 'Ego identity status and family environment: a correlational study', *Psychological Reports* 69: 1203–1212.

Winnicott, D. W. (1953) 'Transitional objects and transitional phenomena: a study of the first not-me possession', *International Journal of Psychoanalysis* 34: 89–97.

Wires, J. W., Barocas, R. and Hollenbeck, A. R. (1994) 'Determinants of adolescent identity development: a cross-sequential study of boarding school boys', *Adolescence* 29: 361–378.

Yates, M. and Youniss, J. (1996) 'Community service and political-moral identity in adolescents', *Journal of Research on Adolescence* 6: 271–284.

Yoder, A. E. (2000) 'Barriers to ego identity status formation: a contextual qualification of Marcia's identity status paradigm', *Journal of Adolescence* 23: 95–106.

Youniss, J. and Yates, M. (1997) *Community Service and Social Responsibility in Youth*, Chicago: University of Chicago Press.

Youniss, J., McLellan, J. A. and Yates, M. (1997) 'What we know about engendering civic identity', *American Behavioral Scientist* 40: 620–631.

Name index

Adamson, L. 202
Adams, G. R. 4, 37, 38, 40, 41, 42, 43, 44, 46, 47, 73, 78, 144–5, 146, 201, 202, 207
Aichhorn, A. 54
Akers, J. F. 42
Albee, E. 156–7
Alisho, K. C. 147
Allen, J. P. 145, 146, 147
Andersen, H. C. 53
Anderson, S. A. 82
Anthis, K. S. 43
Archer, S. L. 48
Armon, C. 113
Armstrong, J. G. 82
Attanucci, J. 108

Bagnold, E. 24
Bailey, J. M. 146
Bartle-Haring, S. 44, 83
Bar-Yam, M. 180
Baumeister, R. F. 2, 4
Baxter Magolda, M. B. 179, 187
Bell, D. C. & L. G. 201
Bellew-Smith, M. 80
Benson, M. J. 78
Bergman, I. 32–3
Bergman, R. 115
Berzonsky, M. D. 40, 46, 47, 51, 73, 146, 201
Bettelheim, B. 35
Beykema, S. 180
Bjornsen, C. A. 79
Blasi, A. 36, 46, 114, 130, 131, 137, 140–1
Blass, R. B. 71

Blatt, M. 119
Blatt, S. J. 71
Blos, P. 8, 10, 11, 17, 38, 53–89, 93, 124, 157, 173, 190, 191, 193, 194, 195, 198, 200, 205, 206, 207
Blum, L. 121
Blustein, D. L. 40, 45, 49, 78
Boles, S. A. 81
Borders, L. D. 154
Bosma, H. A. 43, 202, 206
Bowlby, J. 38
Boyes, M. C. 40, 41, 42, 109
Brandt, D. E. 72, 87
Breger, L. 8, 9
Brenman-Gibson, M. 50
Brickfield, L. 73
Broughton, J. 142
Brown, L. 108
Browning, D. L. 145
Buber, M. 30
Burlingham, D. 54, 77

Cameron, K. A. 41
Campbell, D. 125
Campos, B. P. 43, 149, 202
Candee, D. 115
Caplan, P. J. 35
Carlozzi, A. F. 154
Carlsson, V. 149
Carpendale, J. I. 109, 110, 112
Carroll, J. L. 113
Cebik, R. J. 154
Chandler, M. 40, 41, 42
Chapman, J. W. 73
Chavira, V. 43, 44
Choi, K. H. 83, 88

Ciaccio, N. V. 34
Cohn, L. D. 144, 145
Coimbra, J. L. 84
Colby, A. 93, 94, 99, 101, 104, 109, 112, 113, 116, 119, 120, 199, 207
Coleman, J. C. 80–1
Coles, R. 17
Constantinople, A. 34, 36
Cooper, C. R. 40, 41, 42, 78
Coppolillo, H. P. 62, 63
Costa, M. E. 43, 149, 202
Costa, P. T. 142
Costello, J. L. 70
Costos, D. 146
Côté, J. E. 4, 5, 8, 34, 41, 45, 46
Cramer, P. 43, 73, 147, 149, 207
Cushman, P. 3
Czyzowska, D. 112

Danielsen, L. M. 202
Darley, J. 115
Davidson, W. B. 79
Dawson, T. L. 113
Day, J. M. 110–11
Dekovic, M. 43
Denton, K. 109
Dewey, J. 118
Diessner, R . 114
Dill, D. L. 152, 153
Dixon, J. W. 177, 180
Doehrman, M. J. 69–70
Dolan, B. M. 75
Donovan, J. M. 73
Dostoevsky, F. 67
Douvan, E. 8
Dreiser, T. 61
Dreyer, P. H. 51
Dubow, E. F. 145, 146
Dunkel, C. S. 43, 202
Durkin, K. 139, 142, 143, 144, 148, 152–3, 196
Dyk, P. H. 41, 42, 44

Edgerton, J. 81–2, 87–8
Edwards, C. P. 111, 113
Einstein, A. 14
Ellis, A. 151, 186
Enright, R. D. 78
Erickson, V. L. 152
Erikson, E. 1, 2, 8, 10–11, 15–52, 54,
56, 64, 74, 78, 86, 93, 113, 125, 127, 157, 184, 190, 191, 193–4, 195, 196, 203, 205
Esman, A. H. 54, 55, 72, 77
Evans, R. I. 20, 29, 30, 31

Fairburn, W. R. D. 57
Feldberg, A. 86
Fitch, S. A. 40, 43, 144–5, 146, 202, 207
Fleming, W. M. 82
Flum, H. 45
Foster, J. D. 43, 200
Frank, M. 73
Frank, S. J. 41, 42
Franz, C. E. 35
Frenkel-Brunswik, E. 125
Freud, A. 17, 38, 53, 54, 61, 77
Freud, S. 16, 17, 18, 24, 25, 26, 27, 29, 31, 38, 58, 63, 64, 66, 77, 92, 163
Friedlander, M. L. 82
Friedman, L. J. 16, 17
Friedman, M. 41
Fromm, E. 123, 124, 130, 138
Frost, R. 190
Furman, E. 53

Garmon, L. C. 116
Gergen, K. J. 6
Gfellner, B. M. 114, 139, 145, 147, 148
Gilligan, C. 35, 71, 99, 107, 108, 116, 181
Ginsburg, G. P. 6
Ginsburg, S. D. 40, 73, 146, 147
Gjerde, P. F. 145, 196
Glaser, W. 151
Glodis, K. 36, 46
Gnaulati, E. 83
Goldman, J. A. 43
Goossens, L. 43, 45, 80
Green, K. 43, 72, 75, 146, 180, 181, 201
Greenberg, J. R. 57, 77
Gregg, V. 114
Greif, E. B. 106, 107
Grotevant, H. D. 40, 41, 42, 78
Guntrip, H. J. S. 57
Gutmann, D. 39

Haan, N. 114–15

Hamachek, D. E. 36
Harré, R. 107, 110
Hartmann, H. 38
Haslett, S. J. 40, 41, 42, 72, 73, 74
Hauser, S. T. 139, 141, 143, 147, 148, 196
Heine, B. J. 83
Henderson, A. F. 185
Henton, J. 82
Hesse, H. 15, 22
Heyert, Murray 168
Hickey, L. 120
Higgins, A. 119, 120
Hitler, A. 17, 54
Hock, E. 83
Hodgson, T. O. 180
Hoffer, E. 130
Holmbeck, G. N. 75, 79, 81, 82, 88
Holt, R. R. 137, 207
Hopkins, J. R. 17
Horner, T. M. 58
Hotch, D. F. 82
Hsia, L. C. 180
Hughey, K. F. 84
Hult, R. E. 114, 200
Humphreys, C. N. 79
Hunsberger, B. 45
Hurtig, A. L. 147
Huxley, A. 157
Hy, L. X. 138, 143

Ignelzi, M. 187
Isay, R. A. 72
Ivey, A. E. 49

Jacobson, E. 38, 57
Jahoda, M. 138
James, W. 19
Jennings, W. S. 120
Jensen, M. 202
Johnson, P. 73
Jones, R. M. 51, 78
Jordan, D. 73
Josselson, R. 7, 8, 40, 41, 42, 43, 70, 72, 73, 142

Kacerguis, M. A. 40
Kalsner, L. 83
Kaly, P. W. 51
Kaplan, A. 71,

Kaufman, K. S. 180
Kegan, R. 8, 10, 13, 93, 137, 156–89, 190, 191, 193, 194, 195, 196, 198, 199, 200, 204, 205, 207
Keljo, K. 111
Kernberg, O. 57
Kerr, J. 79
Kierkegaard, S. A. 33
King, M. L. 102
Kitchener, K. S. 114, 144, 147, 201
Klein, M. M. 79
Kohlberg, L. 8, 10, 12, 13, 90–122, 124, 127, 137, 150, 152, 157, 159, 163, 164, 165, 166, 169, 170, 172, 174, 175, 181, 190, 191, 193, 194, 195, 196, 198, 199, 200, 203, 207
Kohut, H. 57
Korn, J. H. 80
Kraemer, D. L. 82, 87
Kramer, R. 101, 106
Krebs, D. L. 109, 115, 116
Krettenauer, T. 145, 149
Kroger, J. 40, 41, 42, 43, 47, 50, 51, 71, 72, 73, 74, 75, 82, 86, 145, 146, 148, 171, 180, 181, 196, 200, 201, 205, 207
Kuk, L. S. 51
Kunnen, E. S. 43, 202, 206
Kurtines, W. 106, 107
Kutnick, P. 115

LaForce, B. 43, 200
Lahey, L. L. 174, 175, 176–7, 179, 181, 187, 188, 205, 208
Lancaster, S. 82
Langford, P. E. 116, 121
Lapsley, D. K. 75, 78, 80, 81–2, 87–8, 115
Larson, R. W. 81
Lasky, B. 115
Leake, C. 81
Leaper, C. 147
Lee, H. Y. 84
Leming, J. S. 120
Lerner, R. M. 4, 5
Levine, C. 4, 5, 8, 34, 41, 46
Levine, J. B. 75, 76
Levine, M. P. 82
Levinson, D. 125
Levitz-Jones, E. M. 42, 80

Loevinger, J. 8, 9, 10, 12–13, 93, 113,
    114, 123–55, 157, 176, 181, 190,
    191, 193, 194, 195, 196, 198, 200,
    201, 203, 207
Logan, R. D. 35
Lourenço, O. 111
Luther, M. 65

McAuliffe, G. J. 187
McCabe, M. P. 40
McCarthy, J. B. 77
McClanahan, G. 75, 79
McCrae, R. R. 142
McCullers, C. 1, 3–4
Macfarlane, J. W. 125
McGrath, D. 187–8
McKinney, J. P. & K. G. 45
Mahler, M. S. 11, 38, 57–8, 59, 60, 61,
    64, 72, 76, 77, 85, 87, 128, 157, 173,
    205, 206
Makros, J. 40
Manners, J. 139, 142, 143, 144, 148,
    152–3, 196
Mansfield, K. 28
Marcia, J. E. 35, 36–50, 71, 72, 73, 86,
    114, 181, 191, 193, 198, 199, 200,
    202–3, 205, 207
Markstrom-Adams, C. 36, 45, 51
Marsden, P. 82
Marshall, S. 4
Maslach, C. 74
Maslow, A. H. 128, 135, 138
Masterson, J. F. 10, 63, 70
Mazor, A. 79
Meeus, W. 43
Michel, C. 112
Michener, J. 209
Miller, I. U. 147, 148
Millis, S. R. 80
Milne, L. C. 82
Milofsky, E. 35
Mitchell, S. A. 57, 77
Mitchell, V. 142, 143
Moore, D. 82
Moustakas, C. E. 30
Munch, E. 63
Munro, G. 202
Muraven, M. 4

Narvaez, D. 119

Neill, A. S. 48, 117
Nelson, J. R. 114
Nettles, E. J. 146
Nicholls, J. G. 73
Niemczynski, A. 112
Nin, A. 128, 130–1, 132, 133–4
Noam, G. G. 142, 148, 149, 152,
    153–4, 160, 175, 176, 177, 207, 208
Novy, D. M. 144, 145, 147

O'Brien, K. M. 84
Offer, D. 8, 70
Offer, J. 8
Orlofsky, J. L. 40, 41, 42, 73, 80, 146,
    147
Oser, F. K. 121
Osgood, C. 180

Palmer, T. B. 154
Papini, D. R. 40, 42, 73, 200
Pearson, K. 175
Perls, F. 186
Perosa, L. M. 73, 78, 200
Perron, J. 44
Philips, S. D. 40
Phinney, J. S. 43, 44
Piaget, J. 13, 91, 93, 94, 99, 105, 106,
    107, 112, 113, 118, 157, 158, 159,
    163, 164, 165, 166, 172, 173, 176,
    181, 198
Pine, F. 58, 71
Pinquart, M. 78
Pistole, M. C. 83
Podd, M. H. 40, 42, 73, 113
Ponte, L. da 53
Prager, K. J. 146
Pratt, M. W. 181, 201

Quintana, S. M. 78, 79

Rapaport, D. 38
Raskin, P. M. 49
Rattansi, A. 6
Recklitis, C. J. 149
Redmore, C. D. 138, 145, 196
Rest, J. 91, 92, 113
Rhodes, B. 82
Rice, K. G. 78, 80, 81
Richmond, M. B. 70
Rierdan, J. 153

Robins, C. J. 146
Rogers, A. G. 145, 147
Rogers, C. R. 48, 49, 151, 184, 186
Rosenthal, D. A. 36
Rossi, J. A. 121
Roth, D. M. 82
Rowe, I. 40, 42, 113, 200
Rubin, K. H. 106

Saintonge, S. 75, 79
Salyer, B. K. 180
Sanders, J. L. 45
Sanford, N. 125
Santos, P. J. 84
Sartre, J. P. 63–4, 204
Schachtel, S. 138
Schafer, R. 71
Scharf, M. 83
Scharf, P. 120
Schenkel, S. 41
Schilling, K. M. 147
Schwartz, S. J. 54
Schwarz, K. 146
Selles, T. 42
Selman, R. L. 93, 175, 181
Serson, J. 17
Seymour, R. D. 180
Shaw, G. B. 90, 94–8, 100
Shea, J. A. 146
Shulkin, A. 73
Shulman, S. 79
Siegel, S. M. 82
Silbereisen, R. K. 78
Silverberg, S. B. 78
Simmons, D. D. 36
Simpson, E. L. 107, 108
Sklansky, M. A. 70
Skoe, E. E. 40, 41, 42, 44, 114, 116, 147, 201
Skorikov, V. B. 45
Slugoski, B. R. 6, 41, 42
Smith, M. 45
Smolak, L. 82
Snarey, J. 93, 111, 112, 113, 127, 137, 140, 141, 142, 143, 146, 201
Sochting, I. 44
Socrates 102
Souvaine, E. 173
Speicher, B. 175
Sprinthall, N. A. 152

Stegarud, L. 202
Steinberg, L. 78
Stephen, J. 41
Sterling, C. M. 40
Stern, D. N. 58
Streitmatter, J. 43
Strimple, R. E. 44
Sullivan, E. V. 107, 108
Sullivan, H. S. 126
Sullivan, K. & A. 82
Swensen, C. H. 150–1, 152, 154

Tappen, M. B. 110–11
Teo, T. 110
Tesch, S. A. 41
Thoma, S. J. 104
Tokar, D. M. 84
Triandis, H. C. 5
Trotter, K. T. 106
Tupuola, A. M. 5–6
Turiel, E. 99, 100, 101, 119, 206

Vaillant, G. E. 35, 137
Van Buskirk, W. 187–8
Van Hoof, A. 36, 46, 47
Van Horn, K. R. 40
Vartanian, L. R. 80
Verhoef, H. 112
Vermeulen, S. C. 116
Villegas-Reimers, E. 177, 180
von der Lippe, A. L. 114, 116, 147, 148, 201
Vondracek, F. W. 45

Walker, L. J. 108, 109, 113, 115, 116
Walker, S. J. 177, 180
Wallerstein, R. S. 38, 39
Walsh, C. 92, 116
Wandrei, M. L. 81, 82, 88
Wasserman, E. 117
Waterman, A. S. 34, 43
Waterman, K. K. 40, 42
Welker, J. N. 27
Wessler, R. 127, 138, 139
Westenberg, P. M. 139, 143, 145, 149, 196
Whitbourne, S. K. 34
White, K. M. 35
White, M. S. 152
White, R. 38

Willemsen, E. W. 40, 42
Winnicott, D. W. 38
Wires, J. W. 43
Wolfe, T. 10

Yale 17, 92

Yates, M. 121
Yoder, A. E. 45, 203
Youniss, J. 121

Zahaykevich, M. K.
142

Subject index

abandonment 86, 178; affiliation versus 191, 193
ability: to fantasize 27; to imagine 26
abortion 107
'abstinence' message 186, 187
abstractions 61
acceptance 44, 130, 147; child-rearing styles characterized by 146
accommodation 99; responses associated with transition 144
accomplishment 28, 59, 60, 78; failure to recognize and reward 29
achievement 24, 28, 37, 39–40, 42, 58, 73, 83, 146, 193; characterized by intrapsychic organization 72; ideal in educational opportunity for 48; ideological 51; measured against own standards 133; progressive movement to 43; providing opportunities for 184; secure in attachment style 74; social lip service to 48; strivings 134
acting-out behaviors 148, 153, 154
adaptation 4–5, 154
adaptive balance 26
adaptive processes 38
adjustment: college 81, 88; good 137; minority group 44; psychological 81; psychology of 138; psychosocial 81, 82; relationship optimal 83; social 78, 138
Adolescent Individuation Measure (Sabatelli and Williams) 74
Adolescent Separation Anxiety Test (Hansburg) 74
adult identities/states 3, 7

advertizing 3
affect 13, 157; heightened 68; relationship between cognition and 158–9; trainee 154
affective states/structures 57, 163; disorders 153; response 81; transformations in processes 7
affiliation: abandonment versus 191, 193; ideological 170; institutional 170, 172; interpersonal 165
age 114, 127, 135, 144; moral judgements become more advanced with 113; normative ranges 174; restrictions of 4; tasks related to 93–4; tolerance of solitude with 80–1; trends in ego development 145
agency 191; self-conceptions of 146; sense of 168
agents: active 4; external 85, 129; independent 11, 184; social 185; socialization 84, 93
aggression 154; directing against self 153
alienation 64
aloneness 81, 87; ability to tolerate 80; ultimate 31
ambiguity 134, 135
ambivalence 40, 73, 80
androgyny 40, 146
anger 170; excessive, freedom from 76; lifelong denial of 18
anxiety 12, 40, 41; avoiding or attenuating 126; capacity to tolerate some degree of 68; disorders 153; engulfment 79; generated by

residual trauma 65; keeping at bay 126; little room for 42; Oedipal 70; pre-adolescent 67; separation 179; separation 63, 77, 79, 81, 83; signal 77; test 152; working through 86
approval 131; group 132, 151; need for 12, 94, 170; parental 76, 86; seeking 41
arousal: impulse 67; sexual drive 85
arrest 7, 9–10, 12, 55; guides as to the most useful means of unblocking 190; separation- individuation 63
assertiveness courses 170
assessment 104; construct 179; meta-analytic 145; social cognition 181
assimilation 99
association 146; potential for 85
attachment 40, 42, 71, 78; conflicted 82; emotional 82; infantile 60; mixed profiles 41; non-autonomous 83; non-secure 74; parental 84; quality unaltered 60; romantic, extra-familial 60; secure 74, 81
attention: channeled outward 27; inescapable demand for 123
attention-deficit disorders 153
attitudes: adult, crucial 86; authoritarian 41; child-rearing 125, 140; collectivist 88; complacent 33; conformity to 13; ethnic, preexisting 44; generative 32; interpretation of 184; mental 19; moral 19, 117; mothers', 117; mothers', towards problems of family life 139–40; orders regulate 47; particular reference group 174; psychosocial 34; relationship 76; self very vulnerable to 169; sex role 40, 146; therapeutic 49
attributes 50
Austin Riggs Center 17
authenticity 151
authoritarianism 140
authority: adherence to 95, 103; group 165; obedience to 98, 99, 104; subject to question 105
authorship 193; self 170, 171, 179, 184
autism 58, 128; infantile 72
autobiographical writing 180
automotive senses 63

autonomous functioning 57, 86
autonomous self 12, 28; people with no sense of 118; successful establishment of 11
autonomous stage 128, 134, 134–5, 151, 152, 194
autonomy 40, 87, 107; developing a greater sense of 68; ego 69; families which have parents supporting 40; fathers' displays of 146; foreclosure 41; from external agents 129; individual 118; low 42; moral 106; primary and secondary 38; relationships which supported 79; respect for 135; shame and doubt/ will versus 25–6; threats to 171; training in 152
avoidances 65, 95, 98, 131, 132, 149
awareness 99, 134, 162; 'cutting edge' of 184; external objects 58; genuine limitations 29; mother's existence 59; potentially productive 54; *see also* self-awareness

'bag of virtues' approach 117, 118, 174
'barriers' concept 45
behavior therapy/strategy 151, 152
being 33, 116; newly emerging way of 159
beliefs 118, 176, 186; changed 171; ideological 49; irrational 151; moral 116; personally satisfying 151; political 37; religious 3, 37, 45; sex role 36
Berkeley 17, 125; Free Speech Movement 114–15
bias 116, 174; class 142; cultural 35, 107, 142; gender 106, 108
big brothers 79
biology 19, 29, 54; concern with early oral experience 24; role in personality development 18
body build 9
boundaries 29; common 58; internal balancing and rebalancing of 10; irreversible 65; managing 186; me-not me 188; protected 68; self and object/other 60, 159, 194; very defined 171; violation of 174
boys 35, 94; fond of talking in school

among themselves 67; girls achieve milestones in ego development earlier than 144; SCT for 138 'breakthrough' concept 162

California Youth Authority 154
capabilities 16
capability 168
capacities 65, 68, 118; cognitive 40, 58; cultural expectation and 186; developmental 162; ego, adaptive in environment 16; favoured 35; gap between demand and 180; mental 186; perceptual 58
care 108, 114, 116, 147; and concern 107
caring 31, 33
cathexis 16
causation 4, 34; psychological 128, 135
cause-effect relationships 186
chance agreements 37
change 13, 46, 119, 133, 171; capturing the essence of 162; cognitive 93, 163; creating conditions to disallow 181; demonstrated 120; developmental 43, 44, 80, 91; ethnic identity 44; future 39; individual 43; interpersonal 77; intra-individual 149, 179; intrapsychic 77, 85; linear or non-stage view of 8; model's sensitivity to 46; necessary forerunner of 99; opportunities for 33; personality 20, 144; physiological 29; pubertal 68; qualitative 7, 125–6; self open to 172; structural 148, 205–6
character 108, 115; Blos's different usages of the term 70; building 118; consolidation 194; development 144; healthy structure 68–9; moral 103, 115, 116; sketches 42
character formation 66, 68, 78, 126; nature of 55–6; optimal 64, 65, 77; phenomenon critical to 65; positive and negative effects on 64; reactive 65
character type 8–9
child rearing 42–3; attitudes towards

140; communal 35; diffusions' environments 73; ecologies 83; independence in 41; mothers' attitudes toward 125; styles 145–6
childhood antecedents 7
childhood 'I' 34; loss of 11
choice 35, 65; career 187; freedom of 4; friendship 42; greater alternatives for 50; moral 111, 120–1; negative identity 21; opportunity for 5; partner 30; self-determined 50, 51; structured 50; vindictive 21; vocational 17
client-centered approach 184
closeness 76, 184; renewed efforts for 87; withdrawal from 86
closure 50, 69; abrupt 67
Cluster school approach (Kohlberg) 121
cognition 12, 13, 146, 157; affect and 158–9; development of 12, 93, 105, 157; ego stage and 147; social 181; trainee 154
cognitive-developmental framework 90–122, 157, 158, 159, 160, 161, 162, 167
cognitive differences 39
cognitive distortion 115
cognitive functioning 113, 119, 127, 176; disequilibrium in 99; physical-mathematical 147; social-interpersonal 147
cognitive performance 181
cognitive processes 7
cognitive structure 99, 147, 163
cognitive style 12, 144; less integratively complex 42
coherence 50; losing 159
collectivist societies 5, 88
commitment 23, 30, 36, 185; career 78; external influences on 45; foreclosure, direct challenge to 50; identity defining 39; ideological 191, 193; individuals unable to make 42; moral 117, 120–1; no willingness to question 42; organizational 172; premature, rewarding 50; professional 54; protective factor against floundering inability to make 78;

relationship, reluctance for 40; religious 45; sexual 191, 193; shying away from 41; two distinct types of 37; vocational 191, 193

communion 31; self-conceptions of 146

community 47–8; absence of 3; desire to adhere to rules 98; enemy agents' 130; importance of 5, 10; just' 120; provides recognition 24; relationship to 97; services to 45; way in which it distributes its desirable assets 103

competence 28, 79; limitless 29; moral 109

complexity 142, 163, 177, 179; cognitive 41, 126, 135, 140; conceptual 131, 133, 137; developmental 153, 207–8; inner life 132; integrative 181; meaning construction 174–5

compulsions 65

concerns 186; cultural 187

concrete operational thought 105, 164, 168

conduct disorders 153

conflict: affiliation versus abandonment 193; autonomous stage, ability to transcend 135; bipolar 23; effectively facilitating 187; externalized 49; failure to resolve favorably 50; final stage of development 32; frequently externalized 134; identity 19, 43; inferiority 29; instinctual 68; integrity versus despair 33; internal 134; intrapsychic 61; irreconcilable 18; justice 103; likely to cause distress 151; love and work 176; moral 110; optimal resolution to 47; perceived 43; possible ways of negotiating 29; psychosocial alternative creating 31; resolving 47, 48, 152; toddler's 59; unconscious 30; value 107

conformist stage 127, 130–1, 132, 136, 137, 138, 139, 142, 145, 150, 151, 193

conformity 13, 40, 98–9, 124, 130–1, 133; interpersonal 96; norms 124, 138; parents encourage 42; peer pressure 137

confrontation 86

confusion 156; commitment and 37; identity and role 36, 191

connectedness 78

connection 173, 191, 104

conscientious stage 127–8, 131, 132–4, 136, 138, 142, 151, 152, 153

consciousness 173; 1st order 166; 2nd order 168, 185; 3rd order 169, 185; 4th order 170, 180, 185, 186, 187, 188; 5th order 172

consequences 82, 105; avoiding breakdown in the system regardless of 97; long-term 86; maintaining expectations regardless of 96; negative 187; physical or hedonistic 95; social, adaptive 109–10; statistics on 186 consistency 106, 110; clarifying the meaning of 176; epistemological 176; implying 112; inter-item 175; internal 37, 104, 116, 139; self 126; work and intimacy 177

constructive-developmental framework 165, 178; confirming and joining guest's meaning-making system 184; current directions in research 180–1; exploration 188; historical backdrop to Kegan's model 175–6; implications for/from 163, 184, 187

constructs 39, 69–71, 80

context 9, 14, 16, 148; bridging 186; business 109; cultural 5, 18, 35, 47, 50, 78, 83, 149; ethnic 83; great discrepancies in demands of 6; historical 18, 23; importance of 11; interpersonal 13, 171; provisional 187; safe 50; self-embeddedness 165; shared 171; situational 110; social 17, 19, 23, 33, 84, 110, 125, 169, 185; therapeutic 158; university 72, 145; work 183

continuity 19, 21, 35; attachment to parents 78; ego 56; inner 24, 56; loss of 18; spatial and temporal 36, 46

contradiction 119, 182, 183, 183; internal 116

control 171; bodily functions 25; earliest opportunities to exercise 25; impulse 12, 124, 127, 129, 168, 191; locus of 4, 73; parental 82; primary conscious preoccupation 129; self 151
coordination 69
coping 68, 80, 176
counseling 48, 49, 86, 87–8, 150; career 187; efficacy 154; often regarded as panacea 182; university centres 152; vocational 50
creative space 188
Cronbach's alpha 37, 76, 139
cross-cultural studies 92, 111, 149
cross-sectional studies 111, 112, 113, 135, 147; hospitalized adolescents 149
cultural relativism 106
culture(s) 4, 27, 93, 109, 180; adolescent developmental stage foreign to 6; collectivist 83; communal 19; contemporary 108; diversity 109; folk 112; importance of 5; inheritance 186; interrelation of identity and 45; organizational 187, 188; predetermined roles 21; pre-literate and semi-literate 111; technologically advanced 7
curriculum 163, 185; academic psychology 138; dilemma 48; 'hidden' 117, 163; identity enhancing 51; narrow focus 145; relevant to genuine needs 49; traditional, role and abilities of students in 187

dating 37
death 32
debasement 64
décalage notions 141–2
decision-making 12, 37; career 78, 84; cooperative 183; planful, rational and logical strategies 40; *see also* moral decision-making
defenses 67, 87, 171, 176; effective 35; mature 73; mechanisms of 38, 149, 177; solidifying of 50
de-idealization 86
Deliberate Psychological Education programmes 152
delinquents 47, 114, 153
demands: context 6; cultural 180, 185; infantile, for immediate drive satisfaction 63; institutional 186; parental ego 60
denial 6; dependency 79; lifelong 18; physical needs 21; self 15
dependency: conflictual 88; denial of 79; family, shedding of 60, 71; infantile 85; less, on external sources of support 60; objects of 129
depression 153, 154; capacity to tolerate some degree of 68; freedom from 79; pubertal girls 153; relationship between subject-object balance and 178; symptoms of 82; three types of 178–9
desires 13, 160; reflection of 69; rules used in the service of one's own 129; teenage 186
despair 22, 32–4
destabilization 119
detachment 42, 64
development 5, 6, 9, 12; cognitive 12, 93, 105, 157; importance of mutuality to 24–5; intellectual 111; male and female 35; deviant 60; epitome of 31; evolutionary stages in 92; moral 91, 92, 106, 109, 112, 120, 144; moral judgement 104; moral reasoning 93, 94–101, 108, 110, 111–16; optimal 26, 29, 53, 74; orientation towards 174; personality 126; phallic stage 26; pre-Oedipal 38; progressive 87; proper rate and sequence of 23; psychosocial 114; regressive 87; slow, gradual, and unremarkable 70; stimulation 118; women's 71; *see also* ego development
developmental approaches 6–10
developmental contextualism 4, 5
developmental crises 59
developmental deficits 42; underlying 51
developmental stages 25, 32, 66–7
deviant foundations 54
diagnosis 126

differentiation 56, 78, 128, 173, 175, 193; contradiction to encourage 182; encouraging 185; environmental host must promote 184; gradual 172; increasingly complex 136; inhibited 86; inner 133; internalized object ties 71; intrapsychic 57, 58, 74; normative 72; optimal 79; premature 86; process begins of its own accord 86; self 12, 57, 73, 88; self-object 72, 74, 184; subphases 73

Differentiation of Self Inventory (Johnson *et al*) 73

diffusion 37, 42, 44, 45, 49, 50, 113, 146, 191, 193; decreased 51; individuals remaining stable in 46; little opportunity for internalizing parents 73; progressive movement from 43; relationships with family and peers 74

dilemmas 12, 101; abstract 109; curriculum 48; existential 178; far removed from real-life experiences 107; hypothetical 94, 103–4, 105, 107, 119; integrative complexity codings of 181; more pervasive 29; person-in-context 6; personal life 181; psychosocial 24, 191; real-life 109, 120; reasoning about, in a business context 109; standardized 114; transpersonal 110; updated 105; *see also* moral dilemmas

disapproval 98; group 130

discomfort 43; inner 15; seeds of 21

discontinuity 6

discrimination 69

discrimination units 175, 177, 179

disembeddedness 97, 98

disengagement 60

disequilibrium 99, 144, 148, 152, 153, 196; potential sources of 119

disobedience 91, 131

disorganization 148, 196

displacement 67

dissociation 82

dissolution 68

distance 64; understanding of new needs for 86

distancing: anxiety about 83; efforts at

87; emotional 73–4; intrapsychic techniques 63

distinctiveness 11

distortions 177

distress: conflict likely to cause 151; troubled individuals seeking relief from 54

DIT (Rest's Defining Issues Test) 103, 104, 105, 114

divorce 79

doubt 26

dread 33

drinking and driving 109

drives 62, 77; aggressive 67, 191; ego besieged by 7; immediate satisfaction 63; infantile 61; organization 68; procreative 31; sexual 67, 68, 85, 191

drug and alcohol culture 180

dynamic balance 23–4, 25

eating disorders 82

ectomorphs 9

education 48, 91, 111, 150, 185; civic, most appropriate goal of 102; failure to complete 187; medical 158; moral 116–17, 118, 119, 120, 174; psychological 49; secondary and tertiary 49; social 119; statistically significant relationship between ego development and 14; tertiary 137; without failure 169

ego: adaptive capacities/processes 16, 38; besieged by drives 7; cataclysmic changes 8; conflict among id, superego and 77; consolidation 66; decrease in control 67; defense mechanisms 38; established 38; growing control over instincts 67; helping to shape 10; important element of 194; inadequacy 61; independence of 87; indivisible 142; massive failure 50; mature organization 65; mediating 67; modal organization of 13; nature of 125–7; parental 7, 60; relatively intact 61; social conditions of choice promote development at puberty 35; structuralization of 74, 77

ego continuity 56, 65
ego development 12, 68, 73, 181;
environmental influences on 77;
Loevinger's paradigm 123–55;
moral reasoning and 113, 114;
social conditions of choice promote
35
ego functioning 12, 67, 69, 91, 176;
excessive responsibility for others
134; health versus illness not at
issue in Loevinger's model 137;
stages 128–37, 152; subdomains of
93, 102
ego ideal 67, 69
ego identity 23, 55, 72; 35; measuring
35–8; nature of 18–19; rudimentary
sense of 24
ego structure 131; qualitative change
in 7
ego synthesis 37
embeddedness 13, 159, 160, 161, 162,
164, 166, 167, 170, 172; cultures of
169, 182, 183; host culture of 184;
self 165, 168, 193; *see also
disembeddedness*
emotions 59, 61, 73, 176, 184; ability
to differentiate 132; constancy of
68; integrated dimensions of 175;
mixture of 179; parental 83;
rationality is devoid of 110
empathy 147, 184
encouragement 48, 87; gradual 50
endomorphs 9
energy 26; libidinal 27; sexual 67;
unlimited 32; vocational 29
engulfment 79; fear of 80, 86
environment 23, 77, 150; adapting to
24; home 28–9; social 27
EOM-EIS-II (Objective Measure of
Ego Identity Status-II) 37–8
epigenesis 20, 23, 35, 36, 38
equilibrium 100, 162; cognitive 99
esteem 169; *see also* self-esteem
Ethic of Care Interview 114
ethics 12, 91, 98–9, 103, 107, 116, 133,
147; care and justice reasoning 147;
peer 170; group 83
ethnicity 43–4; separation-
individuation and 78
evaluation 92; self 132, 186

evolutionary theory 101, 109, 163,
166, 169
evolutionary truces 160–1, 162, 164,
168, 171, 172; transitions between
178
excitement 107; sexual 67
existence 18; early months of 166;
meaning of 19, 33; own, no escape
from 15–16; previous 21; problem
of 123
existential issues 33, 151, 152
expectations 148, 169; androgynous
role 146; cultural 112, 163, 186;
failure to live up to 179; 'hidden
curriculum' 163; important others
in the social milieu 25; maintaining
96; mutual interpersonal 96; others'
interpreting the world via 127;
prescribed role 49; societal 19, 108,
185
experience 21, 157; can become the
source of sexual excitement 67;
external 168; infant interpersonal
56; internal 126, 168, 184; openness
to 4, 39, 41, 78; personal
organization of 19; personally
salient 152; pre-Oedipal 54;
subjective, following successful
individuation 11; unique 50
experimental schools 48, 54, 77
experiments 35, 47; social and sexual
roles 27
exploration 36, 43, 87, 129; career 49;
external influences on 45; guilt and
fear 86; new opportunities for 48;
open, occupational and ideological
alternatives 50; practising toddler
assisted in 86; self 51; tentative 59
expression: providing opportunities
for 184; self 4, 25; sexual 36, 37,
187; strong push toward 65; verbal
61
external objects 58, 81
externalization 149
externalizing disorders 154
extroverts 9

facilitative response 50
factor analyses 83, 140
failure 29, 50, 179, 184–5; dismal 31;

non-normative 193; schools concerned about education without 169

families 82, 186; authoritarian in ideology 140; communication coding system 148; contributions to discussions 147; extended 35; importance of 5; interpersonal relationships involving 78; negotiation scores 148; reconstituted 16; single-parent 79

Family Problem Scale (Loevinger) 139–40

family romance 167

fantasy 33, 167

fathers 62–3; absent through divorce 79; attachments to 78, 83; availability of 79; biological, search for 16; displays of autonomy and relatedness 146; role in separation-individuation 79

fears 27; engulfment 80, 86; homosexual 67; infantile reengulfment 63; merging and separateness 80; parental opposition 73; reflection 50; societal 186

feelings 133, 178; differentiating more clearly 132; internal, highly differentiated 130; moral 110; reflecting 184; sharing 184; vaguely defined 131

femininity 65, 146

feminist writers 71, 177

feudal structures 123, 124

fidelity 29, 36, 37

foreclosure 21, 37, 40, 41–2, 44, 45, 49, 49, 73, 74, 86, 146, 191, 193; daughters' ratings 83–4; decreased 51; direct challenge to commitments 50; individuals remaining stable in 46; progressive movement from 43; sons' scores 84

formal operational thought 113, 147, 164, 173; full 172

fragmentation 6

free associations 167

freedom 4, 76, 79; moral 118; new-found 123

frenetic activity 61, 68

friendships 13, 37, 180; choices 42; new, change as a result of 170; opposite sex 30; same-sex 67, 68

frustration 31, 161

functioning 101, 137; contributing to ego development 126–7

games of skill and knowledge 164

GAP Report (Group for the Advancement of Psychiatry 1968) 78

gender 43–4, 79, 148; bias 106; differences 114, 144, 180; orientations related to morality 116; restrictions of 4

generational issue 19

generativity 31; versus stagnation/care 31–2

genesis 20

genital maturity 29, 31, 54

genitality: fully developed 29; infantile 26

girls 35; achieve milestones in ego development earlier than boys 144; development of moral reasoning for 108; pubertal, depressed 153; SCT originally developed for 138

goals 15, 16, 26, 101–2, 186; far-reaching 27; long-term 132, 133; moral 115, 118; occupational 49; refusal to sacrifice own 138; self-evaluated 132

gratification: direct 67; drive 61; impulse 167; narcissistic 86; self 95

guidance 30, 32, 53, 124

guilt 133, 153, 178; excessive, freedom from 76; explorations of 86; initiative versus 26–7; potential for 27

habits 168

happiness 20, 118

hedonism 95

heterosexuality 66, 68

hidden curriculum 117, 163

historical approaches 2–3, 7, 56

holding environments 167, 187; institutional 172; natural 182; optimal 182, 184; successfully fulfilled functions 183

holding function 169, 183
holism 12, 13, 124, 127
home-leaving strategies 82, 83, 88
homosexual fears 67
hope 25
hopelessness 42
human rights 98, 114
humanistic approach 152
humiliation 179
humor 39

'I' and "Thou" concepts 30, 87
id 16, 38, 55; conflict among ego, superego and 77
idealization 61, 67
ideals 133
ideas: ability to unite and integrate 135; elaborated 147
identification 10, 16, 20, 37, 146; earlier 22, 24, 34; generative individuals provide models needed for 3; identity reached through 49; object relations models focus on 77; positive 28; previous 21; significant 11, 35; social roles 124; striving to provide new models for 50
identity: basis of 124; firm sense of 80; gender 65; health or pathology of 101; Kegan's view of 158–63; Kohlberg's view of 93–4; moral 98, 116, 120; negative 21, 64; positive 21; problem of 1–14, 29, 123–4; religious 45; role confusion/fidelity versus 29–30, 191; self-determined 118; sex role and ego development 146; structural indicator of 94; unique 73, 123; vocational 17, 28, 45
identity crisis 17, 24, 29, 37; caused 87; conditions for 35
identity formation 3, 12, 24, 29, 33, 113; adaptive 50; agency and 45; appreciation of 7; array of empirical inquiries into 35; contextual implications and 5; developmental theories of 135; different dimensions of 36; distinguished from childhood processes 20; epigenetic scheme of 35; Erikson's approach to 16;

ethnic 43, 44; examining the nature of 17; gender differences 43, 44; healthy 56, 173; lifelong challenge of 8; longitudinal study of 171; most meaningful basis for 47; optimal 10, 23, 53; published studies of the process 36; research findings on 39–45; sexual 56; straightforward 6; understanding 4, 9, 14, 18; vital step toward 78; *see also* meaning-making
identity statuses 36–51, 72, 113, 114, 146, 181, 191, 193; statuses, psychosocial 72
identity synthesis 10–11, 15–52
ideologies 19, 63; cultural 4; family, authoritarian 140
idolization 61
image 160; incorporation of another's 20; internalized 10, 11, 53, 85; maternal 59
imaginary audience phenomenon 80
immigrants 2, 128
imperial balance 174, 185, 191; growth and loss of 168–9; making meaning from 183
impressions 16, 17
impulse arousal 67
impulse control 12, 124, 127, 152; through desire for social acceptance 130
impulses 13, 127, 129, 160, 164, 166; aggressive 139; coordinating 168; growth and loss of balance 166–8; inability to separate self from 161; instinctual 67; self subject to its own 167
impulsive stage 129, 139
impulsivity 153
inconsistency 109; contextual 112, 113
incorporative phase 166
independence 56, 78, 83, 87; attitudinal 76; conflictual 76, 88; declarations of 85; emotional 76, 134; field 73; functional 76; psychological 186; transition to a new form of 170
individual differences 131–2, 144; recognition of 134

individualism 95, 164
individualistic stage 128, 134, 151, 152
individuality 13, 152; coexistence of
    connectedness and 78; increased
    sense and appreciation of 134;
    lifelong 59; savouring of 135; strong
    sense of 128
individuation 74, 78; human
    aspirations for 10; infant 71; second
    11, 53–89; successful, subjective
    experience following 11
Individuation Scale (Maslach) 74
industry versus inferiority 27–9, 191
infancy 59; character origins begin in
    56; foundations of 'I' formed in 1;
    internal representations of
    relationships during 38;
    introjection during 10; master trait
    of personality comes into being
    during 12; newborn, state of affairs
    for 128; psychoanalysis and 140;
    reflexes 166; relatedness beyond 71;
    separation and individuation 11;
    subphases of 58, 85, 86; trustful
    interplay with parental figure
    during 20
infantile objects 71
inferiority 26; industry versus 27–9,
    191; perpetrators of 29
influences 3, 5; technological 4
inhibitions 65, 86
initiative versus guilt/purpose 26–7
injury: emotional 64; re-experiencing
    56; serious 86
injustice 92, 100
inner life 127, 130; complexity of 132;
    describing 132; descriptions of 131,
    132; rich 133
inner space 34, 35
inpatient samples 153
insight 48, 54, 85; intrapsychic
    developments 80; mutually
    discovered 161
instincts 67
institutional balance 178, 180, 185;
    growth and loss of 170–2
institutions 172; *see also* social
    institutions
integrated stage 128, 135–7
integration 69, 173; character, reliving

trauma for 64–5; social 68;
    structural 68
integrity 47; versus despair/wisdom
    32–4
intellectual processes 19
intelligence 40, 143; poor measure of
    137; sensori-motor 166; verbal 114
intention 105, 187; making impossible
    any understanding of 164
interaction 106, 182; caretaker-child
    1, 24; challenging 146; family 79,
    147, 148; governed equally by
    internal representations 57;
    individual-contextual systems 5;
    interpersonal 77; person-context 4;
    reciprocal 4; stereotypic or merge
    styles of 42
interdependence 135
interests 20, 49, 68, 168, 169, 185;
    ability to coordinate 169;
    compulsive 67; finding or
    reconnecting with 50;
    interdisciplinary 158; self
    normatively embedded in 13; self-
    protective 191; sexual 66, 67
interindividual balance 194; growth of
    172–3
internal objects 64
internal representations 57, 60, 160;
    restructuring of 57
internalization 43, 56, 112; behavioral
    problems in childhood 149;
    responsibility 136; rules 94, 150;
    successful 20; *see also* parental
    internalizations
internalized object ties: differentiation
    from 71; disengagement from 193
internalizing disorders 154
interpersonal balance 168, 177–8,
    183, 184, 185, 193; demands for
    185; growth and loss of 169–70
interpersonal concordance 164, 170,
    193
interpersonal relationships 126, 169;
    characterized by a wary,
    manipulative mode 129; diffusions
    distant and withdrawn 42;
    foreclosures 'well behaved' 42;
    intensive and responsible 133;
    involving family and peers 78; more

mutual 135; stereotyped and formalized 31; volatility and intensity in 40
interpersonal strategies 149
interpersonal style 12, 144
interpretation 86, 184
intervention 117, 119; appropriate 10; behavioural 152; counseling 150; developmental, generally more effective 51; direct 49; educational 48, 50, 120, 137; implications for 153, 162; justifiable goals for 174; naturalistic models of 182; school-based 51; short-term techniques 48, 51; teacher-induced 120; therapeutic 48, 66, 86, 150, 170
interviews: extensive 105; innovative, qualitative 106; moral dilemma 116; moral judgement 181; semi-structured 103, 174–5; subject-object 179–80, 181
intimacy 29, 35, 40, 44, 80, 184; capacity for 41; consistency within 177; isolation/love versus 30–1, 193–4
intra-personal processes 4
intrapsychic factors/issues 10, 40, 41, 82, 159; differentiation 42, 58, 74; functioning 16; object ties 62; parental representation 53, 56; separation and individuation processes 82
intrapsychic organization 11; achievements characterized by 72; parallels with the symbiotic phase 73; shaken to the core 68; underlying, clues as to 72
intrapsychic restructuring 7, 59, 60; allowing time for it to occur 85; crucial gauge of success in 78; modified application of separation and individuation to 71
intrapsychic structure 59; continued efforts to test 86; undifferentiated from early object ties 81
introjection 20; during infancy 10; generative individuals provide models needed for 31; identity reached through 49
introspectiveness 78

introverts 9
invalidism 32
invulnerability/omnipotence complex 80
IQ (intelligence quotient) 149
ISI (Identity Status Interview) 36–7
isolation 31, 42; intimacy versus 30–1, 193–4

judgement 94; and action 114; mature 32; moral 118; poor 68; reliance on others 41; *see also moral judgement*
justice 101, 102, 107, 108; abstract notion of 98; condition for development to more advanced understanding of 120; conflicts of 103; differing constructions or meanings of 93; ethic of 116; imminent 105; institutional, higher stage of 120; moralities of 105; new and higher stages of orientations to 119; racial 121; reasoning 94; role of superego for determining concepts of 92; social 92, 194; universal 91, 102

kibbutz settings 35, 80, 83, 91
kinship network 2
knowing 108

labels 9, 47, 95, 129
language: constitutes meaning 110; developing 26, 128; tool for communication with others 27; verbal 61
latency 60, 66, 191; earlier relationships, withdrawal from 86; key function of 67; sexual 27
law 91, 92, 94; upholding 103; violation of ethical codes 98
law-and-order orientation 97, 172
leave-taking 82
legal systems 47, 96, 97, 98; requirements 4
libidinal issues: drivers 16; energy 27; needs 35; object constancy 59, 72, 87
life history 18
Likert Scale format 37, 76
linguistic skills/function 25, 27

listening 49
locomotor skills 25, 26, 59, 86
logic 48, 98, 99; based on internalized
    ethical principles 12;
    developmental differences in 163;
    moral 97, 102, 105, 108, 113, 114,
    119, 191, 193; probing questions
    asked to clarify 104; transcended
    97; underlying 99
logical thinking 158
loneliness 42, 107; unbearable 178
longings 173
loss 10; childhood 'I' 11; early,
    multiple and severe 63; ego identity
    19; object 31, 62; sameness and
    continuity 18; to toddler 59;
    transition involves 162
love 30, 69, 108; examined within 176;
    extra- familial 194; satisfaction in
    adult world of 14; sexual 66, 68;
    transcending an idealized notion of
    186
love objects: first, separation from 87;
    internalized, de-idealization of 86;
    new 60
loyalty 95, 185; unquestioning 117–18

macro-sociological factors 45
maladjustment 153
manic depressive 9
manipulation 129
marriage break-up 16
masculinity 65, 79, 146
mass movements 130
mastery 26; desperate attempt at
    regaining 21
maternal incorporation 59
maturation 60, 62, 65, 126, 139; better
    adaptation related to 154; cognitive
    and biological 108; developmental
    patterns of 144; family structure
    capable of supporting and
    encouraging 78; forward surge 60;
    link between higher levels of
    cognitive structure and 147;
    pubertal 67; steady, nontumultuous
    70
maturity 154; career 84; complexity
    and 142; conscientious stage of 119,
    134; further movement toward 9;

genital 29, 31, 54; limits in 135;
    moral 106; most commonly
    occurring state of 136; regression in
    145; religious faith 45
maximalist structural theories 175,
    176
meaning: coherent, search for 127;
    language constitutes 110; literal 20;
    personal, breakdown of 18; shared,
    absence of 3; striving for 126;
    unique 10; social, constructions of
    164
meaning-making 13, 156–89
meaninglessnes 179
mental health: good, no absolute
    model of 174; positive 137, 138;
    relationship between ego
    development and 150, 153
merger 58, 61
mesomorphs 9
metaphysical features 101
micro-sociological factors 45
milieus 38; cultural 19, 29; social 6,
    25, 28, 34
minimalist structural theories 175
minority groups 44
mirroring 79
mistrust 76, 130; trust versus 24–5
MJI (Kohlberg's Moral Judgement
    Interview) 103–4
mobility 62
mood 60, 63
moral action 114, 115, 116
moral decision-making 12, 94, 107,
    109, 115; advanced levels of 120;
    enhancing levels of 91; Kohlberg's
    three levels 115; post-conventional
    reasoning in 113; prime
    considerations in 95
moral dilemmas 99, 106, 107, 109,
    112, 115; care-oriented versus
    justice-oriented 116; hypothetical
    119; teacher-led discussions about
    119
moral judgement 12, 103, 110, 119,
    181; advanced with increasing age
    113; foreclosures 42; inconsistency
    in 109; motives which drive 96;
    objective measure of 104; proposals
    for linking moral behavior with 115

moral realism 94; logic of 105
moral reasoning 12, 40, 44, 91, 127,
 146, 172–3, 181; advanced levels of
 137, 141; alternative explanation
 for discrepancy 110; cognitive-
 developmental framework for
 describing 94; conventional 41, 42,
 96–7, 110; correlations between ego
 stage and 147; development of 93,
 94–101, 108, 110, 111–16, 120, 194;
 higher levels 41, 118, 119; historical
 backdrop to Kohlberg's model
 105–6; measuring 103–5; optimal
 level of 101–2; post-conventional
 40, 97–101, 109, 112, 113; pre-
 conventional 42, 95–6, 110, 113;
 principled 100, 147; programmes
 aimed to stimulate 152; significant
 changes in stage of 119–20;
 transitional 113; understood in
 multidimensional terms 110
moral relativism 94, 105
morale 18
morality 3, 90, 117, 120; attempt to
 incorporate new logic into 99;
 autonomous 106; black and white
 view of 97; centrality in self-
 definition 116; complex
 relationships among different
 aspects of 94; Confucian 109;
 domains of 115; gender-related
 orientations to 116; hedonistic
 orientation towards 169;
 heteronomous 95, 164;
 individualistic views 97;
 internalized 97; narcissistic 102;
 paradigm of social construction
 110; superego 106; 'true' 96;
 understanding 93, 108
moratoriums 37, 40–1, 42, 44, 47, 49,
 146, 193; movement from
 foreclosure or diffusion to 46;
 progressive movement to 43;
 psychosocial 49; vying for power 73
morphology 35
mothers: attachments to 78, 83;
 attempts at 'wooing' 59; attitudes
 towards problems of family life
 139–40; basic trust between child
 and 35; dim recognition of 58;

exasperated 161; experienced as
 separate person 59; external
 medium for infant's evolution 165;
 fathers less involved with offspring
 than 79; fine-tuning of responses
 between infant and 24; 'good
 enough' 86; job of 61; obedience to
 131; ordinary devoted mothering
 85; problems of, with young
 children 125; separation from 87;
 symbiotic fusion with 58
motivation 77, 115, 116; moral 103, 121
motives 96, 126, 176; underlying 132
motor skills 25
mourning 62, 162; earlier internalized
 ties to parents 77; working through
 86
multiple identities 6
mutual regulation 24
mutuality 150, 169; highly invested
 191; relationship 194; importance
 to development 24–5

narcissism 86, 102
narrative approach 110–11
nationality 124
needs 23, 95, 169, 185; conflicting 135;
 declaring more independently 170;
 genuine 48, 49; innermost 22;
 instinctual 77; libidinal 35;
 nurturance 74, 79; others',
 interpreting the world via 127;
 physical, denial of 21; primary 191;
 reflection of 69; self and others 107;
 self normatively embedded in own
 13; sensitivity to 29; stability of 168;
 verbal expression of 61
negative resolution 28
neo-behaviorist critiques 106
neonatal stages 58
nihilism 111
non-being 33
non-commitment 37
non-differentiation 58
non-self 128
normative developmental tasks 3
norms 120, 131; age 142; community
 98; conformity to 124; cultural 35,
 187; group 131; growth 174; legal
 102; social 4, 96, 138

obedience 95, 98, 99, 131
object constancy 59, 60; infant comes gradually to achieve a sense of 128; libidinal 72, 87
object relations 13, 38, 53–89, 157, 159, 160, 193; forerunner to 39; theorists' delineation of ego 158
object representation 73
observation 18, 69; cognitive-developmental 167; extensive 105; healthy mother-infant and mother-toddler dyads 57; theoretical and clinical 72
Oedipus complex 38, 167; anxieties 70; consolidation 67, 191; necessary return for completion of 65–6; reactivation of childhood issues 56; resolution to 54, 58, 66, 68
old age 22, 23; alone in 33; potential for despair in 32; social participation in integrity of 47
omnipotent system 58
openness 42, 119; new experiences 4, 39, 41, 78
opportunism 111, 129
organismic insult 56
organizations 172, 181, 184; intrapsychic 191, 193
outpatient samples 153
overidentification 73

pain 92; object loss 62; self-denial through 15; self-destructive infliction of 21
panic 18
paradigms: developmental 47; guidance in construction of 124; social construction 110
paradox 134
paranoid patients 92
parental internalizations 61, 74; abandoning 86; fear of engulfment 86; ties loosened 67
parental introjects 11, 42, 43; process of disengaging from 41
parental representation 81; failure to internalize 72; internalized 60, 73, 86; significant overlap between self and 85

Parental Separation Anxiety (Hock) 75–6
parenting 180; normative 87
parents 47, 69, 167; attachment to 78; demanding and judgemental 148; differentiation from 78; difficulties detaching from 40; educational level 145; enabling and accepting behaviours 147–8; encouragement of conformity 42; feelings about separation 76; idealization of 61; internalized, loosening of ties with 60; mourning of earlier internalized ties to 77; opposite sex 40, 66; same-sex 66, 78; severing emotional bonds with 71; triangulation and overidentification with 73; wise 28; wishes to individuate from 73
participation 79; token sense of 48
partners/partnerships 31; choice of 30; developmental 47; improbable 31; parent-child 53; people expected to be psychologically independent of 186; suitable 35
PASAS (Parents of Adolescents Separation Anxiety Scale) 83
passivity 61
path analysis 82
pathology 16, 138
PATHSTEP 88
peers 62, 74, 79, 169; high conformity to pressure 137; interpersonal relationships involving 78; prevailing ethic 170; stereotypic relationships 80
perceptions 160, 164, 166, 167; alternatives and exceptions 131; cognitive 88; coordinating 168; distorted or 'selectively inattended' 126; inability to separate self from 161; parenting styles 148
person-in-context orientation 4, 5, 6
personal characteristics 4
personal fable phenomenon 80
personality 39, 69, 78, 111; aspect which patterns responses to stimuli 55; central organizing tendency in 176; change 20; creation of theories addressing development 107;

defined/described 8–9; developing
16, 18, 133, 143; harmonizing the
component parts of 68; healthy
development 54; homogeneous
clusters to indicate various patterns
140; integrated dimensions of 175;
Loevinger's approach to 142; loss
of 178; organization 60; pointing
the way towards a concept of 163;
psychosexual orientation to
development 16; role played by
biology in development 18; typical
and transient characteristics 63;
underlying cylinder of 165; *see also*
traits
phallic stage 26, 60, 65–6
phenomenological dimensions 46
phobias 65
physiological homeostasis 58
post-adolescence 55, 68, 194
post-modernity 6
pre-adolescence 67, 113, 191
preconformist stages 153
prediction 146, 148, 149
predisposing factor 153
'premoral' stage 100
preoccupations 130, 159, 176;
conscious 12, 127, 128, 129, 132,
133, 135
pre-Oedipal experience 38, 54, 85;
object ties 68
pre-operational stage 105, 161, 164,
165, 167
prepubertal impediments 31
preschool years 26–7, 129, 167
presocial stage 128
prisons 120
problem behaviors 51
problem solving 149
procreation 31, 32
prosocial behavior 103
psychiatric patients 47, 178
psychiatry 47, 50, 92, 174; diagnostic
classification 9
psychic issues 56; optimal functioning
68; organization 172;
representation 57
psychic restructuring 61
psychic structure: acquired fixity 68;
loss of 62; urgency for changes in 60

psychoanalysis 16, 17, 18, 38, 39,
53–89, 126, 167; ego development
in 140; ego interpreted in different
ways through rise of 127; person
graduates from treatment 31;
treatment centers 7; usages of the
ego term 12
psychodiagnostic review 39
psychodynamic issues 55, 69, 191
psychodynamic theory 34, 69; classic
11; evolution of 54; general
observations regarding 70
psychological factors 45, 58;
self-employment 171
Psychological Separation Inventory
(Hoffman) 74, 76
psychological tests 39
psychology: academic 138; actions
described in terms of 134;
adjustment 138; adolescent 7;
challenging the prevailing culture in
108; clinical 92; cognitive 158;
constructive- developmental 158,
186, 187; developmental 47, 158;
ego psychoanalytic 38, 70, 157;
explanatory power of various
theories 140; humanistic 174; lack
of attention to women 139;
preventative 182; social 34
psychometrics 12, 125
psychopathology 8, 60, 78, 148;
factors leading to or avoiding 153;
generic vulnerability to all forms of
153; internalized 153; severe 42;
turmoil an indicator of 70
psychosexual development 16, 66
psychosexual stage 31, 140
psychosis 63
psychosocial approach 10, 15–52
psychotherapy 3, 49, 50, 138, 186;
cornerstone of 126; often regarded
as panacea 182
puberty 29, 68, 69; depressed girls
153; maturation 67; social
conditions of choice promote ego
development at 35
punishment 103, 104; avoiding 95, 98,
131, 132; awareness that it is not
inevitable 105; fear of 94;
immediately upon transgression

105; non-authoritarian approach to 146; rewards sought without incurring 151; short-term 129 purpose 26–7; educational 117; instrumental 95, 64

'quality of unselfconscious living' 19

racist views 170
rapprochement 59, 61, 62, 72, 73, 87, 193
rationality 110
reaction 65, 67; maternal 87; non-anxious and unresentful 81; overt behavioral 57; societal 74; stress 152
'real me' 11
reality 48, 58, 118, 161; concrete 167–8; constructing 185; external 57, 85; feeling of 29; innocuous, opposition to 63; meaning-making 187; overdose of 68; physical distance from the mother of 59; screening device which allows us to perceive 12; selectively perceived or misperceived 126; shared 170, 193; social 68; struggle for a feeling of 21; testing 124
reality checks 152
realization 20, 59
reasoning 94; accompany shifts in the quality of 105; dilemmas, in a business context 109; from a perspective of self-interest 95; hypothetico- deductive 164; interpersonal 147; judicial 116, 147; legislative 116; more mature forms, through educational means 150; physical-mathematical 147; transcendent 121; *see also* moral reasoning
reciprocity 169
recognition 11, 26, 31, 59, 162, 165, 184; adequate 172; anticipated 23; community 48; community provides 24; mutual 47; social 20, 28
reflection 47, 64; fears of 50
reflexes 163–4, 166
refugees 91

regression 9, 61, 70, 113, 144, 145, 148–9, 195; infantile demands for immediate drive satisfaction 63; non-defensive 61; normative feature among adolescents 56; structural 100; temporary 177; three different forms 196; unconditionally maladaptive role played by 54
regulation 47
relatedness 58; autonomous 146; beyond infancy 71; fathers' displays of 146; interpersonal 54, 135
relationships 96, 171; ability of subject-object balance to predict 181; adolescent-adult 10; attitudes about 76; basic trust in 50; caring 86; cause-effect 186; client and therapist 150; close 42, 134; cognition and affect 158–9; cognition and ego stage 147; *décalage* 141–2; desire to commit to 30; earlier latency, withdrawal from closeness of 86; early 67; family 74, 78; gradual change in the nature of 69; greater mutuality in 13; 'I' and 'Thou' 87; importance to Freud 77; individuals victimized in 170; intellectual development and ego stage 147; internal representations during infancy 38; intimate 40, 42; loss of 178; love 182, 183, 194; meaning of 108; mutual, self-sacrificing, idealized 184; object to the new 'me' 165; parental 42, 71; peer 74, 79, 80; psychological 111; reciprocal 5, 11, 194; reluctance for commitment 40; romantic 56; safe 20; self-other 80; serious 186–7; sex role identity and ego development 146; social 93, 111; subject-object 160; varied emphases on the role of 38
reliability 37; internal consistency 104; interrater 104, 139, 175; lack of 106; test-retest 37, 104, 175
religion 3, 45, 124
reorganization 9; internal developmental 12; means to

identity 11; pattern of thought 93; qualitative 119, 136, 142
repression 67, 147
resentment 76
resilience 78, 108; defensive and restitutive mechanisms that facilitate 80
respect 26, 86, 98, 99, 102, 169; for autonomy 135; mutual 92; self 134
responses 57, 81; accommodation 144; affective 81; empathic 184; fine-tuning of 24; increasing frequency of 100; mediated, non-intimate forms of 184; moral 99, 110; negative, angry or resentful 81; rationale behind 103; sentence completion 80–1; therapeutic 86; women's 107; *see also* social response
responsibility 26, 60–1, 116, 132, 133; care and 107; conflicting 135; different type towards another 187; judgement of 114; providing opportunities for 184; shifts toward greater internalization of 136; strong feeling for one's own thoughts, values and behavior 127–8; training in 152
retaliation 86, 151; preschool child governed by impulses and fearful of 129
rewards 150, 183; short-term 129; sought-after 151
rightness 95, 97, 103, 105, 118
rights 102; individual 98; parental 118
rigidification 148, 196
risks 153, 154; statistics on 186
role confusion: identity versus 24, 29–30, 191
role models 50
role-taking activities 119, 120; reciprocal 165, 169; simple skills 174
roles 22; acceptable, unattainable 21; ambiguous 7; androgynous 146; biology, in personality development 18; changes of 3; childhood identification figures 37; conflicting 151; consistent 36; criminal or delinquent 47; critical 28; expected 6; identity defining 43; ideological 20, 35, 49; institutional 13; internalized 50; predetermined 21; prescribed 123; religious and vocational identity 45; sexual 20, 26, 27, 36, 37, 40, 49, 146; stereotyped 130; vocational 20, 35, 49; work 23, 28, 49; *see also* social roles
rules 97, 102, 120; application of 116; arbitrary and subject to change 105; community, desire to adhere to 98; conformity to 133; conscientious individual evaluates 133; fixed, teaching of 118; internalization of 94, 132, 150; justification of 116; modifiable by mutual consensus 98; moral, internal representations of 115; obeyed because they are approved by the group 130; scoring 139; used in the service of one's own desires 129

'safe sex' message 186, 187
safety 50
sameness 19, 24, 35, 56; loss of 18
sanctions 27
satisfaction 4, 5, 14; drive 63; loss of 178; self 41; sexual 187
scepticism 39, 41
schizophrenia 9, 39
schools 51, 67, 117, 185; concerned about education without failure 169; primary 27–8, 169, 191
scientific methods 106
SCT (Washington University Sentence Completion Test) 12, 129, 136, 138–9, 140, 142, 143; cross-cultural applications of 149
SCT-Y (Sentence Completion Test for Children and Youth) 139
security 49, 50, 85; attachment 84; capacity for 31
self: autistic 128; birth and rebirth of 173; child's awareness increasing of 25; cognitive dimensions of 175; definition of 47; empty 3, 15; estrangement from 28; evolving 173, 178–81, 182; experience of 12, 58, 127; girls' and women's

conceptions of 108; ideal 132; imperial 183; impulsive 166, 183; incorporative 166, 183; institutional 172, 183; inter-individual 183; internal developmental reorganization of 12; interpersonal 172, 183, 184; intrapsychic 7, 13; needs of 107; organizational 184; outworn 13; overvaluation of 68; physical properties explored 164; previous, attempt to cancel 21; real 10, 132; reconstruction of 183; relational model for identifying 108; sequential stages in transformation of 7; services to 45; structuralization of 38; structured, lost and re-formed 13; *see also* autonomous self; sense of self
self and other/object 10, 11, 169, 170; autonomous sense of 38, 128; boundaries between 159, 194; constancy 193; differentiation 58, 72, 74, 179; internalized, overlap 87; meaning of 159–60; no primitive merging of 71; renegotiation of evolutionary balance between 173; representations 68, 72; thoughts and feelings of 127; *see also* subject-object balance
self-absorption 31–2
self-actualization 128, 135
self-aware stage 127, 131–2, 136, 138, 153
self-awareness 25, 151; exam-anxious 152; increase in 131; more mature state of 13
self-conception 84, 126, 146
self-definition 1, 10, 30; constructed through identity formation 48; gender differences in identity domains most important to 43; labels that may not serve best interests of youths seeking 47; morality's centrality in 116; problems of 4, 7; response to 123; seen through identity substitutes 124; shift in the standard for 3
self-destructive actions 120

self-direction 186
self-esteem 40, 51, 53, 78, 86; blow to 179; greater constancy of 60; heightened 64; low 42; stability of 68
self-evolution 180, 184
self-examination 133
self-fulfilment 135, 151
self-governance 121
self-interest 12; abortion in terms of 107; attention crucial 32; behaving according to 150; isolated 193; primary motivator 13; reasoning from a perspective of 95; recognized and confirmed 183; unconstrained 94; what is best for 127
self-ownership 171, 193
self-preservation 32
self-protective stage 127, 129, 130, 137, 138, 139, 145, 150–1, 191
self-reference 174
self-reports 146
self-serving function 68
self-sufficiency 168
self-worth 109
sensations 163, 164, 166
sense of 'I' 3; changing 7; subjective, alterations to 7; when and how one develops 1
sense of self 6, 34; autonomous 50, 118; cohesive, difficulty in developing 73; collectivistic 88; community contribution to 24; firm in own 63; girls lose 108; integration of morality into 115; losing 159; real, lack of any 42; reworked 33; synthesizes earlier identifications 22
sensitivity 29, 46; heightened 24, 193; moral 103, 110; subject-object balances 163
sensori-motor infants 163, 166
Sentence Completion Test *see* SCT
separateness 173; fears of 80; intrapsychic 80; physical 82; psychological 82
separation 107; genuine beginnings of 67; infantile objects 71; internal 64; intrapsychic 173, 184

separation anxiety 63, 77, 79, 83, 179;
 reflecting 81
separation-individuation 57–8, 59, 82;
 defining the meaning of 71;
 difficulties 63; healthy 79;
 incomplete 63; intrapsychic 77–8;
 measuring 74–7; research findings
 on 77–84; subphases 61, 71, 72
Separation-Individuation Inventory
 (Bartolomucci and Taylor) 74
Separation-Individuation Process
 Inventory (Christenson and
 Wilson) 74, 75
Separation-Individuation Theme
 Scale (Coonerty) 74
severe thought disorder 39
sex differences 108, 143
sexual activity 30; attainment of
 functioning 69; earlier 85; fully
 pleasurable, without intercourse
 187; intercourse 186
sexual identity 37, 56, 65–6;
 established, earlier activity at the
 expense of 85; stabilizing of 68
sexual orientations 23
sexuality 187; allure of 186;
 consummated 31
shame 26
significant others 29, 71, 87;
 experienced as abandoning 76;
 fears of reflection from 50;
 moratoriums more cut off from 73
single-parent families 79
SITA (Separation-Individuation Test
 of Adolescence) 74, 75; nine scales
 76
'situated' identities 6
social class 124, 143; restrictions of 4
social construction 110
social contract 98, 104
social criticism 27
social institutions 4, 48, 49, 110;
 moral atmospheres of 120;
 rehabilitation of 85
social niches 49; individuals
 having difficulty in finding 50;
 meaningful 2
social order 26, 29, 37, 96, 172;
 commitments within 193; doing
 one's duty to maintain 97;

embedded 165; emphasis on 98;
 marginal functioning 137; refusal
 to sacrifice own goals and values to
 138; rules governing 98; sense of
 duty to uphold 193; upholding 102
social perspective taking 180
social rank/status 2, 3
social response 20, 25, 26;
 implications for 47–51, 84–8,
 116–21, 149–54, 163, 182–8,
 198–200; wisdom in 28
social roles 29, 35, 37, 48, 123, 124;
 aptitudes in 24; economic
 self-support 69; willingness not
 to predetermine 47
socialization 25, 84, 118
society 23, 31, 84; institutions 85; just
 102; refusal to provide ready role
 definitions 47
socio-cultural approaches 3–7, 45
socio-economic status 114, 145
sociopaths 9, 169
solitude 80–1; not endured easily 130
space and time 36, 46; one item
 develops on top of another in 20
speech 140; regressive and repetitious
 patterns 147
split-off dimensions 177
stability 9, 69, 126, 168
stagnation 31–2
Standard Issue Scoring system
 (Kohlberg) 101, 107, 113, 115
standards: behavioural, internal
 sources of 151; conscientious
 individual evaluates 133; inner 150;
 internalized 50
stepfathers 16, 17
stereotypes 42, 79, 80, 96, 130
stimuli 67; responses to 55
stress 39, 40, 43; reactions to 152;
 storm and 7–8; temporary
 regression in times of 177
stressors 153
structural-developmental models 112
structural-developmental theories
 176–8
structural equations modelling 84
stylistic preferences 173
subcultures 112
subject-object balance 13, 161, 162,

163, 165, 167, 173, 174; assessments of social cognition to 181; cannot yet be 166; distribution of 180; interrater agreement of 175; relationship between depression and 178; subject shifted to object side 171; underlying basis for cognitive or social-cognitive stages 177; unhinged 183

Subject-Object Interview (Lahey et al) 179–80

sublimations 36

substance abuse 51

suicidal ideation 154

Summerhill 28, 117–18 (Neill)

superego 38, 55, 92; codes diminished 67; conflict among id, ego and 77; dominance partially challenged 69; formation 106; growing control over instincts 67; independence of 87; internalized demands 60; loss of some rigidity and power by 60; quantitatively different controls 93; strong resistance 67

supervision 39, 119, 150, 154

support 53; balance between limit setting and 87; effective 185; emotional 76; less dependence on external sources of 60; organizational 184; parental 73, 87; peer group 62; self 60, 69, 186; social 79, 186

survival 62; basic ingredient of 25; group 41

symbiosis 58, 71, 72, 193

symbiotic stage 128–9

symptoms 31, 138, 153, 177; depression 82

talents 20, 23, 32; finding or reconnecting with 50; opportunities provided by society for 48; sensitivity to 29; special 28

teachers 48; wise/special 28

technological influences 4

teenage pregnancy 186

therapeutic relationship 49, 154

therapy: client-centred 151–2; insight 152; natural 182; rational-emotive 151; self-help 152; successful 182

thought: complexity of structures of 175; concrete operational 105, 164; fantasy-filled, representational, imaginative mode of 167; formal operational 113, 147, 164; moral 110; pre-operational level of 105; qualitative reorganization of pattern of 93; regressive 11; social democratic mode of 102; translating to action 26

threat 178

toddlers 56, 58; ability to incorporate or internalize an image of primary caretaker 11; experience of will 25; loss to 59; practising, assisted in exploration; 86; *rapprochement* 61;

toilet-training episodes 25

tolerance 80–1, 134, 135; social 47

trainee therapists 150, 154

traits: ability to describe individual differences in 132; basic, stable over time 142; homogeneous clusters to indicate 140; master 12, 124, 142, 144; static 9

transcendence 134

transformation 7, 13, 133, 170, 181; meaning- making 187

transition 165, 168, 170, 172, 175, 179, 184; accommodation responses associated with 14; depression the companion of subject-object balance in 178; evolutionary 167; fostering 185; imperial-interpersonal 174; involves loss 162; necessary social supports to assist in 186; oncoming 133; periods 150; structural 185; triumph of 169

transition phases 29, 54, 68, 94, 99–100, 101, 105

trauma 18–19; resolutions to 68; reworking and mastering 56, 64–5

treatment requests 152

triangulation 73

troubled adolescents 21

trust 169; basic 35, 50; infant 33; lacking 130; versus mistrust 24–5

turmoil 7, 68, 70

uncertainty: cultural 3; temporary 24

understanding 7, 99, 111; causal relationships 4; cognitive 173; farsighted 186; moral 92, 97, 115; reflective 32; structural model of 110
undifferentiation 71
unhappiness 16, 42
uniqueness 10, 33, 50, 73, 123, 184
United States 54, 98; absence of community, tradition and shared meaning 3; Bill of Rights 102; ego development 207; fourth order of consciousness 186; governmental policies 157; identity a matter of concern 2; institutional balance 180; 'me generation' (late 1970s) 102; military personnel in Europe 180; modal organization of ego 13, 131; national charter for child and adolescent development 17; psychopathology and storm and stress 8; schools 117; social conformity 202; subject-object balances 180; White House Conference on Children (1950) 17; *see also* SCT
universality 109

vacuum 162, 170; intrapsychic 59, 68
validation 179, 181; construct 39; empirical 34; internal structural 76; three-step procedure 76
validity 106; concurrent 37; construct 37, 46–7, 77, 104, 105, 139, 143; discriminant 143; predictive 37, 47, 104, 105, 143, 148; scientific 35; theoretical-substantive 76
values 19, 20, 23, 176, 186; appropriate 3; authoritarian 41; basic 29, 117; changed 171; childhood identification figures 37; communal 41; cultural 142; diametric contrast 21; family, adherence to 42; group 98; identity defining 43; ideological 41; meaningful 37; moral 97, 117, 165; occupational 37; parental objecting to teaching of 118; personally satisfying 151; philosophy of life 37; political 36, 37; racial egalitarianism 170; recreational 37; refusal to sacrifice own 138; religious 36, 37; sex role 37; social 142; strong feeling of responsibility for one's own 127–8; vocational 41
variables 37, 46–7, 114, 147; affective 181; behavioral 181; complex relationships among 84; constructive 181; dependent 47; family 78; identity status, moral reasoning and cognition 146; mutually influential 5; personality 36, 82, 143
virtues 114, 117, 118, 174
vocalizations 62
vulnerability 64, 87, 129; generic 153; heightened 60

Washington University SCT 125, 137
welfare 120, 130
well-being 23; present and future 31
what-I-am/what-I-ought-to-be 132
wholeness 65; structured 99, 110, 112
'wholism' 176
will 25
wisdom 32, 33, 182
withdrawal 31, 86
women 34, 107, 108, 125; arbitrarily placed in position of disadvantage 177–8; depression in 82; eating disorders 82; older 144; problem of identity definition for 35; psychology's lack of attention to 139; SCT originally developed for 138; theories of human development biased against 116; young adult, intimacy among 80
work 180; consistency within 176, 177; satisfaction in adult world of 14
work-study programs 49
working through 86
wrongness 95, 97, 103, 118

young offenders 154